PArTLy RiGHt

PArTLy RiGHt

RiGHt

Tony Campolo

Thomas Nelson
Since 1798

NASHVILLE DALLAS MEXICO CITY RIO DE JANEIRO BEIJING

Published in Nashville, Tennessee, by Thomas Nelson. Thomas Nelson is a registered trademark of Thomas Nelson, Inc.

Thomas Nelson, Inc. titles may be purchased in bulk for educational, business, fund-raising, or sales promotional use. For information, please e-mail SpecialMarkets@ThomasNelson.com.

Unless otherwise noted, Scripture quotations marked KJV are from the King James Version of the Bible.

Scripture quotations marked NASB are from the NEW AMERICAN STANDARD BIBLE®. © The Lockman Foundation 1960, 1962, 1963, 1968, 1971, 1972, 1973, 1975, 1977. Used by permission.

Library of Congress Cataloging-in-Publication Data

Campolo, Anthony
    Partly right
    1. Christianity—Controversial literature—History and criticism.
    2. Middle classes—Religious life 1. Title
    BL2751 C36 1983   239   85-13843
    ISBN 0-8499-0368-8
    ISBN 0-8499-3138-x (pbk)
    ISBN 978-0-8499-2086-8 (repackaged)

Printed in the United States of America

08 09 10 11 12 RRD 5 4 3 2 1

To my wife, Peggy,
the most interesting and
nicest person I know.

Contents

Preface

THIS BOOK is about the critics of the Christianity of the middle class. It is a review of what they have found wrong with bourgeois religion and why they, in most instances, thought it should be destroyed. Those who would do battle with these cultured despisers of religion should have some idea as to the nature of their arguments. Too often those of us who rant and rage from our pulpits against the materialism of Karl Marx, the sexual preoccupations of Sigmund Freud, and the God-is-dead philosophy of Friedrich Nietzsche know almost nothing about these declared enemies of religion. This book is designed to help overcome that inadequacy. While it does not provide an exhaustive analysis of the thought and works of these anti-church intellectuals, it does provide a basic outline of them. I have tried to make their views and arguments readable, clear, and accurate. I hope that I have succeeded. However, I am aware of the fact that attempts to summarize and simplify inevitably lead to distortions. It is my hope that the distortions in this book will prove minimal and that the reader will take away a limited but working knowledge of the teachings of each of these critics of religion. Intelligent dialogue with non-Christians who are well read and well educated requires no less, and perhaps far more.

Beyond providing some help for those who are interested in religious apologetics, I hope that this book serves an even higher purpose. I hope that by reviewing the critiques of these significant authors, some insights into the shortcomings of the religious thought and practice of middle-class Christian churches might be discovered. A religious group matures and improves only by correcting its flaws, and usually the enemies of that group can help it to see those flaws better than its friends can. The enemies of middle-class religion who are reviewed in this book have provided some of the most brilliant analyses of the failures and weaknesses

of our churches and our theology. There is far more to be learned from
them than from friends who flatter and patronize us, but fail to tell us the
truth that hurts. I hope that by studying the arguments of our enemies
we will recognize our sins, confess them, and work to cleanse ourselves
of them.

Not all of those reviewed in this book are atheists or agnostics. We will
analyze the philosophy of the Danish existentialist Sören Kierkegaard,
who was a passionate believer, and we will give brief consideration to the
Russian novelist Fyodor Dostoyevsky, who was a committed member of
the Orthodox church. However, there is one thing that all of these intellectual antagonists had in common: each was a critic of *middle-class* or
bourgeois forms of Christianity. Each believed that the religion of the
middle class was a detriment to the well-being of humanity.

As you read this book, you will find many negative statements about
bourgeois Christianity, made by our intellectual opponents. In order to
set forth as clearly as possible what they have to say to us, I have presented their arguments in the best possible light, and therefore I argue
their cases with enthusiasm. You may think that I have joined forces
with them in the assault upon bourgeois Christianity. You even may
conclude that I despise, as do they, the religion of the middle class.
Nothing could be farther from the truth. I became a Christian in a
middle-class church. I was educated in a middle-class seminary. I write
books for a middle-class audience. I married a middle-class woman.
Furthermore, I believe that middle-class Christianity is vital and dynamic, and that it has a positive future. One of the reasons I am so
optimistic about the Christianity of the bourgeoisie is that it is open to
criticism and willing to learn from it. That is one factor that led me
to write this book. More important, I believe that bourgeois Christianity has within its ranks divergent movements that can make important
contributions to society and challenge its individual members to enter
into the kinds of personal struggles that lead to growth and maturity.
I find that middle-class Christianity is caught in polar tension between
those who want religion to serve as a conservative influence legitimating and reinforcing the dominant institutions and values of bourgeois
culture, and those who would have religion be a movement which
transforms the existing sociopolitical order for the purpose of creating
greater justice for all. It is my conviction that, to be alive and well, religion should be committed to both of these seemingly opposite objec-

tives. Because American bourgeois religion embraces them both, it is healthy and its future seems bright.

There is one characteristic of middle-class Christianity that is basic to our understanding of its role in our contemporary society: that is, that it is increasingly evangelical. On the one hand it rejects the liberalism that has come to characterize the leadership of the traditional mainline denominations (but usually fails to filter down to the laity in the pews). On the other hand, it rejects the legalistic and subcultural lifestyle associated with fundamentalism.

Evangelical Christians believe in the possibility of personal spiritual conversion. They work hard to bring non-Christians into a personal relationship with the Jesus Christ whom they believe to be mystically present and available for those who want to be "born again." They believe that the death of Christ and His resurrection are the basis for salvation from the punishment of sin, and they believe in eternal life for all who will receive it as a free gift from God. Evangelicals give assent to a literal interpretation of the Apostles' Creed, and perhaps most important, they believe in the authority of Scriptures.

While an argument rages in their midst over whether the Bible is inerrant (i.e., that the Holy Spirit guided the authors so that the original manuscripts were without any errors, any mistaken values, or any intellectual limitations), all evangelicals are what I choose to call "functional inerrantists." This means that while some might grant that biblical textual criticism, which has developed since the time of the Graf-Wellhausen theory (a theory that several authors, rather than Moses, wrote the first five books of the Bible), has created some problems for the inerrantist position, they nevertheless use the Bible as *though* it is inerrant, as they preach, teach, and minister.

This evangelical Christianity, the middle-class cultural lifestyle, and the value system associated with it have become the objects of criticism and attack from a significant number of the philosophers who have come to rule the consciousness of the modern-day intelligentsia. Some have accused evangelical Christianity of having been seduced into the dominant values of the American culture, making it little more than an expression of what the American sociologist Robert Bellah has called cultural religion. Others have demeaned it on the grounds that it renders its participants prosaic rule-keepers of the social establishment, devoid of the passion and heroism that make *Homo sapiens* human. Still others have accused it of offering "cheap grace" to its followers because it does not challenge people to adopt the radical lifestyle required by Jesus and to promote the causes for social justice urged by the Bible. Nevertheless, middle-class Christianity shows no signs of dying. It is more vital today than at any time since the Protestant Reformation. This book is designed to analyze the criticisms of its enemies, test their validity, and explain why bourgeois religion has survived them.

Before we begin our analysis and study, I want to tell you about some of the people who made this book possible. First, there is Pat Wienandt, my patient editor from Word Publishing, who is one of the best in the business. Second, there are the student secretaries who worked on typing this manuscript. They include Judy Landis, Kim Feeser, Carolyn McKee, and Meg Deidesheimer. Third, there is my executive associate, Anne Gray, who did more for me to make this book possible than space will allow me to tell. Finally, there is my wife, Peggy. She knows grammar; she can spell, rewrite sentences, and pick out flaws in arguments; and she has encouraged and prayed for me to make this book happen. I can only say to those authors who are not married to her, "Eat your hearts out."

Introduction: The Triumph of the Religion of Main Street

NOTHING HAS succeeded like the Protestant middle class of the Western world. It has produced unparalleled wealth for itself. Its culture has permeated almost every other nation on the planet. Its religion has been spread to more than half of the earth's people.

Max Weber, a German political economist and one of the founders of modern sociology, has called it the "lead" society of our age. The reason is that all other societies, willingly or unwillingly, have followed its style and adopted its values. The validity of Weber's assertion about the Protestant middle-class culture is easily affirmed by world travelers. What is notable to those who visit the cities of various nations is not how different they are from each other, but how similar. The skyscrapers, traffic jams, neon signs, motion picture theaters, and dress styles seem very much the same regardless of where people go. A monolithic social system, increasingly bureaucratic and technological, appears to have engulfed the planet, and its trademark reads, "Made in the U. S. A."

This "lead" culture, as Weber called it, has not been created by a biologically superior race. The theories that traced social success to the gene pools of races died with Hitler, if not with the collapse of social Darwinism. It has not emerged as a historical accident, as historicists might claim. Rather, it has been created by religion.

Marxists might find that hard to believe. Those materialistic determinists would like to teach us that religion is always invented to serve the interests of the ruling socioeconomic class. They find the idea incredible that religion itself could be a causal factor in creating a social class. Nevertheless, there is much evidence to support the claim that religion did create the Western middle class, and there is valid argument that without the birth of Protestantism there would not have been the birth of the bourgeoisie.

Protestantism, Weber points out, was above all else an attack on the "magical" elements of medieval Catholicism. The Protestant reformers were rationalists who developed logical theological systems and tended to reject any beliefs and doctrines that would not fit into their schemes. This structured way of thinking that characterized the bourgeois approach to all aspects of life reduced salvation itself to a logical judicial process:

1   All humans are sinners.
2   All sinners must die.
3   Jesus, the Son of God, died in the place of sinners.
4   Since He paid "the wages of sin," those who believe in Him are freed from the penalty of their sins.

The miracles, lucky charms, indulgences, and the mysterious powers of priests, so heavily depended upon by pre-Reformation Christianity, were discarded by the Reformers because such things did not conform to their patterns of rationality. Within society as a whole, this rational approach to things eventually swept away traditional societal systems and customs throughout the Western world and beyond.

Protestantism left no room for superstition or magic, but rather made reasonableness a religious virtue. Its followers required that what they believed "make sense." They demanded a pragmatic approach to life and would accept religion only if it provided guidance for living life more successfully.

Once reason and pragmatism replaced superstition and tradition, the way was paved for a rational, technological approach to life and society that became the bedrock for Western middle-class culture. Science moved from being a curiosity understood only by scholars to being an instrument for solving technological problems. In only a short time the rationally prescribed efficiency and inventiveness of Westerners gave birth to increased economic productivity, urbanization, and the semi-affluent bourgeois lifestyle. It was religiosity that made rationality the highest trait of Western character. It was rationality that marked the middle-class approach to everything.

Furthermore, Protestantism encouraged those within its sphere of influence to view their daily work in a new way. The Reformers had declared that work was a divine calling and that their God did not require people to give up "worldly" vocations and flee to monasteries and convents in order to render God-pleasing service. Instead, they claimed that God is glorified by having His people work diligently in the various vocational roles into which they might find themselves called. Scientists believed that they could glorify God through their research. Artisans believed that God could be pleased through their creative labors. Farmers were convinced that in growing food, they were partners with God and that their work was blessed by Him. In all avenues of human endeavor, the Protestant Reformers taught that diligence at work was a religious obligation. Their followers believed that in everything they did, they were carrying out a divine imperative.

The work orientation of the Protestant middle class has been called oppressive and obsessive by its critics. The rational disposition generated by this "lead" group toward all aspects of life, including religion, has made its members seem pedantic to those who consider themselves to be more poetic and imaginatively alive. But when all the critics have exhausted themselves by throwing their darts and hurling their tirades at the Western bourgeoisie, they still must contend with the fact that this social class has not only produced more techniques for better living than any other, but that it also has created more wealth for more people than any other group in human history.

Those who condemn the Western middle-class culture have no desire to be rid of its technology. They are not willing to reject its affluence. Even among the most ardent enemies of Western middle-class culture, its medical advances, labor-saving inventions, and organizational skills are relished and enjoyed.

While some of the anti-Western detractors of the middle class have agreed that the technology and organizational skills of the bourgeoisie might be useful to non-Westernized peoples, they then add that these things should be transferred to the Two-Thirds Nations without those people having to accept the middle-class value system or religion. They want "developing" societies to enjoy the creations of this "lead" class, but they want no part of the mind-set that makes them possible. Such critics do not understand how closely integrated are the technology and organizational genius of the Western middle class with the ethic and thought generated by Protestant belief systems. They fail to see that it is impossible to maintain the former without the latter. Protestantism created the thinking and work styles that became the a priori requisites to all those things that we call modern and efficient. Protestantism, or some other ideology that could create rationality and diligence, was an essential basis for the wonders of our modern technological world.

By the mid-twentieth century, the intellectual elite of Latin America were well aware of the links between Protestantism and Western middle-class socioeconomic success. Consequently, they encouraged the entrance of Protestantism into their countries. They worked hard to end the Roman Catholic monopoly on religious affairs that had characterized their societies since the arrival of the Conquistadors. They hoped that Protestantism might create the same thought patterns and commitments to economic productivity that had made the United States such an admirable success. It was this hope among others that motivated the secular intelligentsia of Latin America to promote the religious freedom so essential for the spread of the Reformers' Christianity.

In the midst of the assaults upon the Western middle-class form of Christianity that have become common since the counterculture years of the 1960s, it is easy to lose sight of its awesome contributions and positive dimensions. Not only did Western middle-class Christianity give rise to technological efficiency and its concomitant wealth; it also provided the world with a morality that gave new meaning to biblically prescribed ethics. By opening the Bible to the masses, Reformation Protestantism introduced people to the things that the Scriptures dictate for everyday living. As individuals scrutinized the Bible, they found guidelines for a lifestyle that was justifiably called Puritanism in England and Pietism in Germany. The moral laxity of the Middle Ages was displaced by a revival of holiness as Protestants embraced the instructions for personal righteousness discovered through Bible study. Drunkenness, debauchery, and cruelty, behaviors common to medieval peoples, were pushed aside by the spiritual renewal that accompanied the doctrinal reforms of the Protestant movement. Sobriety, sexual purity, and kindness increasingly characterized the emerging Protestant population. While the Counter-Reformation and the Council of Trent fostered significant improvement in the normative behavior of Catholic Christians, they failed to generate the personal piety that became the hallmark of Protestantism.

Among the changes wrought by Reformation theology perhaps the most important was in family life. Whereas Catholicism had glorified celibacy and made sex a negative fact of life essential for reproduction, Protestantism glorified the state of marriage as never before and began a program to make sex into something deemed "beautiful." Using biblical instructions, Protestantism regulated and monitored family life in careful and precise fashion. The "double standard" in sexual matters that allowed a great deal of license for men was challenged strongly. Biblical admonitions concerning the roles of parents and children were strictly encouraged. The definition of the father as spiritual leader of the home was taught and learned. Family life changed. Biblically structured families became the bedrock for the newly developed bourgeois class.

During this course of study, many criticisms will be leveled at the Western Protestant bourgeoisie and its religiosity, but let it not be forgotten that this class produced one of the most wholesome, egalitarian, and loving family systems in human history. Furthermore, its family lifestyle may be the best form alive in the world today. I am well aware of how ethnocentric that may seem, but when I compare our family system with those in some of the cultures so lauded by my anthropologist friends, I find ours more desirable. There is less oppression of women in our familial lifestyle. There is less "machismo" employed to prove masculinity among our young men. There is more planning for the welfare of children. I know that among my colleagues in the field of sociology, it is heresy to make such assertions, but I believe them to be true, nevertheless.

There is something admirable about the traditional middle-class bourgeois family, and if radical psychologists like R. D. Laing or David Cooper want to deem it a "sick" institution, I will simply declare them wrong. Strange as it may seem to those who worship cultural relativism, most of the people of the world long for the tenderness between mates that characterizes our ideal for marriage. Women everywhere wish that their husbands would treat them the way Western bourgeoisie husbands are expected to treat their wives. The women of the world look longingly toward the Protestant ideal in which wives are treated as friends and companions.

Just because divorce has become common, we should not assume that the ideals of bourgeois marriage have been relinquished. Divorce may be a frequent occurrence in America *because* people are so committed to those high ideals that they will not settle for marriages devoid of them. Strange as it may seem, the high divorce rate in America may be evidence that the American dream about marriage is as strong as ever and that the ideal marriage stands in judgment of all conjugal relationships that fail to measure up to it.

There is just one last virtue of the Western bourgeoisie created by Protestantism which I choose to cite here, because the list of these virtues could in itself become a book. It is the allegiance to a belief that the kingdom of God is something that can and must be approached within human society. From the time of the Pilgrims, Americans have been imbued with a sense of being on a divine mission. They have believed that it is their calling to establish a society which more closely approximates the will of God than any since the best days of ancient Israel. Americans have sought to hold their institutions to the same ideal for justice that the Hebrew prophets would have commanded, and they have endeavored to establish in their communities a fellowship that imitates the fellowship of the early church.

The American people have not deluded themselves into thinking that they could realize a Utopian dream. They have always recognized that the imagined society that they constructed out of their interpretation of Scripture was an ideal that could never be realized through human efforts. They have believed that only with the second coming of Jesus will the kingdom of God be fully present on earth. Nevertheless, they have preached that it is the duty of all Americans to work together constantly to improve their institutions so that more and more their society might be likened unto that Kingdom which Christ will establish at the eschaton. No matter how good the social system might become, Americans will believe that it has fallen short of the ideal which they find in their biblically defined kingdom of God.

Government in America never has been viewed as simply a necessary evil. Instead, middle-class Americans have viewed it as an instrument through which society could be increasingly perfected. They have viewed government with ambivalence. On the one hand, they have ridiculed its bureaucratic failures and feared its encroachments on personal liberties. On the other hand, they have looked to it with hope, believing that, in spite of all its shortcomings, it is still an instrument through which God's people can work constantly to make America more like that which their God planned for it to be.

Unlike the religions of the East, Buddhism and Hinduism, the religion of Americans has immersed them in the concerns of this world.

Americans have made the transforming of society as holy a task as the sanctifying of the individual. They have rejected any semblance of a religion that was "so heavenly founded that it was no earthly good." Their religion has to be relevant to the social issues of the day. It has to be related to the events on the front page of the morning newspaper. They have no use for an escape into Nirvana, but instead have always prayed to their God saying, "Thy Kingdom come, Thy will be done in *earth,* as it is in heaven" (Matt. 6:10).

The social imperative that Americans found in their Bibles has seldom allowed them to serve simply as "God's ambulance squad," picking up and ministering to the casualties of cruel and unjust social practices. Their religion has required that they attempt to change society, reform institutions, and reconstruct social behavioral patterns so that such cruelties and injustices are diminished. If Americans could have rewritten the story of the Good Samaritan, they would have had the Samaritan not only ministering to the poor man who had fallen among the thieves, they also would have had him establishing a committee to install better lighting along that dangerous highway and organizing a demonstration in front of Herod's palace to demand better police protection for travelers.

The American people seldom have been content to feed the poor; they have endeavored to end poverty. They have seldom been content to clothe the naked; they have tried to establish welfare systems to provide clothing for all of society's citizens. They have seldom been satisfied with charity; they have tried to create a world in which charity could be unnecessary.

The bourgeois culture, created in part by the theologies of Calvin, Luther, and Wesley, has been marked by a religiously motivated activism that tires Europeans who try to keep up with it. Even in its most secularized forms, the altruistic activism generated by Protestantism still remains. Whether it be in a Jerry Lewis telethon or in a benefit concert by the Beach Boys, the spirit of religious activism, if not its overt expression, lives on. Americans believe that they can make the world a better place. They believe that they have been blessed with resources and opportunities which obligate them to such a high and holy task. Repeating the Scripture that reads ". . . to whom much is given, from him much will be required" (Luke 12:48) they charge forth, believing that their manifest destiny is to transform the world into what God would have it be.

The middle class often has been criticized for its activism. Third World peoples have accused Americans of attempting to impose the American way of life on their cultures. Anthropologists have condemned American missionaries for disrupting indigenous cultures. Environmentalists have declared that the Western bourgeoisie has adopted a lifestyle necessitating the rapid exhaustion of the world's nonrenewable resources. While there is truth in all of these accusations, those who make them often ignore the positive contributions of the Western bourgeoisie in general, and of the American middle class in particular. The missionary zeal of this "lead class" has brought the gospel to countless numbers of people around the world. The compassion of the members of the bourgeoisie has led to a global medical program that has cut the death rate of infants, and extended the life expectancy of adults. The institutions of learning established by Americans in the name of their Savior have given opportunities and hope for a better life to those who might otherwise never have dreamed of such options. In short, in spite of all the evils that American middle-class people may have perpetrated throughout the world, the balance sheet of history almost certainly will give the verdict that the human race is better off because they have lived.

The Bourgeoisie under Attack

I have proposed the thesis that religion has been crucial in the creation of the Western bourgeoisie and that it has been particularly significant in the development of the American middle class. This thesis does not necessitate that religious ideas are always the primary causal factor in societal formation. There are times and circumstances in which economic forces are the determinative factors. There are other times and circumstances in which political movements initiate social change, and still other times and circumstances in which history is restructured because of the leadership of charismatic personalities. There is no single cause of social change, in spite of what some prominent spokespersons in the fields of sociology, economics, political science, and psychology may say. We must analyze each situation in the drama of history as separately and objectively as possible, and we should try to observe causal factors without a priori assumptions of what they might be. Only then will we be open to discover what it really is that has given birth to a movement or a process of social change.

I have tried to be objective in my assessment of the creative forces that have given birth to the American middle class and to its culture. While my affirmation of the virtues of this class may reflect a certain amount of bias, I believe that there are few who would deny that religion must be considered seriously when attempts are made to explain the origins of the American bourgeoisie.

The Western nations and, through them, most of the rest of the world, have been dominated by the style, culture, and orientations of the bourgeoisie. The bourgeoisie properly has been called by Marxists the ruling class. However, like most rulers, the bourgeoisie has been subject to criticism and attack by those who resent its hegemony over the modern world and its Weltanschauung (world-view). These attacks have waxed and waned over the years, but seldom have they had more force and credibility than they have had since the 1960s.

During the crazy decade of the '60s, the criticism of The Establishment, as the White, Anglo-Saxon, Protestant cohort was called, came primarily from a counterculture made up of disaffected children of middle-class parents. These critics (some of them "hippies," some of them neo-Marxists) put down the affluent lifestyle of the American bourgeoisie. They condemned the Protestant work ethic, claiming that it made people into workaholics and gave a destructive importance to the accumulation of wealth. They declared that the prosperity of the middle class was achieved only because the rich bourgeoisie of America exploited vulnerable Third World nations. Furthermore, it was asserted that the processes of economic production, utilized to establish the vast capital reserves of the American middle class, dehumanized the working class and left the poor of the urban ghettos alienated and oppressed.

In more recent years, the criticism of the American middle class has come from the spokespersons of the Third World. "Liberation theologians" (the title that the Latin American Christian Marxists often assign to themselves) have created the impression that not only are there flaws in the bourgeois culture, but that God is at war with it. These ideologies dress Jesus in the garb of Che Guevara, and they cast Jehovah in the role of a God who leads His people into violent revolutions against oppressive ruling classes.

The liberation theologians, who have become a presence that cannot be ignored either in our houses of worship or in our houses of Congress, teach that the Bible reveals a God who calls for revolutionary movements against those unjust social elites who enjoy affluence at the expense of weak and downtrodden peoples. They trace the action of Jehovah from the time that

He championed the cause of the Israelites and fought for them against the oppressive ruling Egyptians, to the time He sanctified the Maccabean revolts. They point out that Jehovah has always stood with the downtrodden when they cry for justice. Even within Israel, God would not tolerate the exploitation of the poor. When rich Jews oppressed poor Jews, God sent His prophets to declare His judgment against this social injustice.

The liberation theologians see the ultimate incarnation of their revolutionary God in Jesus, who they believe will establish a new social order. They look forward to a time when God's kingdom will be realized in history, and it can be said of their Messiah, "He hath put down the mighty from their seats, and exalted them of low degree. He hath filled the hungry with good things; and the rich he hath sent empty away" (Luke 1:52–53).

Any of us who have traveled to Third-World countries have become sensitive to the validity of much of what the liberation theologians are saying. We have come to recognize that there is a severely unequal distribution of wealth that defies justification; that there are millions of people trapped in grinding poverty without any opportunities for escape; that there are political and economic structures in place that create obscene oppression. We have become convinced along with liberation theologians that Jehovah is filled with wrath against the societal systems in which such injustices are perpetrated, and that He condemns those whose affluence is derived from such conditions.

However, many of us are not convinced that the violent revolutions encouraged by Christian Marxists are the answer to the horrendous state of affairs that exists in Third World countries. Our tendency to back off from that solution may lie in our fears that, should it succeed, we members of the bourgeois class would be the losers. Or, our opposition to the revolutions of the liberation theologians may be the result of the skepticism generated from watching too many revolutions in Third World countries in which victory has resulted only in the changing of the palace guard. We have seen too many revolutions that have promised freedom and hope for the masses, but have instead resulted in regimes every bit as dictatorial and exploitive as those that they have replaced.

We might buy into revolutionary solutions if we were unacquainted with the insights of Alexis de Tocqueville, the nineteenth-century French journalist and social critic, who explained that every violent revolution necessarily results in tyranny. De Tocqueville explained that if the revolution succeeds, those who have won must suppress and control by military means those who have opposed it. The loyalists to the old regime must flee for their lives. This is true whether it be the Cuban Revolution causing refugees to escape to Florida, or the American Revolution, which caused loyalists to flee to New Brunswick and Bermuda. Over an extended period of time restrictive measures may be relaxed, but often a whole generation must pass away for that to happen. On the other hand, tyranny will also be necessitated should the revolution fail. The ruling elite will have to use military violence to put the unruly dissenters back in their place and keep them there. I am convinced that there must be a better way, and an attempt to outline at least one alternative will be given in a later chapter of this book.

The twentieth-century critics of our American bourgeois society had their antecedents in the intellectual thought of the nineteenth century. Marx, Engels, Saint-Simon, Sorel, and a host of other social philosophers who were disenchanted with the society created by the industrial revolution, attacked the middle class as the culprit responsible for the dire state of affairs they faced in their day. These critics provided extensive analyses of how the bourgeoisie had structured society to unjustly serve their interests, and how this social class had used religion and philosophy to justify their favored position in the world. They punctured the pompous claims to superiority that were all too common among middle-class ideologists and patrons, and they charted courses for the future of society that would do away with bourgeois privilege and pave the way for an egalitarian world in which everyone, regardless of accidents of birth, would have access to lives of dignity and economic opportunity.

These intellectuals provided the ideology for the attack on the middle class that came from those who were below. They provided the arguments and justifications which the poor and oppressed proletarians needed to rally their forces against the painful conditions which they had been forced to accept by the ruling bourgeoisie. They provided the basis for *The Attacks from Below.*

The Attacks from Below

Among those who articulated the suffering and the aspirations of the proletariat, none is more prominent than Karl Marx. His name has become anathema among the middle class, which views him as the satanic creator of the ideology and movement that challenge its dominance in the world. However, by those who champion the concerns of the poor and the oppressed, Marx has been ascribed such titles as "messiah" and "prophet." His Manifesto has become The Declaration of Independence to people who live in the Two-Thirds Nations. His antiestablishment message has resonated through the barrios of Latin American cities. His economic theories have provided the basis for critiquing capitalism and his sociological theories have made revolution seem like the only hope for society's underclass. Not since the time of Mohammed has the presence and thought of one person so altered human history as the life and works of Karl Marx. Christians must take him seriously.

In the modern academic arena, Marx has become a primary figure. His brilliant attacks on the bourgeoisie and his call for a new social order have inspired many to believe that they might as well rise up against oppression because they have nothing to lose but their chains. Marx's attacks have been aimed not only at the practices of the middle class, but also have been directed at the Protestant religious system which supports and legitimates the bourgeois position as the ruling class. The religious spokespersons for middle-class Protestantism have endeavored to defend their faith against Marx and his followers, but unfortunately, their arguments have tended to be unconvincing. The defenders of the Protestant theology and lifestyle have failed to be effective in their opposition to Marxist attacks for three reasons:

1   They seldom have taken the time to master Marx's writings and thought. They attack an oversimplified version of his system, rendering their attack superficial to any who have taken the time to give Marx's works serious consideration.

2   They have failed to acknowledge that many of Marx's critiques of Protestant middle class religiosity are valid and should be heeded. The leaders of Protestantism would do well to repent of some of the sins in their systems of thought, lifestyle, and social practice that Marx pointed out, rather than spending so much effort in trying to refute the accusations.

3   They have failed to outline a plan for social change that is a viable alternative to the Marxist proposal. Instead of clinging tenaciously to their theories of supply-side economics, which seldom allow for wealth and prosperity to "trickle down" to the lowest strata of

societal systems, they would do well to outline workable options for social change that would not necessitate the embracing of communism and its totalitarian tendencies.

In the second section of this book, I suggest how we might go about correcting some of these failures. The legitimate critiques that Marx makes of life in our modern industrial bourgeois society are discussed and given serious consideration. An attempt is made to summarize some of his basic theories and to present them simply and briefly enough to allow those who are harried for time to grasp their significance. Furthermore, alternatives to the Marxist plan for social change are described.

There is no way for the Protestant establishment to respond to the attacks from below without acknowledging that there is serious need for corrections in our bourgeois middle-class economic system and the lifestyle it engenders. There is no way that the poor and oppressed peoples of the world will take our theology and biblical message seriously unless we can outline and initiate a program of social change and a promise of social justice that surpass those offered by the Marxists. There is little chance that Protestant belief systems will remain viable unless we understand and respond to the intelligent arguments formulated by the most serious spokesperson among those who are marshaling the attacks from below.

The Attacks from Above

The bourgeoisie, being the *middle* class, not only faces criticism from those below who view it as an agent of economic oppression, but it also must respond to the accusations and criticism that come from the aristocrats. From the time that the middle class began to assert itself in the meso-European world (all those areas living under the terms of European cultural standards) of the sixteenth century, the representatives of the upper class viewed its members as threats to their rule and affluence. The elitists of this class of landed gentry recognized that, with the Industrial Revolution, power and wealth had begun to slip from their hands and was residing increasingly in a suddenly omnipresent new class of merchants and clerks. The aristocrats not only regretted their loss of prestige and domination of the social order, they also lamented what the new ruling class was doing to society. To many of them, it seemed as though the Puritan Protestant culture of the emerging bourgeoisie was devoid of the pleasure and taste that had marked their lives in the courts and palaces of Europe. As far as the old aristocrats were concerned, the new class of bourgeois shopkeepers and bookkeepers who made diligent hard work a virtue, had made the world into an austere and drab place. With their constant sense of drivenness for work, work, work, and more work, the bourgeoisie seemed to have no time for "the finer things of life." The aristocrats wondered what would happen to the arts in the new bourgeois world. They saw no evidence that the money-grubbing businessmen of the new age would patronize the artists and musicians who had enriched the culture of Western Europe. The new middle class seemed to be committed to efficiency and practicality, leaving little room in their lives to develop philosophical depth or the intellectual sensitivity to grasp the significance of existence or the glory of life. The aristocratic elite looked with contempt on a class that they believed lacked manners, taste, artistic appreciation, intellect, depth, and graciousness in style.

While studying the United States in the early nineteenth century, Alexis de Tocqueville observed that in bourgeois society, social status was not ascribed by birth as was the case in an aristocratic society. De Tocqueville, who was a member of the aristocracy of France, saw that in America social status was achieved through the accumulation of wealth. In a bourgeois culture, birth and background meant nothing, reported de Tocqueville. One's standing in society was achieved by successes in the marketplace. Those whose business acumen enabled them to accumulate significant wealth would rise in social status, while those who failed in economic ventures would fall to the bottom of the system. Status was precarious in the bourgeois world, and those who had done well could not afford the luxury of relaxation. In an unforeseen twist of business affairs or an unpredictable change in the market, they could lose all they had gained. Such a state of affairs, according to de Tocqueville, rendered the American middle class hard-working though mundane, driven though boring, and affluent though without taste. The American middle class made materialism a way of life, and the accumulation of wealth a religious obligation. It all seemed so crass and petty to the debonair elitists of the aristocracy.

The aristocratic contempt for the newly arrived bourgeoisie of the Western world found ample expression in the works of some of the key intellectuals of the late nineteenth and early twentieth century. And the aristocrat of the aristocrats in that era was Friedrich Nietzsche. His disgust for the lifestyle and religion of the middle class led him to write some of the most devastating criticism of the bourgeoisie ever penned. He scathingly denounced its lack of passion, its prosaic lifestyle, its art and music, and most of all, its religion and philosophy.

Nietzsche was not alone in his reactions to the cultural forms of bourgeois society. There were others, whose religious orientation was quite different from his, who joined the attack upon the way of life that had become dominant in Western Europe and America. Whereas Nietzsche was a militant atheist and called himself "The Antichrist," some who deemed themselves Christians were no less critical of middle-class life and religion.

Among the critics within the household of faith, Sören Kierkegaard deserves special notice. I have found that mention of this famous Dane elicits all kinds of negative responses from those of my church friends who are theologically fundamentalistic. Kierkegaard is considered one of the founders of existential theology, and there is great fear of existentialism among those evangelicals and fundamentalists who view this brand of philosophy as the source of secular humanism. Such a quick connection between Kierkegaard and secular humanism is unwarranted. First of all, Kierkegaard was an orthodox Christian who treated the Bible as inerrant revelation. He took Jesus more seriously than most contemporary church leaders, and he ran into his most difficult opposition because he believed that the radical commands of Jesus should be taken literally. His commitment to the directions given by Christ for Christians to totally surrender their wealth, security, and social status in the process of becoming what he called "true knights of faith" set him at variance with the mainstream middle-class churches of his day as well as those of today.

Furthermore, Kierkegaard stressed the "inwardness" of Christianity. Revivalists who talk about "a personal relationship with Jesus" are closer to the emphasis of this founder of modern Christian existentialist theology than most of them would care to admit. For Kierkegaard, the affirmation of the doctrines of the state church of Denmark, and baptism into ecclesiastical membership, hardly sufficed to make the individual into a Christian. In Kierkegaard's words, "something more is needed." This something more was a subjective involvement with the living Christ who Kierkegaard believed presents Himself personally to every one of us. The encounter with Jesus in the depths of the self was the sole basis for salvation so far as he was concerned. It is his apparent emphasis on subjectivity as the basis for Christian faith that has troubled orthodox church leaders down to the present. Those in the church who want the Christian faith to be established on more solid ground than that of personal experience, who look for objective validation for Christian beliefs, and who are convinced that spiritual inwardness can easily be confused with psychological disorders, view Kierkegaard as dangerous.

In this book, Kierkegaard will serve as a proponent of the elitist criticisms of bourgeois religion. He certainly should be considered as representative of the aristocratic mentality that looks down upon middle-class religion, accusing those who embrace it of being superficial and passionless. Kierkegaard despised the bourgeois Christians of his day who seemed to "play church," and who desired a comfortable religion devoid of fanatical commitment. He protested the bourgeois forms of religiosity that watered down the cost of discipleship into the rules of middle-class morality.

No survey of the attacks upon bourgeois religion would be complete without giving some consideration to the founder of modern psychoanalytical theory, Sigmund Freud. After his assault upon middle-class Christianity, the pretensions and pious image of its members were difficult to maintain. Freud stripped away the appearance of self-righteousness that had become a characteristic of many Protestant church members, revealing them to be persons with sensuous appetites and dark dreams. When Freud had finished his analysis of the psyche of the Victorian types who came to him for help, he made it clear that these people were members of a social class that was far removed from the sanctified people of God they sometimes pretended to be.

Religion, claimed Freud, was a delusion created partly out of sexual fantasies and partly out of fear. The belief system that middle-class people held to so dearly was simply an instrument of repression that kept the lustful impulses of seemingly proper people under control. For the sake of emotional and psychological health, Freud wished to do away with bourgeois religion once and for all. He said that Protestant religion was a primary cause for neurosis, and that only as human beings rejected what it said about them and accepted a scientific approach to self-understanding (which he believed that his theories provided) could a higher stage of human development be achieved. Freud functioned like an elitist. He seemed to be saying, "If you knew what I know, you would cast aside your bourgeois religion and affirm a more sophisticated understanding of humanity and society."

The Future Shape of Middle-class Christianity

Attacks upon the Christianity of the middle class have been varied and brilliant. The intellectuals who have formulated these attacks have at times been able to stimulate social movements which gave their arguments political significance. The halls of higher education have echoed with the cynicism generated by the cultured despisers of the faith, while the ghettos and slums of the urban poor have bristled with the anger generated by Marxist organizers. Nevertheless, middle-class religion has survived. What is more surprising, it is showing signs of renewal and growth that signal that its best days may lie ahead.

The death notices for middle-class religion, heralded by the "God is dead" theologians, have proved premature to say the least. Christianity in its bourgeois form has demonstrated an unexpected resilience and staying power. Its critics have not destroyed it, but have toughened it up so that it seems more resistant to its enemies now than at any time since its earliest period of development. Its strength and vitality must be explained. No student of the sociology of religion can ignore the phenomenon of the comeback of middle-class religion in America, its revival in England, and its new beginnings on the continent of Europe.

In his book *One-Dimensional Man*, Herbert Marcuse, a leading neo-Marxist of the 1960s, wrote that the bourgeois social system, including its religion, had become so powerful that movements aimed at overthrowing it or destroying it were doomed to failure. Marcuse believed that prior to the modern bourgeois society, every social system was doomed to death and replacement. This, he claimed, was because every system had failures and inadequacies, and those who were victimized by these failures and inadequacies would create revolutionary movements to oppose the system. According to Marcuse, out of the conflict between society and the revolutionary movements it generated had always come a new social system, qualitatively different from either the original society or the one envisioned by the leaders of the revolution. However, Marcuse believed that this time-honored process had come to an end with the emergence of the modern, affluent, technologically efficient Western middle-class system. He felt that whenever opposition movements would emerge to challenge the bourgeois way of life, the dominant middle-class system would prove able to negate their threats without experiencing any significant damage. The religion of the bourgeoisie, like other elements of its culture, would be able to resist annihilation from any ideology or counterculture movement in the foreseeable future. According to Marcuse, the ability of the bourgeois society and its various cultural components to survive antithetical challenges to its existence was based upon its capacity to control the thinking of its citizens so that descriptions of its shortcomings and failures would be reinterpreted as minor shortcomings, easily correctable by some creative middle-class program funded by some charitable foundation, if not through a government grant. For instance, poor people in America were not viewed as an inevitable result of the failures of the capitalistic economic system, as Marxists would say, but as the consequence of their own inadequate socialization. Educational programs, special social welfare schemes, and perhaps religious conversion, could change these people into successful citizens, according to the leaders of the bourgeois establishment.

Marcuse argued that the poor and oppressed of the modem Western world believed this explanation for their social and economic failures, and readily bought into the programs for personal improvement, not realizing that the real need was for systemic change. The modern bourgeoisie had the capability of always being able to make the failures of their social system seem to be traceable to the inadequacies of society's victims. Instead of becoming revolutionaries, says Marcuse, the poor and down-trodden feel guilty over their condition, and keep promising to try harder to fit into the system which, in reality, is responsible for their dire circumstances. Hence, according to Marcuse, the age for revolutions is over.

I argue that Marcuse, for all his sophistication, is wrong. I believe that the resilience of the middle class is not due to its ability to propagandize its citizenry but is a sign of its greatness. I believe that the middle class is able to overcome its opponents because its people have developed the critical abilities to learn from their enemies. At its best, the Western bourgeoisie is able to hear out its opponents, evaluate their positions and arguments, and then restructure itself to overcome the shortcomings revealed to it by its opponents. When the Marxists point out the oppression of the workers in the capitalistic system, the bourgeoisie reluctantly allows for unions and collective bargaining to correct that evil. When the critics from the Third World decry the unequal distribution of wealth that has caused the people in their homelands to suffer, the Western middle class sends an army of Peace Corps workers, development experts, and engineers. These "do-gooders," as they are often sarcastically called by Marxists, frequently offer more hope for a new economic order than most of the more militant movements that have vied for the allegiance of the people in the Two-Thirds Nations.

When the aristocrats properly point out that middle-class religion is devoid of passion, lacking in heroism, and inadequately representative of biblical requisites, the leadership of the middle class learns from them. It is secure enough to hear out criticism, and actually appreciates honest condemnation of its shortcomings.

This book has been written with these positive convictions about American middle-class religion in mind. I believe that by evaluating and critiquing our critics we middle-class church members can learn some lessons we need to learn, and undergo correctives that will make us stronger. We can learn from our enemies. And we can improve as a people and as Christians as we recognize where corrective measures are needed. I believe the Western bourgeoisie still has a major role to play in the future of Christendom, and I believe that a careful review of its strengths and shortcomings as seen by those who oppose it will help its people to carry out that role with effectiveness.

Part One

Middle-Class Religion

1

Individualistic Salvation

CHRISTIANITY, prior to the Protestant Reformation, encompassed all of life. The church of the medieval era dictated the norms that governed every sector of society and prescribed the requisites of every social role.

The Authority of the Medieval Church

In politics, monarchs ruled by divine right. Those who governed were expected to protect the church, exempt its land holdings from taxation, ensure Christian worship, and even compel citizens into church membership through baptism. In exchange, the church was to instruct the people that those who held positions of power had been given authority by God to rule and that those who opposed their rulers opposed God. The populace was encouraged to believe that when the king spoke, he did so as a representative of Jehovah, and that his pronouncements should be treated as though God Himself had made them.

Education also was controlled by religion. The church determined what constituted truth and prescribed what could be taught in universities. Only doctrines and theories that the church deemed supportive of its world-view were permitted expression. When scholars like Copernicus and Galileo set forth cosmological descriptions that seemed threatening to ecclesiastical theological constructions, they were condemned as heretics and their teachings were indexed and kept from public dissemination. Those who taught in universities were churchmen, and those who learned from them were expected to use their knowledge in the service of Christendom.

The arts were controlled by the church and were used almost exclusively for religious purposes. Cathedrals exemplified the highest form of architectural genius: Paintings told biblical stories and depicted the lives of the saints. Not only was the subject matter of paintings religious, so also was the style.

Author Pitirim Sorokin, one-time chairperson of the sociology department at Harvard University, has pointed out that the style of paintings then was purely "ideational," as opposed to the "sensate" style of the present day. The sensate artistic style glorifies the human body by calling attention to its physical qualities, accentuating motion, and setting the action at a particular place and time. Ideational art forms are diametrically opposed, rendering characters ageless, motionless, and as un-earthy as possible. Anyone who views medieval art at a museum is struck by the unreality of the paintings. The figures are flat, and one gains no sense of the age of the characters. Even the baby Jesus appears in paintings of the Holy Family as a miniature version of a mature person, and there is no evidence that any attempt was made to place biblical scenes in the physical setting of ancient Palestine. The characters have an eternal quality, reinforced more often than not by the halos the artist has given them. The scenes are frozen, depicting a belief in the unchanging nature of the truth being expressed. The overall impression is that what is ultimately real is beyond time and space.

Such art forms were not accidental, nor were they the result of the limited abilities of artists to capture reality as we see it. Instead, medieval paintings reflected the control of art by a church that believed its purpose was to help people to transcend nature and history and to accept the church's version of an ultimate reality, spiritual and eternal.

Economic institutions and behavior also were strictly regulated by religious requisites. Money could not be lent for interest. Peasants were bound by religious obligation to their agricultural roles. Artisans belonged to guilds which were viewed as divinely instituted organizations. Religious traditions dictated what could be produced, how it was produced, and what constituted a fair price for products. The accumulation of capital was considered greed, and investment financing was considered the sin of usury.

The church made some of its most encompassing demands upon the family. Familial obligations, acceptable sexual practices, and the determination of who could marry whom were all carefully delineated by religious formulas. The clergy claimed the prescribing of family practices as its primary function, and the laity never doubted the right of church leaders to instruct them in these matters.

The Protestant Church and Secular Society

The monopolistic control over all aspects of daily living began to come to an end with the Protestant Reformation. Contrary to popular opinion, this movement was not simply religious in nature. Prominent sociologists such as Max Weber and R. H. Tawney pointed out that economic factors also helped to bring about the Reformation. Endeavoring to escape the economic control exercised by Rome over Switzerland and Germany, the ruling princes in these countries realized that the religious revolt generated by Luther and Calvin against papal rule and theology could have positive potential for their own economic interests. They saw that a break with Catholicism would free them to pursue business policies that the church had prohibited. The development of a modern capitalistic economy had been rendered almost impossible by the Roman Church, which condemned both the practice of charging interest for borrowed money and the setting of prices by the law of supply and demand. In exchange for the princes' support in the founding of their new churches, the Reformers granted them and their bourgeois supporters the free exercise of their economic interests without ecclesiastical interference. As long as business was conducted in honesty and contracts were fulfilled, the new church leaders promised to refrain from exercising restraints on the activities of the new and growing breed of entrepreneurs. This trade-off provided advantages for both church leaders and the emerging bourgeoisie.

However, the loss of ecclesiastical control of the business and economic sectors of the societal system was to have far-reaching and unanticipated results. Economic systems are always interrelated with, and often determinative of, political systems. When economic systems change, the associated political systems change too. Consequently, as the economic systems in Protestant nations shifted from religiously prescribed patterns to more pragmatically dictated forms, the political systems soon followed suit. It was only a matter of time before secularized political systems separate from the control of religious institutions would become normative.

The doctrine of separation of church and state was an inevitable consequence of the secularization of economic practices. Since the state required that its citizens be socialized into its value orientation and committed to its causes, the educational system had to be converted to serve its interests. Thus the schooling of children came to be viewed as a function of government rather than of the church. The consequences of a state-controlled educational system were eventually to be realized in a secularized world view and social consciousness, and the focus of the arts, an expression of society's perception of reality, would shift from the religious and ideational to the secular and sensate.

Under the influence of the secularizing process stimulated by the Protestant Reformation, only family life has been left under the sacred canopy of religious legitimation. The church still maintains authority when it speaks on sexual matters or on domestic relations, and the populace of Protestantized countries still acknowledges the right of the church to provide admonition and direction in such matters. Though church members increasingly ignore the directions of the church (e.g., the vast majority of Roman Catholic women practice birth control, and Protestant premarital sexual behavior strays from the official morality set forth by Protestant theology), there are few who would question the right of the church to claim this sector of life as properly within its domain of supervision.

Middle-class Christians often become angry with those members of the clergy who get off on tangents they believe to be outside the concerns of religion (e.g., politics, business, economics). They would rather have preachers keep silent on such subjects as America's foreign policy in Central America, unilateral disarmament, economic discrimination against women, and the role of multinational corporations in the plight of developing nations. The members of middle-class churches often claim that when they go to church, they want something they can apply to their everyday lives. But what many really mean is that they want a biblical message that will still their personal anxieties, eliminate their personal guilt, provide the self-confidence needed to be successful in the competitive world in which they must live, and above all else, guide them on how to get along with their mates and raise their children.

The clergy have very willingly accepted these limitations upon their authority. Furthermore, a significant proportion of them would agree with the circumscribed role that the modern, increasingly rational Protestant society has outlined for them to play. In their seminary training, they prepare for their limited area of jurisdiction. They seldom, if ever, take courses in international relations, economics, business, or political science. Though some of the more "prophetic" types might claim that the gospel applies to all of life (that's part of the rhetoric learned in seminary), they seldom study in areas outside of the normative courses in theology, biblical studies, and introductory social ethics except for the expected courses in pastoral counseling and family enrichment.

I can think of very, very few ministerial students who have taken the time to adopt any course of study that would prepare them for informed analysis of the ways in which social institutions function, and what the Bible has to say about them. Of course, there are members of the clergy who do speak out on social issues, but very often they demonstrate a simplicity and a naiveté that exposes their lack of training in such matters. Their shallow knowledge and their overly simplistic solutions draw some patronizing by those who control the dominant institutions of society, and their opinions are seldom taken seriously. Society's leaders know that on social issues, clergy types are usually not in the same league with them. On the other hand, politicians recognize that when they begin to legislate contrary to the interests of church leaders on such concerns as family life and sexual behavior, they are in trouble. The public is inclined to side with church leaders in these matters. Indeed, politicians who favor liberal attitudes toward abortion and homosexuality are quite likely to be told that they had better shape up or be shipped out of office because they are involving the government in matters that are best governed by the church.

Religious leaders who set up forums and lectures on such subjects as "A Christian Appraisal of American Involvement in El Salvador" or "A Christian Critique of American Business" will generally be ignored by both the general public and the religious community. On the other hand, the evangelical community responds with enthusiasm when offered an opportunity to participate in family-oriented seminars. Let me cite two examples. The outstanding communicator Bill Gothard has attracted hundreds of thousands of people to his three-day seminar program entitled "Basic Youth Conflicts." These lectures give thorough and interesting information supporting the positions of the American Fundamentalist movement on such topics as how wives are to relate to their husbands and what the Bible says about the responsibilities of children to parents. While the role of women suggested by these seminars would seem outrageous to feminists, and the young person's subservience to parental dictates psychologically unhealthy,

the overwhelming number of those who attend the Bill Gothard programs claim to be greatly helped by them. Many report that they "have
been hungry for biblical teachings on family living" and complain that
their pastors ought to develop such programs for local churches instead
of trying to do other things.

Attending a Bill Gothard seminar requires the payment of a fairly hefty
fee. The going rate is thirty-five dollars per person, group plan. That may
not seem like much when compared to the amount charged by the EST
Seminars of Werner Erhard, which promise participants knowledge that
will solve all of their personal problems and guarantee social success, or of
the "Color Me Beautiful" seminars which help people determine what
color clothes they should wear and what color makeup they should use. But
for religious gatherings, which are usually free, this is big money. The fee
is not a rip off by any means. The meeting usually is held at a large urban
auditorium or city hall. Expensive work materials are provided. Hundreds
of auxiliary personnel are required. Such things do cost money.

Upon entering the auditorium where the seminar is to be held, each
participant (and there may be as many as five thousand in attendance) is
given a large loose-leaf study book loaded with charts and graphs sum-
marizing the lecture material about to be presented. There are pages of
questions commonly raised concerning parent/teenager relationships and
husband/wife relationships. Blank spaces are left after these questions
providing ample space to write in the answers as Bill Gothard provides
them. To the best of his ability he will back up each of his answers with
biblical texts. Whatever criticism might be voiced about these programs,
it must be conceded that Gothard makes a strong attempt to relate biblical revelation to family living.

The lights are lowered and a spotlight is turned on Gothard as he begins his series of lectures to an audience he will hold in rapt attention over
the next two and one-half days. At his command are all the tools of modern communication. Charts, graphs, and Bible verses, replicating those
in the study books—will be projected onto a huge silver screen. A gigantic
televised image of Gothard will be projected onto another screen so that
the audience can study every facial expression of the speaker. He speaks
with authority, and the people listen, while middle-class religion is made
relevant to life.

If the Bill Gothard seminars are not as popular in the 1990s as they
were in the 1970s, it is not because the religious focus of the middle class

has changed, but only because religious speakers, like movie stars, come and go. The dominant Christian spokesperson on family affairs and psychological well-being in the 1990s is the popular radio and TV personality Dr. James Dobson, who, like Gothard, is a brilliant communicator. However, his academic credentials are far more impressive and his use of the insights of research materials from the social sciences is far more extensive than Gothard's. His daily radio program, Focus on the Family, is heard by millions of Christian-oriented people across America. He has produced a film series on principles for family living that has been shown in thousands of churches, and his books are best sellers. Dobson, more than any other major Christian speaker, has integrated Christianity with the findings of social science and communicated the result to a middle-class audience that believes he deals with what is essential in religion.

With the middle class, sin is always an individual matter and the world might be set right if enough individuals would accept Jesus as their personal Savior. When theologians talk about corporate guilt or the sinful nature of social systems, the members of the middle class do not so much reject their messages as find them incomprehensible. For them, everything is personal and individualistic. The character of institutions and societal systems is nothing more than the sum total of the character of each and every individual who makes up those institutions and systems. In sociological terms, they are elementarists: they believe that the whole—society—is nothing more than the sum total of its parts—individuals. To the middle class, social systems change when those persons who make up those systems change (i.e., good people create a good system and evil people create an evil system). Accordingly, the members of this class believe that religion is very important because it makes people good. To them, the church need not bother with trying to change the political and business institutions of society. Instead, its leaders should concentrate upon bringing people into a personal relationship with God, which is determined by their individual decisions about Jesus. It is no surprise to find that a favorite hymn in middle-class churches is "I Come to the Garden Alone."

The Rising Voice of the Oppressed

Over and against the individualistic personalism that prevents religion from addressing with authority any societal concerns that transcend family life and private relationships, a new form of religious life and thought is rapidly emerging. It is being given voice by the poor and oppressed, by socially disinherited Christians who have never shared in the American Dream. They have never known the options for success competitively achieved. They have not lived with middle-class optimism. They often come from single-parent homes.

These increasingly vocal Christians are from the social class that Marxists call the proletariat. Usually referred to as the lower class, and in some cases the underclass, they live in the ghettos of American cities and in the barrios of the cities of Latin America. They are the poor people on the African continent who are emerging with a new identity and dignity generated by nationalism and independence. They are the people who have escaped what leftist politicians call the false consciousness of the bourgeoisie and who have affirmed a perspective on social reality that serves their own aspirations and hopes. These previously "wretched of the earth" have come to the awareness that they constitute a distinct social class with interests and cultural values different from those of the middle class. This increasingly assertive subculture affirms those who formerly were looked upon with condescension.

The religion of this subculture stands in diametrical opposition to the American middle-class culture, because it sees sin as being evidenced in the very structure of social and economic arrangements, as well as in individuals. It refuses to see the social, psychological, and spiritual failures of poor people as simply the results of personal failure or poor family life. It argues that the socioeconomic systems in which such persons have had to live are more responsible for their plight than are any decisions made or actions taken by them as individuals.

When a socioeconomic system provides no legitimate means for persons to provide sustenance for their loved ones, is it any wonder that illegitimate means are utilized? If a mother is left with no other means of feeding her children than to sell her body in prostitution, is she to be condemned? If children are orphaned and abandoned, are they to be judged as evil because they steal bread? The middle-class religionists might answer a cautious "yes" to each of these questions, but the theological ethics of the proletariat would declare that it was an evil social system, rather than individuals, who should be condemned. It is quite possible that the proletariat might consider the actions of such persons to be acts of revolution, defying societal structures that are obviously demonic.

Christianity, as understood by the proletariat, is a movement that God has ordained for liberation from oppression. Salvation is viewed as the realization of the fullness of humanity, and sin is anything that prevents that from happening. Middle-class conservatives readily criticize this emphasis, labeling the liberation theology of emerging Third World peoples as a version of "humanism" that ignores the need for individuals to undergo personal deliverance from the consequences of "original sin." The oppressed proletariat argues in rebuttal that the condition of persons is more determined by the social conditions under which they must live than by traits inherited from Adam. People are largely conditioned by the societal systems in which they are reared and in which they must live. The oppressed proletariat claims that there is no way in which people can be expected to be righteous individually as long as they are under the social and psychological domination of a society that predisposes them to anti-biblical behavior.

The liberation theology of the proletariat has focused attention on various biblical themes that are conveniently overlooked in the hermeneutics of the bourgeoisie. For instance, they recognize that Christians are supposed to struggle not only against the lusts of the flesh (as emphasized in the personal piety of the middle class), but are also supposed to struggle against the "principalities and powers." There are conflicting interpretations as to what the apostle Paul is teaching in Ephesians 6:12:

> For we wrestle not against flesh and blood, but against principalities, against powers, against the rulers of darkness of this world, against spiritual wickedness in high places.

The traditional middle-class hermeneutics suggests that Paul's statement about principalities and powers refers to evil spirits under the direction of Satan. This interpretation sets forth the doctrine that in the struggle to live a godly life, the Christian must deal not only with the human weaknesses that stem from sexual appetites and tendencies to pride and power, but also with demonic spirits (i.e., fallen angels) who are constantly endeavoring to seduce and discourage them.

Those with a theology of liberation have a very different interpretation of such Bible verses. They contend that Paul's reference to principalities and powers refers to all suprahuman realities that impose themselves on the human condition. Such suprahuman realities include political and economic systems that deny certain groups of people the opportunity to make those decisions that determine their own destinies; commercial advertising that leads people to make great sacrifices in order to obtain artificially created wants while they ignore their real needs; an educational system that leaves hordes of Hispanic and black young people illiterate while it grants them graduation diplomas; an interpretation of history and the arts that leaves minority peoples with no sense of having meaningfully contributed to the progress of society; and a system of jurisprudence that delivers one kind of justice for the rich who can pay for lawyers and bail, and another kind for the poor who cannot afford such luxuries. The hermeneutics of the poor and oppressed lead them to view the principalities and powers as the social institutions controlled by the ruling middle class and serving bourgeois interests while keeping the proletarian masses from actualizing their human potentiality.

One spokesperson for the oppressed, who surprisingly has become a popular speaker on many of the campuses of evangelical colleges, is Tom Skinner, author of *Black and Free*. Skinner calls upon Christians to attack structural evil (i.e., evil that results from the ways that social institutions function). He claims that this is involved in following the admonition of the apostle John who calls upon Christians to "destroy the works of the devil." Satan, according to Skinner, is destroying God's people by controlling their destinies through oppressive social institutions. As a case in point, Skinner cites apartheid in South Africa as "a work of the devil" which Christians should be committed to destroy. He believes that apartheid prevents the black people in South Africa from living with the dignity and economic well-being essential for the realization of human fulfillment. For Skinner, it is not that personal righteousness is unimportant, but that it is something that is to be realized in the struggle for social justice. If personal righteousness is a goal, it leads to pride. However, when the people of God commit themselves to eradicating the evil inherent in social structures, they develop lifestyles characterized by piety and holiness. Personal righteousness becomes a means to an end rather than an end in itself. When Christians seek holiness not for their own sakes but in order to be better fit to work for the realization of the kingdom of God in history, holiness emerges as a basic trait in their character.

During the civil rights era of the 1950s, I became very aware that it was possible to achieve a high level of personal righteousness while participating in the maintenance of a sociopolitical system that had demonic characteristics. During that time I witnessed revivalistic movements sweep through various communities in the deep South. In each case the lives of a host of individuals were significantly changed. Repentance for personal sins was pervasive, as people turned from sexual deviance, materialistic lifestyles, and egotistical behavior. However, regardless of their achievement of personal righteousness through religious conversions, these people continued to be part of a Jim Crow system that perpetuated racial segregation and discrimination. While those whites who were converted might be motivated to treat blacks with compassion and tenderness, they nevertheless did little, if anything, to challenge the social system that relegated their black brothers and sisters to second-class citizenship and diminished their humanity. Such persons might feel pangs of guilt if they hurt black people individually in face-to-face encounters, but they seemed to feel no guilt from their collective support for a political economic system that attacked the dignity of blacks. Social justice did not necessarily follow the creation of individual righteousness through personal conversions. As far as the oppressed were concerned, the demonic system continued to exercise its evil in spite of the exorcism of evil from the individuals who created and supported the devastating system of racial segregation. The oppressed readily realized that the exorcism of evil through personal conversion might make white people more loving, but only a revolution that would replace the existing social order with one characterized by social justice could provide the fullness of salvation from demonic destruction.

Such interpretations of sin and salvation are significantly removed from the concepts of sin and salvation promoted by middle-class theology. But it is this middle-class theology that is being increasingly threatened with critiques and attacks. As proletarian voices reach an ever higher pitch, the middle class can no longer evade or ignore them. The theology of the middle class must be modified to encompass the added dimensions of sin and salvation discovered by interpreting the biblical revelation from the perspectives of the poor and oppressed proletarian Christians.

2

Hegel: The Pope of the Middle Class

IT HAS BEEN pointed out that the much heralded Death of God predicted by a select number of avant-garde theologians during the 1950s never happened. Religion, contrary to the expectations of many, is more vital and dynamic than ever before. Believers in God are still convinced that the Almighty is alive and well. The significant political power of the "New Right" in the U. S. and the revolutions in Latin America, stimulated by the liberation theologians, give ample evidence that people take their religious beliefs seriously and are ready to translate their convictions into effective social movements.

I have argued that religion and belief in God are likely to continue into the foreseeable future. However, I have claimed at the same time that the ways in which religion is expressed and the structures that institutionalize it probably will be displaced and changed. I believe it is possible that in the next few decades we are going to witness the passing of what has been referred to by many contemporary intellectuals as "bourgeois religiosity." It may be that, while religion will be with us indefinitely, the theologies and the organizational system developed to express the religion of white, middle class, chauvinistic Protestantism will become things of the past. Already the signs of the demise of middle-class religiosity are evident. The mainline denominations are declining and losing influence, while religious groups that embody the sentiments of people in the bottom part of the socioeconomic system are demonstrating rapid growth in size and significance.

The religion of the white middle class has been such a dominant expression of Christianity and has been so readily imposed upon other ethnic groups and economic classes that it has become synonymous with Christianity itself. However, white middle-class Christianity is only one way to express the gospel. Furthermore, there is ample evidence that it really may distort it. Contrary to the Gilbert and Sullivan operetta, God is not an Englishman. Nor is God an American. For that matter, God is not even a middle-class representative of occidental culture. The worship of God need not take place in churches which have Episcopalian, Presbyterian, or even Congregational forms of polity. God can be talked about in other ways and through other institutional instruments than those prescribed by middle-class WASPs.

As Western white middle-class males lose their dominance over the world, the religion that they have espoused (which in many ways has provided a rationalization and glorification of their dominating role) is likely to lose its hold over the consciousness of others. The passing of the "Religion of the Great White Race," as the famous racist author Madison Grant would have called it, was predicted and even encouraged long before there was any evidence of its impending demise. Critiques and condemnations of this variety of religiosity were brilliantly evident in the late nineteenth and early twentieth centuries, and those critiques and condemnations are finding growing popular support as we close in on the twenty-first century. On the one hand, the intellectual aristocrats (i.e., Nietzsche, Kierkegaard, Wagner) criticized its prosaic, dispassionate artificiality and its repression of the potential for the actualization of the individual. On the other hand, the protagonists of the socially disinherited peasants and factory workers (i.e., Dostoyevsky, Tolstoy, and Marx) condemned its arrogant disregard for the plight of the poor and oppressed. All the critics of middle-class religion commonly oppose its rationalizing tendencies, which have intellectualized Christianity into a philosophical system devoid of humanizing potentiality and insensitive to social oppression.

Hegel's Philosophy: The Expression of the Middle-class Mind-set

Any survey of the intellectual critics who have attacked middle-class religion over the last hundred years will reveal that they had at least one thing in common. Each of them made the philosophy of Georg Wilhelm Friedrich Hegel the target of his attacks. Hegel richly deserved this dubious honor because, in many ways, what he wrote exemplified the middle-class mind-set and the middle-class version of Christianity. It is difficult to underestimate the importance of Hegel during this period.

His writings came to control the curricula of European universities. His philosophy both expressed and helped to create the intellectual disposition of "the Great White Race" that had come to dominate the world from its European citadel. His work symbolized for both aristocratic and proletarian critics all that bourgeois religion was about. He provided a rational explanation of the history of humanity that was to these critics the epitome of middle-class ideological thinking. To them, his work embodied in its most perfected form the mind-set of middle-class entrepreneurial, ethnocentric, intellectual arrogance.

Hegel's philosophy was symbolic of what the foes of bourgeois religion were out to destroy. It was Hegel's God that existentialists viewed as the frustrator of human potentiality. It was Hegel's God against whom the Marxists would rant as "the enemy of the people." Furthermore, it is my contention that it is Hegel's God who is dying. It is his middle-class version of Christianity that is becoming passé. Recent intellectual critics of Christianity have understood this. Dietrich Bonhoeffer so predicted, and in our own time we are seeing it happen. An understanding of Hegel's thought is consequently prerequisite to any excursion into the intellectual consciousness of our time and to any comprehension of what is happening to religion in our present age. Morton White, in his thorough review of early twentieth-century philosophy, correctly states that all contemporary thinking is but a postscript to this great German. White was probably right.

Born in Stuttgart in 1770, Hegel was destined to provide the most comprehensive ideology the middle class has ever had. This one-time student for the gospel ministry was a protégé of the historian Schiller and a friend of the romantic philosophers Fichte and Schelling. He became the most important source of philosophy for European and American universities for more than a century. Pontificating from his chair of philosophy at the University of Berlin, Hegel spun out a theology and theory of human history that seemed to synthesize all knowledge and led many to think that the middle class of the Germanic peoples was the bearer of all that was good, true, and beautiful in the world.

Hegelian Idealism and the Doctrine of the Geist

According to Hegel, in the beginning was the *Geist*. This German word can be translated as "mind," "spirit," "idea," and "soul." When

Hegel spoke of the *Geist* he meant all of these things, because for Hegel the *Geist* was God. Hegel, who considered himself to be an orthodox Lutheran, believed that his philosophy would provide a basis for a Christian theology that would make the doctrine of God reasonable to modern scholars. However, Hegel's *Geist* hardly correlates with what traditional evangelical Christians believe about God. First, traditional Christians believe that God existed before there was a physical universe. Hegel did not. Second, traditional Christians believe that God was always a self-fulfilled Being with no need for creating a universe of humanity. Hegel disagreed. Third, traditional Christians believe that God has always been the same, from everlasting to everlasting, unchangeable. This was not Hegel's view.

Hegel teaches that the *Geist* is a Spirit. However, his *Geist* is not an Aristotelian unmoved mover nor an eternally established Platonic archetype. He is not an absolute Being who is the same yesterday, today, and forever. The *Geist* of Hegel is a God who is emerging, developing, and expressing Himself in richer and fuller ways throughout time and throughout human history. Even as advocates of the human potential movement claim that every human being has a drive to be self-actualized, fulfilled, and fully expressed, so Hegel would say of his God that He has a need to express Himself in ways that allow Him to achieve His highest levels of fulfillment. Hegel's doctrine of God proves strange to evangelical Christians who adhere to the traditional creeds of the church. Hegel teaches that the *Geist is* a subjective being driven to express His selfhood and His ultimate fulfillment of self-realization.

The *Geist,* according to Hegel, did not create the physical universe, as traditional Christians believe. Instead the physical universe coexisted with the *Geist.* Even as a human being could not exist and express himself/herself without a physical body, so the *Geist* needs the physical universe as a vehicle for His self-expression. The physical universe, according to Hegel, was structured for the specific purpose of providing the means through which the *Geist* could work out his potential for self-actualization and self-fulfillment.

To the modern reader in Southern California it might seem that Hegel's God could be a candidate for the human potential movement. Certainly, what the advocates of that movement (best represented by the psychology of Abraham Maslow) hope will happen to each human personality comes fairly close to what Hegel believes will happen to the *Geist.* This subjective spiritual being, according to Hegel, has been struggling to achieve self-awareness, self-realization, and self-actualization. Hegel's God is trying to become an ultimately perfected expression of Himself.

Hegel contended that the advent of human beings on the planet Earth represented a new and special epoch for the expressive drive of the *Geist.* With humanity the *Geist* had a rational vehicle for His self-expression, according to Hegel. Human beings could think, reflect, artistically create, and achieve self-consciousness. Hegel taught that in all of these activities there were possibilities for the self-expression of the *Geist* that until then had been impossible. The objective physical universe was resistant to the expression of the *Geist.* The *Geist* was limited in the ways He could fulfill Himself in rocks, rivers, trees, flowers, and even in animals. There were limits to the ways in which the *Geist* could form the inorganic elements and even the organic creatures to give expression to whom and what He wills to be. But with the emergence of humanity there were fantastic new possibilities for the self-expression of the *Geist.*

Hegel believed that all that humanity created was really the *Geist* at work in and through humanity. He taught that the culture of any society—its art, its music, its ethics, its social institutions, and, most of all, its philosophical ideas—were expressions of the *Geist* manifesting Himself and realizing His potential for self-actualization. The genius of humanity demonstrated throughout cultural history is to be understood, according to Hegel, as traces of the *Geist* at work struggling to externalize His subjective nature through this promising rational vehicle. Hegel believed that cultural history is the history of *Geist.* Philosophy, which is the highest cultural creation, according to Hegel, provides the best means within any given society for the *Geist* to demonstrate the highest expression of His selfhood. Hegel also contended that the human race is resistant to the expression of the *Geist.* Dialectical tension results as the subjective spirit endeavors to fashion objective humanity to its own ends. Nevertheless, the *Geist* relentlessly presses on toward the mark of its own high calling—which is its own perfected self-expression.

The Volksgeist: God Expressing Himself through Ethnic Communities

The *Geist,* according to Hegel, does not express His dynamic creative presence in all sectors of humanity simultaneously. Instead, Hegel believed that the *Geist* expresses Himself through a succession of ethnic communities, realizing His potentialities through their respective cultures. For instance, at one stage of His development, the *Geist* expressed Himself in the Egyptian people and through the Egyptian culture. The music, architecture, poetry, social institutions, religious thought, ethics, philosophy, and military conquests of the Egyptians were nothing more and nothing less than the *Geist* expressing Himself in His fullest manner possible to date. The Egyptian people were, during that time, the vehicle or instrument through which the *Geist* developed. The expression of the *Geist* could be witnessed in all that was transpiring in the consciousness of the people in the Egyptian society. The cultural creations of the Egyptians—the sphinx, pyramids, the religion of Ikhnaton, the hieroglyphics of the scribes, the irrigation systems of the farmers, the discoveries of the astronomers and mathematicians, and the efficient government of the pharaohs—were all expressions of the *Geist* creatively evolving within that ethnic culture. At that stage of human history the *Geist* grew and blossomed within the Egyptian people, and at that stage the cultural system of the Egyptians was the manifestation of His spirit.

Hegel taught that, as long as the *Geist* was expressing Himself through the Egyptian community, the Egyptian culture flourished. However, there came a time, he believed, when the potential for a growing self-expression within that community was exhausted. The dialectical tension generated as the subjective *Geist*, struggling to express Himself through the objective Egyptian community, led to an eventual "burn-out." Hegel taught that at that point in human history the *Geist* had to move on and make His dwelling place with a new ethnic community.

Historically, the *Geist* next lived among the Greek people. All that the *Geist* had gained in the Egyptian period was taken up by the Greeks and made part of their culture. The Greek culture then became superior to the Egyptian culture. In its beginnings it possessed all of the magnificent achievements previously expressed through what Hegel called the Egyptian *Volksgeist*. The starting place for the Greeks was what had been the climactic crescendo of Egyptian cultural accomplishments. The *Geist* then found in the Greek culture and in the Greek people a new instrument through which He could realize greater possibilities for self-expression not attainable during His sojourn with the Egyptians.

During the Greek stage of the expression of the *Geist*, the culture of Greece became dynamic and creative, while Egyptian culture gradually became lethargic and static. As the Greek stage of the *Geist* evolved, the whole world had to look toward Greece for vitality and innovation. It was the Greeks' turn to express in their culture all that the *Geist* was becoming. Greek sculpture and architecture then transcended any that had hitherto existed. Greek poetry and drama surpassed that of all previous cultures. Greek philosophy was the highest form of rational reflection in the world.

But the time of the Greeks would also pass. The Greek culture, like the Egyptian culture before it, would become an exhausted vehicle for the emergent creativity of the *Geist*. For the Greeks, too, glory would become only a memory. The *Geist* would pass and move to another culture that had more potential for growth and development than could be expressed in the flourishing of the Hellenistic culture.

Within the Greek stage, the *Geist* achieved something hitherto unknown. Except for the special case of the Jewish people, which Hegel handles as an unusual group possessing a unique revelation from God, the *Geist* had always been an ambiguous entity. With the Greeks that ambiguity was transcended. With the Greeks, as with the Jews, the *Geist* expressed Himself not only *through* human beings but as human beings. In previous cultures the *Geist* had been nonpersonal. Among the Chinese He was the Tao. Among the Indians He was Brahma. Among the Persians He was light. But among the Greeks, as with the Jews, the *Geist* was expressed in human beings.

Hegel pointed out that for all of its superiority over earlier expressions of the *Geist* there was a significant weakness to what occurred among the Greeks. Their human incarnations of God were too parochial. They lacked expressions of the *Geist* that had universal appeal. The other peoples of the world could never identify with the gods of the Greeks because each of them represented a specific city. The national state had not yet been born as a historical reality so the gods of the Greeks expressed the mind of Athens, or the mind of Sparta, or the mind of Corinth. In short, while the gods of the Greeks, being human incarnations of the *Geist*, were superior to the ambiguous amorphous concepts of ultimate reality existent in other earlier cultures, the Greek gods were too small.

Jesus: The Perfect Expression of the Geist

Hegel found in Judaism a culture that was outside the mainstream of the historical development of the *Geist*. He recognized that with the

Jews, the *Geist* became a person with universal dimensions. However, even with the Jews there was something lacking. For while the Jews believe God to be personal and universal, overcoming the parochialism of the gods of Greek mythology, He still lacked the ultimate objective expression. The wholly subjective *Geist* was not yet fully expressed in human flesh. It remained for Jesus of Nazareth to accomplish this ultimate revelation of God. Hegel believed that in Jesus the *Geist* finally achieved perfected self-fulfillment and awareness. In Jesus the *Geist* was able to experience self-reflection and become fully conscious of His selfhood. Jesus was the *telos,* the purpose of history, the glorious expression of the potentiality of God—the fulfillment of the *Geist.*

Hegel contended that it was necessary for Jesus to die. The self-actualized, self-realized, self-fulfilled, and completely expressed God had to die, rise again, and go to "The Father." By that, Hegel meant that the *Geist,* who had fully expressed Himself in Jesus, had to rise beyond that immediate incarnation that was located in a specific time and place in order to make His fully expressed Spirit available to all peoples, at all times, everywhere. Thus, said Hegel, the *Geist,* who was perfectly expressed in Jesus, ascended from His specific locale in space and time and then returned to humanity as the Holy Spirit.

The Time of the Romans and the Birth of the National State

Something special happened in Rome, according to Hegel. In Rome there was the embryo of the modern national state. This modern national state with its rational bureaucratic organization presented a vehicle through which the Holy Spirit could establish the kingdom of God. Until there was a rationally prescribed national state, history could not fully express the *Geist.*

While the Roman Empire emerged in history prior to the time of Jesus, it was not until Christianity invaded the empire that it had the potential to give the *Geist* His full range of expression. Hegel believed that through Christianity the *Geist* might have been a transforming influence in the Roman Empire, molding its various institutions in accord with the will of God. However, for all of its greatness and possibilities, the Roman Empire had one basic flaw: the empire did not allow for the freedom of the individual. Rather, the Roman government called for the subjugation of individual freedom for the good of the state. The state was oriented to a totalitarian system that would curtail the creative possibilities of individuals.

The *Geist* had always been seeking the freedom to fully express Himself, and He had accomplished this goal in Jesus. Following Jesus, He seeks to express Himself in other men and women. Thus, according to Hegel, the *Geist* seeks individuals who will allow Him full expression in their creative works and thinking. And, the *Geist* wills a society that allows individuals the freedom to build and dream, and most of all to philosophize. In such persons, Hegel contends, the *Geist* can repeat what He did in Jesus. Through individuals who express the mind of Jesus, the institutions of the national state can gradually be transformed until they perfectly express the Mind of the *Geist*. Hegel looked forward to a time in history wherein there would be a community created by the *Geist* working through free, fulfilled individuals, a community through which the *Geist* would create as the kingdom of God a national state that would allow for the fullness of God to be lived out on earth.

The Glory Time for the Germanic Peoples

Hegel believed that, after Rome, the *Geist*, who had come to personal self-realization, self-consciousness, and full expression in Jesus, established Himself within the Germanic peoples. According to Hegel, those people who swarmed over the Roman Empire and brought on the Dark Ages were programmed to build a national state that would be based upon the freedom of the individual. These barbarians recognized no authority and hence were conditioned to love individual freedom. It would take them centuries to reinstitute the genius of the national state created by the Romans, but, according to Hegel, eventually that would happen.

Hegel believed that the Germanic peoples were to receive Christianity, and through the Spirit of Jesus, generate the institutions and the modern rational government that would be the epitome of the national state. Analyzing the history of the Germanic peoples (including all those who constituted the barbarian hordes, not just those who made up the state of Germany), he traced in his lectures and writings the ways in which they gradually began to awaken to their time of greatness. He pointed out that Catholicism, the earliest form of Christianity, was inadequate to inspire them to their final greatness. Catholicism, contended Hegel, was not subjective enough; it was too sacramental and lacked sufficient subjective spirituality and personal freedom. It was too confining and materialistic for a people who would give perfect expression to the *Geist*, who had freedom as part of His self-realized nature. However, with the dawn of Protestantism among the Germanic peoples, the stage was set for a climactic expression of the *Geist*. The Reformation allowed for the subjective Spirit of God to flow freely through a community which had all the traits essential for the emergence of the kingdom of God as a historical reality.

One may ask: Is there any conclusion to this process? Will there ever be a culmination of the expression of God in history? Is there any culture in which the *Geist* will express Himself so completely that He will have no need to leave it for another? Is there any ethnic group with so much potential for growth and development that it cannot be exhausted?

There was no reason for Hegel to conclude that the *Geist* would stay with the Germanic peoples forever, but Hegel gives no reasons why He should ever leave. Everything necessary for His full expression within a cultural community was available within the Germanic peoples who inhabited northwestern Europe. The Prussian Lutheran state was a prime example of what the *Geist* is able to do among a people who are so viable as objective vehicles for the expression of the self-expressed *Geist*. It seemed plausible to Hegel that because the Germanic peoples were the latest to be the primary actors in the drama of history, they would possess all that was of worth from earlier cultures. For Hegel and his followers, there would be no music greater than Germanic music, no art greater than what Germanic peoples could produce, and no social structures superior to the Germanic institutions. Furthermore, according to Hegel, the Prussian society seemed to be the most receptive objective reality available within the Germanic peoples for the work of the *Geist*.

The Prussian government, in which his father had been a civil servant, was viewed as the pinnacle of rational organization. The political system of the nineteenth-century Prussian middle class, with the state bureaucracy, was viewed as superior to any that had ever existed. The Prussian bourgeoisie was thought by Hegel to be "the universal class," the bearer to the rest of the world of the highest state of consciousness and the highest forms of knowledge the world would ever know. He was convinced that the Prussian entrepreneurial middle class was endowed with good and honorable intentions and, by its very nature, could only be a blessing to lesser nations and inferior ethnic breeds. The Prussian middle-class culture was, to Hegel, the bearer of the greatest achievements of human reason and it alone possessed in the modern world the capacity for the rational organization that was required to create God's Kingdom. Hegel was convinced that the way in which the German middle class spent its wealth would promote the general good of humanity and provide material progress for all other peoples. He was sure that the emergence and dominance of the Prussian bourgeois culture would assure happiness for the rest of the nations and all other peoples.

The Far-reaching Influence of Hegel

From our contemporary "enlightened" perspective, it seems that Hegel and his followers were both naive and arrogant in their assertions about German culture. But we cannot underestimate the importance and wide acceptance that his philosophy gained throughout Europe in the nineteenth and early twentieth centuries. That ethnocentric German nationalists would buy into such a system is understandable, but Hegelian thought reached far beyond them. Even in America, Hegel's views were given credence.

Perhaps what was responsible for the popularity of Hegelian thought was Hegel's magnificent systematizing of all knowledge into one philosophical system. Maybe it was the fact that Hegel was able to place all national cultures and all of human history within one unified scheme. It may have been that the intellectuals of his time were mesmerized by the host of original insights his philosophy provided. But whatever it was, until the twentieth century Hegel's thinking reigned supreme in Europe, and to a lesser degree in America. Scholars from other nations traveled to Germany to learn, believing that only in the German culture could the fullest expression of truth be grasped. Musicians flocked to Germany, certain that only in that country could the best symphonies be written. Theologians considered German universities to be the only places in which their craft could be developed properly. After all, if the *Geist* was God, as Hegel had taught, then God could best be known within the context of that ethnic culture which was its most complete expression. German theology was the only theology worth knowing, and as the rest of the occidental world sought theological instruction, it was to the Germans that they turned. Thus the works of such German scholars as Friedrich Schleiermacher, D. F. Strauss, A. E. Biedermann, and Julius Wellhausen dominated the theological thinking of the nineteenth century.

It is impossible to understand the trends in twentieth-century theology without a comprehension of the role of Hegelian philosophy as their antecedent. The theological thinkers that gave us "modernism" took their inspiration from Hegel's writings. Among the German theologians who dominated intellectual thought during the twentieth century there was, as a consequence of Hegelian philosophy, an abandonment of the belief in a transcendent God. For theologians from Schleiermacher to Karl Barth, there was the general assumption that God could not exist apart from the universe. God was *immanent,* not transcendent. There was no God beyond the universe. There was no God outside of time and space. The basis for naturalism was firmly established. God, according to the Hegelians, was expressed through nature. There was no room for revelation breaking into human history from the "outside" because there was no God "outside." The salvation of God was the unfolding of the *Geist,* first through the structuring of the physical universe, and later, magnificently, through the history of humanity.

Because of Hegel, the orthodox beliefs that God was before time and space were created and that God created the cosmos and would exist after the cosmos was no more, were abandoned by many. It would not be until Karl Barth, the Swiss proponent of neo-orthodox Protestant theology, brilliantly reaffirmed the radical transcendence of God and made the case for a God who is "totally other than man" that the stranglehold of Hegelian philosophy upon Protestant theology was broken.

It was Hegelian philosophy that gave birth to the doctrine of postmillennialism, a doctrine severely condemned by fundamentalists, and to a lesser degree by evangelicals. Postmillennialism in its theologically liberal form is the doctrine that there is no need for Jesus to return in power, leading an army of angels, in order for the kingdom of God to be established on earth. Theological liberals contend that God is expressing Himself within history and that the kingdom of God will gradually emerge through what God accomplishes through humanity. The postmillennialists have no need for a Second Coming of Christ, nor do they believe there will be such an event. As far as they are concerned, the saving force of the *Geist* is working itself out in human history. Divine intervention from a heaven and from a God who transcends time, space, and humanity is both unnecessary and untenable.

A Note on German Fascism and American Jingoism

Sometimes people wonder how it was possible for Hitler to seduce a people as highly educated and culturally sophisticated as were the German people of the twentieth century. They want to know how Fascism could find a home in a nation sensitized by the music of Bach, the writings of Schiller, and the theology of Schleiermacher. They are puzzled that a society so steeped in religion as to give birth to the Pietistic movement could be the locale in which Nazism emerged.

Those who ask such questions have not given proper consideration to the ways in which Hegelian philosophy conditioned the values and perspectives of the German people. Hegel had told the Germans that their culture was superior to all the other cultures of the world. He had convinced their intelligentsia that the German arts and sciences were the best possible. The leadership of the German nation had been led to believe that its society represented the highest and last stage of the evolution of the *Geist*. In short, Hegel, even if he had not intended to do so, had encouraged the German people to believe that God was a German and that their society was the beginning of the kingdom of God.

When, a century later, Hitler claimed that Germany was about to usher in a millennium that he called the Third Reich, he did so within an intellectual milieu that warranted such expectations. It is easy to understand how the cultural nationalism generated by Hegelianism was the soil in which one of the most diabolical political movements of all time could develop. Indeed, it would have been surprising if something like the Nazi movement had not emerged among the German people. Hegel himself would have despised the Nazi movement. Hitlerism contradicted all that he believed about the freedom of the individual, and he would have viewed a totalitarian state in which individual self-expression was not allowed as a context in which the *Geist* could not be expressed. Nevertheless, Hegelian thought, or at least some twisted versions of it, provided a basis for the Third Reich.

A Warning for America

Most people think that what happened in Germany during the 1930s could never happen here. Most are convinced that a country like America could never become insanely committed to the kind of fascist mentality that was manifested in Nazism. And yet there are disturbing signs in contemporary America. A cultural religion has emerged within this land that gives evidence of providing an ideology for a fascist movement. The mistakes of Germany could be repeated here. It is important that we learn from the mistakes of the past lest our tomorrow be a hideous repeat of Germany's yesterday.

There is in America a new burst of nationalism that increasingly resembles a distorted Hegelian mind-set. It plays upon the worst ethnocentric tendencies of the American people and encourages us to think in megalomaniacal ways. More and more we are hearing claims like these:

"Americans are the best people in the world!"

"Only America can save the world!"

"Our way of life is superior to all others!"

"There's no political system as good as ours. The rest of the world should realize that what is best for them is to do things our way."

"America has been chosen by God to be His instrument for saving the world."

"An America with a strong military is essential for the survival of Christianity."

"America is prosperous because it is an elect nation which God has blessed in a special way."

"Extremism in the name of patriotism is no vice."

Such statements not only ring from the rostrums of political conventions, where such rhetoric is expected and understood to be hyperbole, but they also can be heard from American pulpits. Documentation of this fact has been available since the end of the 1950s when Will Herberg wrote his book *Protestant, Catholic, Jew*. Herberg made us aware that most Americans have been seduced into a religion of Americanism which increasingly is confused with and substituted for evangelical Christianity. Herberg showed us that, all too often, American Protestant churches have become primarily propagators of American social values rather than advocates of biblical values. In such churches, Christianity is turned into a religion of prosperity, guaranteeing the fulfillment of the American Dream to those who live according to biblical principles. It becomes a religion that casts America as the only instrument available to God for the destruction of "atheistic communism," thus justifying an obscene arms buildup. It is a religion that incorporates patriotism into its lifestyle to such a degree that outsiders are left wondering whether loyalty to America is the same thing as loyalty to God.

This nationalistic religion is gradually developing a doctrinal system of its own. Its theology may lack the grand intellectual systematizing of a genius like Friedrich Hegel, but it is, nevertheless, beginning to take a definite form. It may not have the support of the intelligentsia, but it is, nevertheless, gaining wide acceptance among the general populace. It may not gain support outside the confines of the nation, but it is, nevertheless, an ideology that holds remaking the world in the image of America to be a divine imperative. Too many Americans are coming to believe that God is most fully expressed in the American culture, and, concomitantly, that God is an American.

Partly in reaction to our national humiliation over the Vietnam War, and partly because of the ridiculing of our institutions and way of life by the counterculture of the 1960s, Americans have moved toward an affirmation of their institutions, values, and way of life that, while it might be positive in some ways, in other ways has dangerous possibilities. Some of our most prominent television evangelists have become shrill proponents of an America that has Messianic qualities. Our politicians have learned that there are votes and money to insure their reelections if only they will promise to make America, once again, a Christian nation.

There is nothing wrong with good citizenship. The Bible commands it. There is nothing wrong with a people having a positive image of themselves. It's healthy! There is nothing to condemn in a belief that America has something wonderful to offer the rest of the world. It does! What is dangerous is to equate America with the kingdom of God; to view our nation as the new Israel; to believe that the fullness of God's will for the world is manifested through our institutions and in our way of life.

We have a responsibility to share the blessings of God with other people, but we must learn the humility that will allow us to receive from them a host of blessings that we lack. To believe that America is a glorious and wonderful country in which to live does not necessitate the opinion that other nations are somewhat inferior and that we must remold them in the American image.

We must not deify our nation, making its actions infallible. Especially in this nuclear age, we must be careful not to fall into blind patriotism. We must learn to question the behavior of the American government, and not to assume that God is on our side in international affairs. When our armies march into battle, we must not assume that the Lord of history identifies with our cause. We must recognize that American military activities are not necessarily expressions of the will of God. We have been known to be morally wrong in war. If you don't want to make that judgment about the Vietnam War or the war in Nicaragua, then try evaluating the justice of our cause in the American Indian Wars or in the war with Mexico.

Our economic system is not necessarily of benefit to all other nations. Try tracing the consequences of what some of our multinational corporations have done in Latin America, and you will discover negative effects that, in many cases, outweigh any good they have done.

Our cultural values are not superior to those generated by other societies. As difficult as it may be for some of us to accept, not all the other peoples of the world want to become like us. They admire our technology and even envy our wealth, but they also are aware of our spiritual poverty and our disintegrating morality. If we are to avoid the kind of cultural religion that led Germany into fascism we must be on guard against nationalistic extremism. Let us be suspicious of religious leaders who in any way even imply the following:

1   That the American middle-class lifestyle is biblically prescribed.
2   That God has ordained America to establish in other nations the kind of political system we espouse.
3   That capitalism is necessarily Christian and therefore should be the only economic system to exist.
4   That the manifest destiny of America is to give its way of life and values to the rest of the world.

The middle-class American cultural Christianity that is commonly evident in the religious media and in some of our churches often expresses such doctrines.

It is this American middle-class religiosity that has come under attack in this last part of the twentieth century, and rightly so. It is the God of this cultural Christianity who is dead, or to be more accurate, who never lived.

If this kind of religion is what is being attacked and condemned by radical intellectual critics, we ought not to condemn the condemners too readily. Instead, we should listen to their criticisms of cultural Christianity so that we might be the more able to eliminate its blinding and binding influence upon us. Perhaps then we will be free to grasp biblical Christianity with clarity.

Part Two

The Attack from Above

3

Nietzsche: The Glorious Antichrist

FRIEDRICH WILHELM NIETZSCHE was born October 14, 1844. His father, a Lutheran clergyman, died when Friedrich was not quite five years of age and the boy was raised by his extremely religious mother and sister. It was generally assumed that this precocious child would one day follow his father and enter the ministry of the church. There was an attractive piety about the young Nietzsche, and it has been reported that when he was called upon to read the Scriptures during the chapel hour at his school, he did so with such feeling that tears were brought to the eyes of his listeners. However, his spiritual piety slowly died and he gradually abandoned his early religiosity for skepticism. No exact time or special occasion marked Nietzsche's abandonment of his faith, but by the time he started his university training at Bonn, those who knew him could recognize his antipathy to religion.

At Bonn he met and studied under one of the most important theologians of his time, Friedrich Ritschl. However, the negative attitudes of Ritschl toward any beliefs about the deity of Christ and doctrines of a transcendent God provided little stimulus for Nietzsche to become a Christian. It was Ritschl who first recognized the genius of Nietzsche and encouraged him to pursue an academic career. And it was primarily through Ritschl's influence that Nietzsche was appointed a professor of philology at the University of Basel at the age of twenty-four.

Philology is a discipline that concentrates on the Greek classical writers. And while Nietzsche would later endeavor to make a transition into philosophy, it was his acquaintance with the Greek classical dramatists that largely provided the framework for the development of his thought. It is amazing that he received such a prestigious academic appointment so early in life, especially in view of the meaning of a professorship within the context of the European universities. Furthermore, Nietzsche gained this position without having written a doctoral dissertation or having earned a doctor of philosophy degree. Later the University of Leipzig granted him a Ph.D. on the basis of some essays he had written in undergraduate days, but it is evidence of his brilliance that one of the most prestigious universities of Europe welcomed him to its highest academic circles even though he lacked the proper credentials.

His contributions as a teacher were limited. Almost from the beginning of his academic years, he was haunted by poor health. He was constantly sick, regularly canceling classes, and thereby hindered from providing inspiration for his students. His seminars declined in popularity. Few students paid attention to this sickly philologist, and his distinguished beginnings did not lead to the fulfillment of what had at first appeared to be a promising academic career.

After a few years of struggling with his teaching duties, Nietzsche gave up and retired from the classroom. A small pension provided by the university allowed him to live out the rest of his life in some degree of comfort and, most important, allowed him the opportunity to write.

The Shaping of Nietzsche's Thought

Undoubtedly, his mother and sister conditioned his thinking. They had raised him, and their religious orientation conditioned Nietzsche to give serious consideration to the ultimate meaning of human existence. The religious training they had provided was not sufficient to induce Nietzsche to embrace the metaphysical presuppositions of Christianity, but it did orient him to ask religious questions throughout his life.

As he came to study the writings of the Greek dramatists, he was introduced to two Hellenistic gods that provided motifs for his analysis and philosophy of human existence. In the figures of Dionysus and Apollo he found symbols of two orientations to life; two styles of philosophy; two ways of facing the tragedies of existence.

Nietzsche viewed life as tragic. For him there was no transcendental God who could make everything turn out all right in the end. Those Christians who quote Romans 8:28 in times of trouble are people whom he would despise because of their unwillingness to acknowledge that life does not work itself out in a happy resolution. Nietzsche did not find in human existence the hope that justice and goodness would triumph, nor did he cynically believe that evil would ultimately express itself in history.

Neither God nor the devil are involved in being human, so far as Nietzsche was concerned. And it is in the face of these realities that he held out the Dionysian lifestyle as worthy of noble emulation.

The way of Dionysus is an attempt to stop the passing moment. It is a lust for knowledge, beauty, youth, and superhuman power. The Dionysian spirit calls for a "tragic optimism" in the face of tragedy. It enables us to look confidently into the agony of human existence and empathize with the craving for survival and its terror in the face of impending destruction. Nietzsche moved beyond the romanticism of Rousseau in his affirmation of life. He saw that a person could transcend despairing nihilism only by yielding to that spirit of Dionysus which has a superabundance of creative energy and craves change and "becoming." The Dionysian spirit was, for Nietzsche, the overcoming of the overly optimistic *Geist* of Hegel. It was a rejection of the confident belief, so evident in Hegelian philosophy, that all contradictions are ultimately resolved in a positive fashion. As he embraced the Dionysian spirit, Nietzsche found the means to overcome personally the despair of nihilism, not with the Pollyanna pretense he perceived in Hegel, but in an affirmation of the potentiality for self-transcendence. In notes that were made late in his life, he wrote this description of the Dionysian spirit.

> . . . an ecstatic affirmation of the totality of life as what remains constant—not less potent, not less ecstatic—throughout all fluctuation; the great pantheistic sharing of joy and distress which blesses and endorses even the ghastliest, the most questionable elements in life, the eternal will for regeneration, fruitfulness, recurrence; the awareness that creation and destruction are inseparable.

The Dionysian spirit rejects the cold rationality of the Hegelian system, and calls for a passionate embracing of life and its incredible possibilities for euphoria and explosive joy. It gives expression to the lust for realizing one's potentiality by going beyond what life is supposed to provide in the way of gratifications. It is feeling, emotion, dynamism, ecstasy, sensuality, aliveness—all of which carry the worshiper into a state of personal transcendence that leaves behind the prosaic "good life" prescribed by bourgeois virtues.

Nietzsche, for a few years, thought he had found in the music of his friend Richard Wagner the instrument for stimulating these Dionysian passions. He himself tried to write oratorios and operas that would lift involved listeners out of the mundane passionless rational existence of middle-class society. But Nietzsche's limited artistic ability betrayed his hopes for musical genius. Instead, he attached himself to Richard Wagner, and sought in the music dramas of this man, who temporarily became the father he never had, the instrument for release from the deadened consciousness of those confined by the requisites of respectable society. Wagner's operas seemed to gather up listeners in a whirl of crescendos that infused them with a sense of power. Through Wagner's music, the Dionysian ecstasy of abandonment, self-transcendence, and mastery could be experienced. Through identification with Siegfried, the main character in Wagner's famous *Ring* operas, deliverance from the societally imposed constraints of human emotions, lusts, and hunger for power could be achieved.

Wagner disappointed him. Nietzsche watched with disillusionment as his one-time idol gradually was seduced by public acclaim and yielded to the temptation to produce music for general consumption rather than for the liberation of the soul. The elitist mind-set of Wagner gave way to the pay and benefits derived from the adoration of the masses whom Nietzsche had come to detest.

Without Wagner to provide the way of salvation, Nietzsche looked elsewhere. Bizet's opera *Carmen* gave him some cause for rejoicing. He was particularly overwhelmed by the closing scene of the opera in which Don Jose cries out, "Yes, I have killed her, I—my adored Carmen." This, according to Nietzsche, captured the tragic passion of love and life. He went to twenty performances of the opera and each time was intoxicated with the Dionysian passion he experienced in Bizet's music.

Finally, Nietzsche turned to his own artistic talent to portray the glory of Dionysus and the highest expression of human transcendence. He used his incomparable skill as a poet to write the literary masterpiece *Thus Spake Zarathustra*. His story and description of this fictitious Persian prince allowed him to give the world a vivid picture of what a person who transcended typical human nature and realized the depth and passion of the Dionysian spirit would be like. Zarathustra is the savior who preaches self-transcendence and prophesies a future in which humanity can live without God. In the story, Zarathustra comes down from his mountain retreat in order to challenge humanity with his message. It is a message of hope that will equip humanity to look into the abyss of nothingness that results from an end of religious faith and make it ring with laughter. He wants to overcome pessimism through the sheer force of the will. Zarathustra calls his listeners to a higher stage of humanity in which the fullness of humanness is realized. He is awed by the potential of humans, but cries over their failure to live up to their capacity for abundant living. The contrast between the shallow, passionless, orderly, rational lifestyle of petty and vulgar people and the fullness of life among the ancient Dionysian Greeks shocks him.

Nietzsche is noted for having urged human beings to realize that they are only a stage in the evolutionary process. Having read the works of Charles Darwin, Nietzsche was convinced that just as it was the nature of apes to be transcended by the emergence of humankind, so it is the destiny of the human race to be transcended by a new order of beings which he calls the *supermen*. This human transcendence would not be crudely biological. It would not come from the process of natural selection described by Darwin. Instead, the next stage of evolution would result from an exercise of the will. Humans would have to will the next stage of development. This transcendence would come as humans take their innate "will to power" and turn it into a process of self-mastery. Human beings have an innate drive to exercise power and dominate others, according to Nietzsche. The determination to use that "will to power" to remake themselves into superior persons is essential for the emergence of the higher form of humanity. Zarathustra exemplified this next stage of evolution. For Nietzsche, Zarathustra was the symbol of human transcendence. He was an expression of the superman.

Nietzsche believed that human beings achieve their highest state of self-actualization when they aspire to be heroes. To be heroic requires that persons attempt to accomplish things hitherto reserved for their gods. Those who would be heroic must transcend the highest expectations prescribed by society. They must seek aesthetic achievements that defy ordinary imagination. The heroes daringly rise above what is done by ordinary people who are governed by rational morality. They write music, paint pictures, fight battles, challenge nature, and attempt feats that call for superhuman qualities. Heroes usually reach for goals that prove unattainable and, consequently, fail. Tragedy is the glorious end of the hero.

Unfortunately, contends Nietzsche, there are few, if any, tragic heroes left in the world. The age of the ancient Greeks was full of tragic heroes, but our age is full of pathetic persons. Those who make up "the herd" (Nietzsche's title for the German middle-class citizens whom Hegel viewed as the highest expression of the *Geist*) live and die without the passions that motivate acts of heroism. These inferior specimens of humanity also fail, but because their aspirations were so paltry and their hopes so limited, their failures lack tragic dimensions and, therefore, their lives can only be labeled pathetic. "The hero," says Nietzsche, "lives dangerously; he builds his cities at the foot of Vesuvius." Zarathustra is that hero whom Nietzsche wishes to be born in our time. If Wagner was the father he never had, then Zarathustra was the son Nietzsche wished he had had.

Christianity and the Apollonian Way

Even as Dionysus represents, for Nietzsche, all that rings of ascendancy, heroism, exuberance, and passion, the Greek god Apollo represents cowardice, stagnation, loss of creativity, and the death of the human spirit. In his discussions of the Greeks, Nietzsche points out that their glorious period of history, which was marked by Dionysian dynamism, was followed by an Apollonian period in which their culture moved through senility toward death.

The Apollonian age was marked by rationality and conformity to the morality of the herd. It was the age of Socrates, Plato, and Aristotle. Surprisingly, Nietzsche did not admire these so-called giants of Greek philosophy. Instead, he viewed them as men who were incapable of living life to its fullest, unable to express the exuberance of lust and human desire, devoid of the passions for the affirmation of life. In Nietzsche's view, these men developed theories of life that would restrain human passion, because none was left in them. They constructed ethical systems that would restrain the heroes, because they themselves were incapable of heroic acts. They talked of eternal essence and ultimate "being" because their lives were static and empty of the capacity for "becoming."

To Nietzsche, philosophical reflection occurs when the ability to act has been lost. Humans develop "systems" when they have lost the craving for excitement. He taught that philosophy is not the highest expression of humanity, as Hegel had thought, but rather is evidence that the people who produce it are almost dead. And the death of any culture is marked by the cold rationality of the Apollonian way of life. The end of heroism is reached when humanity can no longer face the realities of life and death without the promise of a happy ending. The Apollonians cannot face the absurdity of existence with honesty. Instead they look for some philosophy that comforts them with the delusion that everything works out for good in the end, and that the "virtue" of complying with the morality of the herd will be rewarded. Nietzsche despises such a morality and lifestyle. He longs for the rebirth of heroism, the salvation of the superman, the rekindling of the spirit of Dionysus.

The Nietzschean Hatred for Christianity

It has been said that it is better to have an enemy who understands you than a friend who does not. If that is true, then Christians should be pleased to have Nietzsche in their world. He sees Christianity for what it is and rejects it for what it is. Not many preachers of the gospel grasp the meaning of the message of Jesus as well as does this atheistic existentialist. If Nietzsche does anything for us that is worthy of our serious attention, it is this: he makes us clearly aware of the teachings of Jesus. He takes us beyond the watered-down versions of Christian morality espoused by the middle class. He forces us to see Christianity stripped of the cultural accretions that have been provided by the bourgeoisie to make it acceptable to "the comfortable herd that fills the churches."

A careful reading of the Sermon on the Mount (Matt. 5:7) sets forth the main emphasis of the teachings of Jesus. Nietzsche condemns these teachings with hatred. Jesus taught that the blessed are those who are willing to give up their wealth to feed the poor. For Nietzsche, sacrifice to preserve the unsuccessful specimens of humanity is always a mistake. The wretched of the earth who lack the courage and strength to assert themselves in the face of insurmountable odds do not deserve the sacrifices of the *Ubermensch* (anyone who would aspire to be a superman). Nietzsche says that Christians have preserved too much of that which ought to perish—and that they have brought about the corruption of the European race. He claims that Jesus calls His followers to commit themselves to meet the needs of the hungry and to minister to the oppressed. In opposition to such doctrine, Nietzsche believes that each human being should be committed to his/her own self-transcendence. Instead of self-sacrifice, Nietzsche calls for self-assertion so that the individual might do something worthy of a tragic hero. Nietzsche calls for the fulfillment of one's potential rather than the self-denial required by Christ.

While Nietzsche condemns the teachings of Christ, he admires His honesty. Jesus does not conceal the meaning of discipleship. Far more despicable to this philosopher, who called himself the Antichrist, was the religiosity of the Lutheran middle class so affirmed by Hegel. Middle-class Christianity did not challenge people to the heroism of the self-asserting superman on the one hand, nor did it call for the radical self-sacrifice of Christ on the other. Nietzsche was disgusted with a church that lacked the honesty to admit that its Lord really required that those who would call themselves Christians be more like Mother Teresa and Saint Francis than like the well-heeled businessman in the posh pew of the institutional church.

Nietzsche finds in Jesus the antithesis to his own beliefs about power. Whereas Jesus requires that His followers empty themselves of power and assume the role of servants, Nietzsche calls humanity to an exercise of power for the purpose of achieving self-glorification. Nietzsche understood Jesus well when he claimed that the Nazarene would make humanity into a Kingdom of people who defined themselves as slaves and understood happiness to be the result of service. He saw this and rejected the plan.

Nietzsche despises the church of the middle class which conceals the message of Christ in its bourgeois theologies. The middle-class Christianity so typical in the Germany of Nietzsche's day, and so typical in American Protestantism, refuses to face up to the fact that Jesus calls for the abandonment of power. "Resist not evil" is core to the gospel. "Love your enemies" is a paramount doctrine of Christ. Yet the church is unwilling on the one hand to be pacifist, and on the other, it is unwilling to call people to express the will to power in self-mastery. Nietzsche reacted to the church as Jesus Himself might react. One can almost hear the philosopher echoing the words of the Lord as He says, "I wish you were for me or against me! I wish that you were either hot or cold! But because you are lukewarm I spew you out of my mouth!"

Christ died in a way that perfectly manifested His nature: He resisted not evil.

There is a consistency in Jesus that Nietzsche did not find in His successors. Jesus calls people to suppress those traits which Nietzsche believed were the glory of our humanity. Jesus would have us tame the lusts of the flesh and the craving for personal glory. However, the middle-class church refuses to pay the price of discipleship on the one hand, yet refuses to affirm humanity's true nature on the other.

Nietzsche had a strange admiration for Jesus even as he rejected His teachings as a negation of the human spirit. He saw Jesus in mutiny against the social order of His day, and as an enemy of the mediocrity of the established religion of the Pharisees. Jesus, so far as Nietzsche was concerned, was not a representative of the "herd morality" that typified the masses in ancient Israel. However, Nietzsche believed that the apostles disfigured the image of Jesus and made Him into something He was not. Whereas Jesus taught that all humans could become sons of God (supermen, in Nietzsche's terms), the followers of Jesus turned his teachings into what could be called a theology of resentment. According to Nietzsche, the followers of Jesus were resentful people who developed the doctrine of the elect. These twisters of Jesus, said Nietzsche, created a religion which protects them against the powerful who reach for self-conquest and self-actualization. Being weak slave-types, they cleverly transformed Jesus into a punisher of those who would transcend their humanness and become like the *Ubermensch*. Nietzsche believed that they made Jesus into a God who would not only protect them but also prevent those who are superior from exercising their powers. He believed that the Scriptures were deliberately written by the disciples to change Jesus into a symbol of a religion of resentment. Those who succeeded Jesus delighted in the doctrine that they were "the saved" and all others were "the lost." With despicable malice they condemned to Hell those who would not yield to them and their confining herd morality. They created a religion out of Jesus which would enable the inferior to gleefully squeal to those who aspire to heroism that if they do not give up their dreams for greatness they will be punished by God. Beneath such a theology Nietzsche saw the resentment of slaves who envied those who could throw off the yoke of a herd morality that prevented the exercise of human powers and the lust for life. He called upon those with sufficient character to reject this religion and cast aside the belief in the God of the resentful. He called for an abolition of the religion that promised so much after life because it had nothing to affirm in life here in this world.

A Christian Appraisal of Nietzsche

A review of Nietzsche's attack on middle-class religion would generate some approval from many thoughtful Christians. The affirmation of mediocrity, the lack of passion for life, and the static rationale so characteristic of bourgeois religiosity make it a poor substitute for the challenging, emotionally explosive and dynamic spirituality introduced by Jesus. Nietzsche was correct in his assessment of Jesus because the philosopher recognized that the lifestyle He prescribed required the sacrificing of wealth in order to meet the needs of the poor, a willingness to love one's enemies and an assumption of the servant role toward everyone. The transformation of Christianity into a religion that expresses neither the radical commitment to sacrificial love required by Jesus, nor the total abandonment to the spirit of Dionysus called for by Nietzsche is deserving of condemnation. Insofar as Nietzsche assumes the role of the destroyer of the cultural religion that is so typical of middle-class churches, his condemnation is, in the minds of many, a positive thing. Too often the religion of the bourgeoisie is such a watered-down version of the message of Jesus that His early followers would be hard pressed to recognize it as the faith for which they were willing to die.

Many people who become Christians discover that membership in the church is not a call to express their individuality in creative and positive ways but, rather, carries the expectation of conformity to the requisites of a religious institution. Too often the church has a host of legalistic requirements, and compliance with those requirements is considered essential before persons can confirm themselves to be "true born-again Christians." Usually proof-texts are used to prove that compliance with the stifling norms of this middle-class religiosity is required by God. Sermons in some churches are moralistic admonitions to submit to these norms rather than inspiring challenges that call the listeners to realize their highest potentialities and to live life to the fullest. When this is the case, religion deserves to be rejected in favor of something more life-affirming.

When, as a teenager, I became a Christian, I was attracted by the challenges of church youth leaders who told me that my new lifestyle was to be one of nonconformity. I was told that the world would not without trouble allow me to live the "higher" life to which I had become committed. I would be pressured by worldly people who would view my new life in Christ as a judgment of their own lifeless, meaningless conformity to values and expectations of society. The world, so I was told, would do its best to bring me into conformity with its ways.

In reality my secular friends hardly gave me any trouble at all. Some of them looked upon my new faith and lifestyle with curiosity. Others looked upon it with respect.

I remember carrying my Bible when I went to school. I made sure it was prominently displayed on top of my other books. One day my Jewish friend, Jerry, noticed my ever-visible Bible and casually inquired, "Hey, Tony! What's that?"

"That," I told him, "is my Bible. I've committed my life to Christ and from now on I'm going to live according to the principles of God's Word."

I waited for his response. I was sure that he would laugh at me in derision; that he would ridicule my religious commitment; that he would begin to "persecute me for righteousness' sake." Instead, he responded with genuine respect, "Gee—that's really neat!"

I didn't know how to handle that. I had been led to expect a different response. I had anticipated social sanctions designed to bring me into conformity with "the ways of the world." But I discovered, much to my chagrin, that the world could not care less about my newly adopted lifestyle.

My new life was not free from social pressure to conform, however. As a matter of fact, I soon learned that I was about to experience group censure and control beyond anything I could have imagined. But that pressure to conform did not come from the secular society; it came from people in the church. Those who had promised me "new freedom in Christ," now pressured me to conform to a confining lifestyle. They expected of me a piety which led me to pretend that I was something that I really was not. So I pretended that I was no longer "turned on" by sexual desires; that I was free from appetites for "worldly pleasures;" that my mind was purified and my motives were holy. I quickly learned that there was a certain way in which I was expected to talk, that there were certain views I was supposed to articulate, and certain beliefs I was supposed to espouse. I learned quickly and I adapted well. I allowed myself to be swept into the religiosity of the church.

This is the sort of thing that Nietzsche despised. He condemned the willingness of men and women to allow themselves to be controlled by the expectations of "the herd." He railed against those persons who deny their true humanness in order to gain the approval of a group that has neither the will nor the courage to be authentic human beings. He looked with disgust upon those creatures who could be "supermen," but refuse to pay the price demanded of those who break with the conventional mores of the prevailing socioreligious system. To Nietzsche, the confinements of religiosity were instruments for the denial of humanness.

Jesus would have concurred with Nietzsche's condemnation of "the herd morality." Jesus called men and women into a new era in which they would go beyond legalism and allow an indwelling spirit to make them into nonconformists, alive to the possibilities of a new and higher life.

My argument is that Nietzsche did not so much reject Jesus as reject what middle-class religion had done to Jesus. Nietzsche was not even aware of the fact that the Jesus whom he opposed had come to declare a message of liberation from the impossibility of living under the oppressive confinement of religious law. The philosopher failed to understand that Jesus had come to call humanity beyond religiosity and mundane living to become "sons of God" (John 1:12) and "joint heirs together with Christ" (Rom. 8:17). The middle-class religion of his German youth did not reveal to Nietzsche that Christianity is basically a call to achieve a higher level of being than our present humanity. Religion as he saw it failed to communicate to him the awesome implications of the biblical good news: "It doth not yet appear what we shall be" (1 John 3:2). There are infinite potentialities in human beings, and Christ came to deliver us from the things which would frustrate us from realizing those potentialities. Nietzsche failed to see in Christianity a call to reject the confining and oppressing religiosity of the ruling social classes and to express the spiritual dynamism that waits for the possibility of full expression.

Christianity is an antiestablishment movement that the ruling classes of society have always endeavored to suppress because of its revolutionary dimensions. Jesus himself was put to death by the ruling establishment of His day because He posed a threat to the socioreligious order of Israel. His enemies recognized that Jesus was committed to destroy the religion that confined the human spirit and established regulations that ensured social order at the expense of human spontaneity. On the cross, Jesus exposed the socioreligious system of His day for what it was, and His death clearly demonstrates that the socioreligious system of our day is also His enemy. If the cultural religion was really what it claimed to be—an expression of God—it would not have led its adherents to crucify the Son of God. As the apostle Paul says: "When He had disarmed the rulers and authorities, He made a public display of them, having triumphed over them through Him" (Col. 2:15, NASB).

This is not to say that there are no major differences between the doctrine of Nietzsche and the teachings of Christ when it comes to ways by which to fulfill human potentialities. Nietzsche believes that the basic drive of human personality is the "will to power," and he teaches that the gratification and fulfillment of human destiny comes through breaking restraints and exercising that will. On the other hand, Jesus teaches that personal fulfillment comes through being loving. By living according to the way laid down by Jesus, human beings reach their highest level of existence. The transcendence of their "old nature" and their greatest sense of joyous freedom comes through being loved and pouring out love toward God and others. By being open to the capacity to love that comes from God, we are empowered to express love. Jesus taught that it is in expressing love that we transcend our present nature and realize the fantastic possibilities that lie inherent in our humanity. However, we would lack this capacity for self-transcendence without His gift of grace: "We love because He first loved us."

Both Nietzsche and Jesus call us to transcend our present condition. Both pass negative judgment on the religion of the middle class because of its legalistic bondage of the human spirit. Both teach that humanity is called to live with exuberance and joy in the face of the tragedies of existence. But Nietzsche and Jesus have opposite ways of responding to these challenges. Seldom has the antithesis to the way of Jesus been so clearly defined as in the way proposed by Nietzsche. Those of us who would break out of the confinements of a middle-class ecclesiology that stifles human potentialities must choose between these two ways. We must decide whether salvation lies in "the will to power" or in the love that comes through the grace of God.

As for me, I am committed to the way of Jesus. The decision to be so committed is not simply an arbitrary one on my part. It was not simply a "leap of faith" made without empirical support to justify the choice of the one option over the other. I believe that both history and personal experience provide ample evidence that love is greater than power.

Nietzsche's call to heroic living proves very attractive to many Christians. I wish with all my heart that the church would do more to explore the call for heroism and self-transcendence that is set forth in the Bible. It seems to me that a careful reading of Scripture would show that Jesus calls us out of the ordinariness of typical "religious" living to explore the possibilities for greatness that lie inherent in our humanity. I believe that Jesus came to establish the basis for a new kind of personhood that can be realized only insofar as we shed the securities of socially prescribed religiosity and dare to take the steps of faith leading to authentic salvation. I believe that now, more than ever, Christianity should reemphasize the heroic dimension of the biblical revelation. True Christianity would be a more than adequate response to the Nietzschean complaint that Christianity discourages heroism.

Jesus calls for a commitment that challenges people to abandon courageously the securities of family, friends, and ecclesiastical legitimation in order to follow Him into the glories of a higher lifestyle and quality of being.

The elect of Jesus are few in number, although the call to become children of God is for everyone. There are very few who are willing to pay the price. The rich young ruler was not (Mark 10:17–22); King Agrippa was not (Acts 26:28), Ananias and Sapphira were not (Acts 5:1–11). Jesus required a radical commitment, and He indicated that those who would share in His Kingdom must realize the full ramifications of this commitment. Jesus said that no person can serve two masters and that, ultimately, everyone is required to decide whether or not to totally embrace the lifestyle of His new Kingdom.

While the rewards of such commitments will not be worldly wealth, power, and prestige, Jesus promises far more:

> Jesus said, "Truly I say to you, there is no one who has left house or brothers or sisters or mother or father or children or farms, for My sake and for the gospel's sake, but that he shall receive a hundred times as much now in the present age, houses and brothers and sisters and mothers and children and farms, along with persecutions; and in the world to come, eternal life. But many who are first, will be last; and the last, first."
>
> Mark 10:29–31, NASB

The 1960s' television series *Star Trek* was my all-time favorite. The series featured Captain Kirk of the Starship *Enterprise;* his first officer, Spock; and a collection of other strange, exotic, and wonderful crew members. This show always began with the *Enterprise* zooming into outer space, as a hidden spokesman told the viewing audience that these heroes were challenged "*to boldly go where no man has gone before.*" In so many ways that simple line captures for me much of the meaning of an authentic Christian commitment. Instead of becoming a simple conformist to a religious lifestyle prescribed by the church, the Christian is called by Jesus to go where no one has ever gone before, to do what no one has ever done before, and to be what no one has ever been before.

In authentic Christianity, each Christian is called to realize that he or she has a particular mission to live out for God. To transform this world into the world that ought to be, there is a crucial role that God has preordained for each individual to play. Jesus would have the world realize that there can be cosmic significance to the life of any individual who realizes what God has planned for him/her "from before the foundation of the world" (Eph. 1:4), a task worthy of a "child of God."

Christianity is an invitation to do battle with "the principalities and powers and rulers of this age" in the struggle to realize a new social order built upon justice and love. What Jesus seeks is far more dramatic than simply to make humanity into a herd of "nice" people who conform, more or less, to ecclesiastical requisites. He would have each person aspire to a heroic place in the history of the world's salvation. Christianity at its best does not attract people with "cheap grace" promised to those who give minimal intellectual assent to certain theological propositions and offer a semblance of obedience to religiously prescribed behavioral expectations. Instead, true Christianity is a challenge to offer up one's life to live out a heroic calling of eternal significance.

In preaching I regularly invite people to sacrifice everything that the world can offer in order to live out a heroic mission for God. The response to this kind of invitation exceeds, by far, the response to an invitation that simply promises heaven after death. I have discovered that a Christianity built on heroic challenges is far more attractive than a middle-class religion that promises comfort and good fortune to its adherents. All in all, I am convinced that Christianity loses far more by expecting too little of people than it would by challenging them to sacrifice everything in heroic ventures for God.

As Nietzsche struggled to set forth his call to heroic living he had to make one essential assertion about the nature of the universe. He had to postulate a "doctrine of recurrence." Nietzsche came to teach that everything that "is" will repeat itself many times. He believed that every event, every person, every molecule that "is," would happen over and over again, even as it had in the past. It is Nietzsche's doctrine of recurrence that gives the individual the full meaning of his/her heroic action.

Nietzsche claims that only by optimistically willing to embrace life with all of its tragic dimensions can an individual be considered truly heroic. He believes that humans who would say "yea" to life must do so in the full awareness that whatever is suffered in willing self-transcendence will be repeated again and again. It is the willingness to affirm the potentialities of humanity in spite of the repetitious pains associated with making such an affirmation that turns individuals into heroes. There must be an eternal significance to the tragic suffering of heroes in order to give them the cosmic and ultimate meaning that their commitment requires. And Nietzsche finds that eternal significance in their willingness to suffer the agonies of self-transcendence even with the awareness that those agonies will repeat themselves endlessly.

For Christians there is also the need to establish their heroism in some manner that gives their commitments and actions eternal significance. They find their significance in the fact that what they do is essential to the cosmic purposes of God. Christians come to believe that the entire universe is poised and waiting for them to live out their potentialities, transcend their present state of being, and become incarnations of a new and higher humanity.

> For we know that the whole creation groans and suffers the pains of childbirth together until now. And not only this, but also we ourselves, having the first fruits of the Spirit, even we ourselves groan within ourselves, waiting eagerly for our adoption as sons, the redemption of our body.
>
> Romans 8:22, 23, NASB

The universe longs for each of us to be what we are called to be, and by living in such heroic fashion to deliver it from its "groanings and travail." Christians should be led to believe that it is not simply for personal fulfillment, but for the redemption of the cosmos, that they have been called to be heroes.

Nietzsche might find some value to Christianity so described. But he would claim, nevertheless, that the fullness of heroism could not be achieved within the Christian system because in the end it is too

Apollonian. It is too neatly tied up in the end, according to Nietzsche. He says that Christianity turns all suffering and tragedy into joy and blessedness in the end, robbing them of eternal significance. While the divine missions to which Christians are called can give their lives heroic dimensions, Nietzsche claims that only heroism that is eternally tragic, yet full of optimism, is capable of providing the self-transcendence that makes for supermen. Everything becomes happy and glorious in the eschaton of the Christians. When people believe in such an end to things, the courage to live heroically is not too much to ask. For Nietzsche, true heroism comes when such Apollonian theodicies are set aside and those who aspire to greatness embrace the task of self-transcendence without any promise of heavenly reward.

I agree with Nietzsche that his way is far more courageous than the way prescribed by Jesus. Indeed, the way laid out by Jesus leaves us with very little in which to find personal glory in Nietzsche's terms. Insofar as self-glorification is a positive value for Nietzsche, Christianity proves to be the extreme opposite of his expectations. On the other hand, I wonder whether any human beings are capable of the tragic heroism outlined by Nietzsche. He, himself, by his own admission failed to become a superman. Furthermore, he knew of none who had achieved this kind of greatness. He saw the self-transcending humanity as "yet to come." The heroism of Christianity is realizable by the grace of God. The heroism of Nietzsche is unrealized in human history because of the frailty of the race. It is up to each of us to decide whether it is better to embrace a realizable heroism that, brings glory to God or an impossible heroism that brings glory to the not yet existing superman. It is up to each of us to decide between a heroism that is possible for everyone and a heroism that is possible only for an aristocratic elite that has not yet come into being.

4

Kierkegaard: The Disturbing Dane

SÖREN KIERKEGAARD lived between 1813 and 1855, but it was not until the twentieth century that the fullness of his genius was recognized. He was not a world-renowned philosopher, for two reasons. First, he wrote in Danish, a language unfamiliar to most other Western nations. It was not until after World War II that English translations of his works were readily available. Second, he wrote about a culture that was just being born. The modern secular society with its bored and anxiety-ridden citizens was not to burst into full bloom until a century after his death. He was truly a man ahead of his time.

This "Gloomy Dane," as he is sometimes called, was well known in his native city of Copenhagen. He wrote for the local press, published a variety of books, and was very much a part of the "in" social circles of the community. He was known about town as a dilettante. Few suspected that this witty, life-of-the-party bachelor was really a brooding philosopher preoccupied by guilt and threatened by death. He made it a practice to appear in the lobbies of the Copenhagen theaters prior to performances. When others took their seats at show time he would hurry to his apartment and feverishly write his books and articles. At intermission he would be back, laughing and joking for all to see. Then he would again return to his flat to work once the intermission was ended. He did this because he wanted to conceal the fact that he was writing what proved to be some of the most caustic critiques of Danish society and religious life.

Kierkegaard was the antithesis of Friedrich Hegel. He criticized Hegel's work because it did not address the ultimate question of life: "How can I become a Christian?" Hegel had developed a grand system of rational philosophy which explained how God manifested Himself in history, but that was not important to Kierkegaard. Objectively demonstrated knowledge, according to Kierkegaard, could not provide salvation.

Truth, he contended, was something inward that could be known only subjectively, and as such was beyond anything that Hegel discussed.

For Kierkegaard there are two kinds of knowledge. One is objective knowledge, such as that handled by scientists and mathematicians, and the other is religious knowledge, that can only be grasped inwardly. Kierkegaard argues that truth that answers the ultimate questions of human existence is not available to the detached speculative mind but is experienced only by those who struggle and suffer their way toward an understanding of life. Whereas objective knowledge consists of facts that can be handled as objects of interest, existential truth can be grasped only by the individual who is passionately committed and who, in desperation, is willing to risk his/her life for it. God, according to Kierkegaard, cannot be described as a historical force, discernible to all who objectively observe human history, as Hegel had described Him. Instead, God could be known only after the individual inwardly struggled through the meaningless agonies of human existence, and in total despair received God as a gift. Kierkegaard felt that the philosopher, ideally typified for him in Hegel, treated God as One who could be understood rationally. For Kierkegaard, philosophy was folly, because God is not a thing to be analyzed as He weaves His way through history, but a Person to be encountered in the depths of one's being.

Imagine a man suffering with cancer. The pain and agony of the disease racks his body. He has always believed that there was a God out there someplace. He had gone to church in better days and heard about God and sung hymns about Him. But now it seems as though this God is punishing him. As he lies in his hospital bed, he asks, "Why?" The pain in his body is nothing compared to the inward agony that seems unbearable. Preachers come and tell him that "all things work together for good for those who love God and are called according to His purposes." He listens to discourses on how his suffering is really part of some wonderful cosmic plan of God's. He tries to make sense out of his suffering from the well-honed theological and philosophical knowledge that is standard fare when questions about suffering are asked. He does not refute the answers of the preachers and teachers, but their answers do not work for him. Maybe they have helped other people. Maybe other people have understood God's will because of these propositions that seem so logical. Yet these are not answers that satisfy him. He wants a truth to satisfy an inner longing in his heart, and theologies and philosophies do not accomplish what he needs. He is passionate and desperate. He trembles as he hangs suspended in an emotional abyss. Then one day, people notice that the struggle is over. There is a Buddha-like smile on his face, a smile that smiles inwardly. With a depth to his voice he says, "I know." "What do you know?" we inquire.

"I know that I know!" he mutters. There is a strangeness about him that only Zen Masters might feel. He knows something that he cannot say. He knows God—not the god of the philosopher, not the god of the astronomers, not the god of the logicians and mathematicians, but the God that Isaac knew when he wrestled all night on Mount Bethel—the God that Isaiah met when he went into the temple to pray in the year that King Uzziah died. There are no new facts that proved that this God exists. There is no new philosophical argument that has resolved the questions concerning the essence of God. But there is another kind of knowledge—the kind that comes to those who suffer and suffer until they reach despair, the kind of knowledge that comes *only in the midst of despair*. It is not a knowledge that is grasped by reason, as Hegel might have tried to grasp it. Instead it comes as a gracious gift. It is a revelation, an inward truth. And because of this truth, known only subjectively, this man is a new creature and he has a reason for everything, which reason cannot know.

This is the truth that Kierkegaard praises. He calls Hegel "That Comic Philosopher" because Hegel is ridiculous enough to think he has grasped the truth about God within the concepts of his system of knowledge. Kierkegaard writes his condemnation in a book entitled *Philosophical Fragments*. It is his way of mocking Hegel's philosophical system.

I have always admired my wife, whose thinking shuns philosophical speculation or theological explanations. When tragedy strikes she refuses to believe that it is all part of some grand and glorious plan of God. She views tragedy as absurdly without rhyme or reason. Taped to the back of one of the cupboard doors of our kitchen is the photograph of a young woman we know who became paralyzed in an accident during her teenage years. My wife tells me that her answer to tragedy is not in some philosophy or theology but in the conquest over despair that has characterized this young woman following her accident. The woman surrendered to God and in God became triumphant. This woman has faith in God rather than an explanation for her tragedy.

There is no objective truth, according to Kierkegaard, only subjective encounter with a personal God who says that *He is* the truth. Truth is a person not a proposition. Truth is learned through suffering and despair. Truth is not composed of facts. Instead, it gives meaning to the facts.

Kierkegaard on Becoming a Christian

Middle-class religion is uncomfortable with Kierkegaard's method for truth. The middle class likes things under control. Its people are rational and want a religion that makes life easier and happier. They buy religious books that reduce Christianity to a reasonable plan for successful living. They seek out churches that promise a healthy, optimistic Christianity. Kierkegaard seems diametrically opposed to all of this. His religion is a call to suffering. His truth is discovered through despair. His form of Christianity is out of sync with the culture. Middle-class religion explains what a person is supposed to think, but it fails to make people into Christians. It invites a person to accept reasoned-out, propositional statements about God but leaves him/her unconverted. It deludes people into believing that they are Christians if they give intellectual assent to theological statements. Kierkegaard contends that one can believe that there was a man named Jesus who lived two thousand years ago, was crucified dead and buried, rose again on the third day, and is coming again in glory—and still not be a Christian. He would ask the would-be Christian if he/she knows Jesus personally if he/she has, through despair, come to a point in which there was a total surrender to a transforming encounter with the Jesus who is resurrected and therefore waiting to be encountered here and now. A major thrust of Kierkegaard's writings is an affirmation of the good news that Jesus is alive and is therefore the individual's contemporary. The Jesus who saves is not the Jesus who is talked about by historians, but the Jesus known personally in the present moment. When fundamentalist evangelists talk about "knowing Jesus as your personal Savior," they are talking about a relationship with a divine subject who confronts the individual as a lover in the "now."

Above all else, Kierkegaard wants to show us how to have a personal relationship with the risen Lord who is a contemporary of every person who has ever lived. Coming to know Jesus is no easy process like walking down the aisle of a church during an "invitation." Knowing Jesus does not come about by uttering a little prayer requesting Him to come into the heart. Kierkegaard would have only scorn for those evangelists who would reduce the ultimate Christian experience to something less than the crucifixion of one's selfhood. To take the suffering and despair out of the salvation experience is to strip it of its power and validity. The struggle that leads into a saving encounter with Jesus takes the individual through three steps. Kierkegaard understood them well because he went through two of them himself and may have entered into the third, although he denies that he did.

The Aesthetic Stage

The first stage of life is labeled by Kierkegaard as the aesthetic stage. In it the individual seeks his/her salvation through pleasure. This is not necessarily the pleasure that comes from the titillations of a sensate lifestyle. The pleasure that is sought can be more refined. Listening to good music, watching quality theater, viewing masterpieces of art, and reading or listening to poetry can satisfy the higher appetites. The aesthete becomes a dilettante who samples all that life can offer and tries to taste all of its joys without becoming personally involved or committed. The aesthete may be shrewd, making brilliant observations about the human condition and the state of society. He/she may seem to know a great deal about everything and give the appearance of being very "cultured." However, the aesthete is only a spectator, evaluating and discussing religious beliefs and ideas. He/she remains detached from life and never becomes passionate about anything.

The aesthete is a skeptic because skepticism is a way to avoid commitment. If one idea or religion is as good or as bad as another; if there is no certainty about anything, then there is no need to give one's life to anything or anyone. In the skeptical aesthete's thinking, only crazy fanatics become totally committed. "How can I become a Christian," the aesthete will ask, "since there is no way of knowing if the Bible stories are true?" He/she appears so sophisticated in this detachment that there are few who suspect that the cynicism and skepticism are evasions of responsibility. The aesthete does not want to believe in the truth because then he/she would be required to act.

Don't all of us know people like that? Don't we all know some who escape the call to Christ with a condescending word about admiring, simple-minded folk who seem to be able to accept Him? Such people find Christianity an interesting philosophy of life that is worthy of the further reflection they plan to give to it when they have more time.

The personality and lifestyle of the aesthete is most fully described in the first volume of Kierkegaard's major work, *Either/Or*. In that volume he tells the story of a young man whom he calls The Great Seducer. The story allows us to get a glimpse of the thinking of this young man, and we cannot help admiring his wit and cleverness. He demonstrates the utmost ingenuity and sophistication as he goes about the seducing of a certain young woman. His manners and cultured style are most attractive, and we know as we read the story that the poor woman does not stand a chance of resisting him. His plans for seducing her affections are both devious and brilliant. It is only a matter of time before she falls hopelessly in love. But when she does surrender herself to The Great Seducer, we learn the truth about him—he is incapable of making a commitment to her. He must move on to a new conquest. He is desirous of demonstrating his abilities and powers but unwilling to become passionately involved.

In a sense, members of the middle class have certain similarities to The Great Seducer. They brilliantly play with Christianity. They can, in a detached manner, enjoy its beauty. But all too seldom do they become passionately involved with Christ. They do not act. They do not commit themselves.

Kierkegaard tells the delightful story of a make-believe land in which only ducks lived. On Sunday morning all the ducks got up, brushed their feathers, and waddled to church. After waddling down the church aisle and into their pews, they squatted. Shortly the duck minister waddled in and took his place behind the pulpit. He opened the duck Bible to the place where it spoke of God's great gift to ducks—wings. "With wings," said the duck preacher, "you ducks can fly. You can mount up like eagles and soar into the heavens. You can escape the confinement of pens and fences. You can know the euphoria of complete freedom. You must give thanks to God for so great a gift as wings."

All the ducks in the congregation agreed and shouted, "Amen!" and then—they all *waddled* home.

This is the kind of parable that Kierkegaard used time and time again to poke fun at the "Christians" of Copenhagen who could listen to the gospel in a detached and proper manner, give intellectual assent to its message, but remain uncommitted and unchanged by it. Religion was approached by the middle class in an aesthetic manner, and it was this bourgeois approach that he scorned.

Eventually the aesthetic stage is passed. It is abandoned, not for intellectual reasons, but for emotional ones. The dilettante tires of his/her pleasures. The museums lose their fascination. The theater becomes tedious, and there comes a time when even the music of Beethoven fails to satisfy. Boredom sets in, and little by little the boredom becomes more than he/she can stand. The dilettante yawns in the midst of the most superb performances, and eventually the yawn turns into a scream. Life loses the capacity to entertain, and the aesthete is left empty. Kierkegaard writes:

I do not care for anything. I do not care to ride, for the exercise is too violent. I do not care to walk, walking is too strenuous. I do not care to lie down, for I should either have to remain lying, and I do not care to do that, or I should have to get up again, and I do not care to do that either. Summa summarum I do not care at all.*

It is emptiness and boredom that ends this stage of life. It is the despair that follows the exhaustion of pleasure that drives the aesthete to look for salvation elsewhere. Kierkegaard says that in the aesthetic stage each of us is like a smooth flat stone that a boy throws across the surface of a pond. The stone dances along the surface until it runs out of momentum. Then it sinks into nothingness. So it is with each of us. Kierkegaard writes in his diary of the time in his own life when this moment came: "I have just come from a party of which I was the soul; witticism flowed from my mouth, all laughed and admired me, but I went away—and there should be a dash as long as the radius of the earth's orbit——and wanted to shoot myself."

The Ethical Stage

The ethical stage is characterized by duty. The seducer gets married. The hippie gets a job. The skeptic joins a church. The aesthetic stage of detachment is followed by the individual's making a commitment. He/she decides to do what is moral, and to try to live out the requisites of the Bible and the laws of God. He/she becomes diligent in the task of doing

---

* Carl Michalson, ed, *The Witness of Sören Kierkegaard* (New York: Association Press), p. 32.

what is right. Salvation is sought through obedience to the rules established by church and society.

The ethical stage of life is akin to what Hegel, and especially his successors, have made out of Christianity. They have taken the Lord of Eternity who broke into history as the Jesus who was crucified and resurrected and is ready to encounter each of us here and now, and have reduced Him to an ethical ideal. The teachings of Jesus are used to provide the principles to guide people into a lifestyle that becomes the highest expression of human potential. The life of Jesus is taken as an example of the kind of person we are all trying to be and as the inspiration to help us to aspire to moral greatness. All that God would have us become, according to Hegel, was expressed in Jesus, and now it only remains for us to become like the Master.

But Hegel and others who believe that becoming a Christian is assuming the lifestyle prescribed by the ethical stage seem to forget one important thing: that we humans are incapable of living up to the moral requirements of God. Kierkegaard mocks the propagators of the middle-class religion of morality and ethics by pointing out their blindness to the fact that all of us are cursed by original sin. According to Kierkegaard's understanding of original sin, all of us, as children of the first Adam, are separated from God so completely that our perception of what is right and good is perverted. As heirs of Adam, we are cursed with a spiritual blindness that keeps us from grasping the truth about what we are supposed to become. Furthermore, even if we knew what righteousness God required of us, as "fallen creatures" we lack the capacity to fulfill His expectations.

Kierkegaard's depressing views about human nature came out of his own personal experiences, particularly his relationship with his father. His father, in a moment of lonely anguish during his own youth, had shaken his fists at heaven and cursed God. It was the belief of both Sören and his father that this sin was the unforgivable sin described by Jesus (see Mark 3:28–29). Consequently, Kierkegaard was convinced that both he and his father were under the condemnation of God and that God's curse upon the family would doom them all. He saw himself in a spiritually hopeless condition, and what he sensed about himself individually, he believed about all members of the human race in general. According to Kierkegaard, each of us is under a spiritual curse because we are children of Adam. Each of us is separated from God by an unbridgeable gulf. No efforts at being righteous can undo our fate nor reestablish unity with God.

What amazed Kierkegaard most about the middle-class Hegelian religiosity of his day was the seemingly arrogant self-sufficiency of the Germanic people. Thinking themselves to be a people through whom the *Geist* (God) had expressed Himself most fully, they believed themselves to be in possession of the power to live lives of godly righteousness. Kierkegaard ridiculed the "proper" religious people of Copenhagen for their lack of awareness of their spiritual and moral impotence and their incapacity to live up to the ethical principles of the New Testament. The typical churchgoers, according to Kierkegaard, were able to perpetuate this self-deception only with the help of the clergy. The rational theologians who occupied the bourgeois pulpits had reduced the impossible demands of Jesus, as set forth in the Bible, to a set of rules that were relatively easy for any socially proper person to uphold. The radical requisites of the gospel had been reduced, by the clergy, into a reasonable set of socially acceptable regulations which could be kept without too much trouble. Thus, by obeying this watered-down version of Christian morality, the self-righteous middle-class church members could delude themselves into thinking that they were true Christians.

Kierkegaard's anger toward what the church had done to Christianity and the biblical message exploded following the death of Bishop Mynster, an old family friend and the bishop of Zealand. As part of the memorial service for the bishop, Hans Larsen Martensen, who had once been Kierkegaard's theological professor, preached a eulogy. Martensen characterized Bishop Mynster as a "true Christian," and claimed that he had lived out to the fullest the teachings of Jesus. The sermon was too much for Kierkegaard. At best he considered the bishop a mediocre man, and to ascribe to him spiritual greatness was, for Kierkegaard, totally unwarranted. It would have been enough to say that the bishop was sincere, but even that should not have earned him the title of "true Christian." According to Kierkegaard, "mediocrity is never so dangerous as when it is dressed up as sincerity." To consider the bishop a true Christian was evidence of the horrible extent to which the demands of the Lord had been reduced in order to make them acceptable to the middle-class churchgoers of Copenhagen. For Kierkegaard, Bishop Mynster lived out the comfortable, reasonable, socially acceptable form of Christianity which was being propagated throughout nineteenth-century Christendom, but his life bore little resemblance to the life that was lived by Jesus. Bishop Mynster was rich, whereas Jesus was poor. Bishop Mynster was an official of his government, whereas Jesus was condemned by His government. Bishop Mynster was a respected man, whereas Jesus was a rejected man. If what is meant by Christian is what the New Testament teaches, then according to Kierkegaard, Bishop Mynster was not a Christian.

With his attack upon Martensen's sermon, Kierkegaard initiated his frontal attack on the church. Hitherto, his message of judgment had been subtle and indirect. He had hinted at what was wrong through the use of parables and aphorisms. But following Martensen's sermon, Kierkegaard began the onslaught with a vehemence unparalleled since the time that Jesus attacked the religion of His day and declared, "Unless your righteousness surpasses that of the scribes and Pharisees you shall not enter the kingdom of heaven" (Matt. 5:20, NASB).

It is hard to imagine the anger and sarcasm that Kierkegaard would vent on the churches of modern America. He would despise the middle-class morality which we propagate as Christian ethics, and ridicule our lack of passionate commitment to becoming what Jesus is.

The controversial author Ron Sider is my friend and a colleague at Eastern College and Eastern Baptist Theological Seminary. A few years ago he wrote a book entitled *Rich Christians in an Age of Hunger*. Kierkegaard would have approved of the book. Sider's small volume does not set forth some new or heretical theological position. It does not propose doubts about the veracity of the biblical revelation nor does it outline some dangerous political ideology. This book simply suggests that Jesus was serious when He said that it is harder for a rich man to enter the kingdom of God then for a camel to go through the eye of a needle (Mark 10:25). Sider claims that to be a Christian is to be radically obedient to the Jesus who tells us, even as He told the rich young ruler, to sell what we have and give to the poor. Sider argues that Jesus meant exactly what He said when He stated: "If any man will come after me, let him deny himself, and take up his cross daily, and follow me" (Luke 9:23, KJV).

The contemporary evangelical church has taken Christ's radical demand and reduced the call to Christian self-giving to tithing. Instead of surrendering all to Christ and giving all to the poor in His name, the middle-class Christian is required only to set aside 10 percent of his/her income, duly receipted for tax purposes, in order to be a faithful disciple of Jesus. When Sider reminds us what Jesus really expects of the church, we call him names, one of which, attributed to him by a popular preacher very much in the Martensen mold, is "closet communist." Kierkegaard expected to be the object of that same kind of condemnation from the church leaders in his day because he believed that the message of Jesus Christ is always an offense to the comfortably religious members of society.

I recently heard a sermon on Mark 10, which contains the story of The Rich Young Ruler. Without so much as a comment to explain what he was doing, the preacher changed the words of Christ to read, "You *must be willing* to sell all you have and feed the poor," instead of the actual words which simply read, "Sell all you have and give to the poor." The preacher went on to say that Jesus *really* does not expect middle-class people to do anything so radical as to give everything away for the sake of the poor. He argued that all that Jesus wanted was for the young man to get his priorities straightened out.

The preacher never explained how the hungry would be fed, the naked clothed, and the sick healed if all that the rich people of America have to do is to get their priorities straightened out. It seems to me that unless we *give* to the poor, they will starve. Jesus called upon us to be radically committed to giving to the poor, not just to change our priorities. It seems to me that Jesus will be less upset with those who reject His message than He will be with those who distort it and weaken it in order to make it acceptable to the bourgeois conscience.

The middle class not only wants to hold onto its wealth, in spite of what Jesus requires of Christians, but it is willing to kill in order to defend what it has. Jesus said:

> Ye have heard that it hath been said, Thou shalt love thy neighbour, and hate thine enemy. But I say unto you, Love your enemies, bless them that curse you, do good to them that hate you, and pray for them which despitefully use you, and persecute you.
>
> Matthew 5:43–44

There is little question in the minds of many people about whether or not Jesus would use a bayonet in battle or drop bombs on an Asian village. However, for most of us, maintaining our positions of wealth and power is more important than imitating what Jesus would do.

Pacifism is unrealistic and unreasonable, we say. (And if there is anything we middle-class types require of our religion it is that it be realistic and reasonable.) No matter that the apostle Paul claimed that to this world the way of Christ would always appear as foolishness. We are committed to a reasonable faith. Kierkegaard would have hard words for us all.

The Disturbing Dane, as Kierkegaard has been called by several modern theologians, condemns Christians who spend millions of dollars on buildings to honor One who told us that He does not dwell in temples made with hands. He sees something incongruous about a church in which people sit in cushioned pews, in sanctuaries where sunlight streams through stained-glass windows, listening to velvet-robed clergymen reading from gilded copies of the Bible "Jesus said, 'If any man would come after me, let him deny himself. . . .'" In the face of such an incongruity, Kierkegaard asks why nobody laughs. He would say that it is one thing to love the wretched of the earth so much that one is willing to sacrifice everything for them, but it is quite another thing to expect to earn $25,000 a year describing somebody who sacrificed everything for them.

It is no surprise that Kierkegaard is considered dangerous by many. He is called an extremist, an antirational, and even an ethical relativist. He stripped bare the pretension of the middle-class clergy. He exposed the smugness of the properly religious. He humiliated Christendom by contrasting its ethics and morality with the requisites of Scripture. He ridiculed the Jesus of the bourgeoisie by contrasting him with the Jesus of history.

Whenever individuals are confronted with the requisites of the Bible and are faced with the call to imitate the real Jesus, they are driven to despair. Whenever they try to live out the real Christian lifestyle, they are left with a sense of frailty and hopelessness. Those who try to live up to the expectations inherent in the ethical stage will be driven to cry out with the apostle Paul:

> For the good that I would I do not: but the evil which I would not, that I do. Now if I do that I would not, it is no more I that do it, but sin that dwelleth in me. I find then a law, that, when I would do good, evil is present with me. For I delight in the law of God after the inward man: But I see another law in my members, warring against

the law of my mind, and bringing me into captivity to the law of sin which is in my members. O wretched man that I am! Who shall deliver me from the body of this death?

Romans 7:19–24

Hegel believed too much in human potential. He, like Socrates, thought that all of us had goodness and truth within us waiting to be developed and brought out. Hegel created a self-confidence in the middle class, helping them to believe that righteousness needed only to be willed. Kierkegaard shattered this Hegelian illusion about the *Geist* waiting to express Himself in everyone. He made us see that all of us are victims of a sinful condition inherited from Adam that renders us too weak to achieve righteousness and too perverted even to understand what it is. Kierkegaard asks us to commit ourselves passionately to the tasks of the *ethical* stage. Then, he says, we will come to realize what we lack. Then we will realize what we cannot be. Then we will grasp our despicable nature and be driven to despair.

The despair about ourselves, created in our exhausted efforts to achieve righteousness, is something that is filled with the potential for wonder. Kierkegaard encourages us to recognize that the suffering that brought us to an end of hoping to achieve the righteousness of Jesus through our own efforts is a precondition to our being "born again" and becoming new creatures. He teaches us that going through the ethical stage of life is not in vain because it prepares us to be truly religious. Without the despair created through our failure, we would not be ready to make the desperate "leap of faith" into being truly Christian. It is ethical despair that poises us to make the great plunge into the religious stage of life.

The Religious Stage

Kierkegaard finds his religious hero in Abraham, the patriarch of Israel. The story of Abraham taking Isaac to the top of a mountain to sacrifice the boy to God is at the center of Kierkegaard's attention in his discussion of what is involved in becoming a Christian and entering the religious stage of life.

Abraham had lived a life of obedience to Yahweh. He left Ur of the Chaldees when God ordered him to do so. By faith he had a son by his aged wife Sarah and was convinced that through that son a new nation would come into existence, whose people would be a blessing to all humanity. Abraham was one who took the ethical requirements of life seriously. This was important to Kierkegaard's thinking because he believed that only those who are absolutely committed to the laws of God are able to transcend those laws in order to enter into a higher stage of life.

One night God came to Abraham in a dream and asked him to do something that was seemingly insane. Yahweh called upon Abraham to take his son, Isaac, to the top of a certain mountain and slay him as a holy sacrifice. The message of God must have seemed unbelievable to the father of Israel. Isaac had been promised to him by God. Through Isaac, the promise of God for the creation of Israel was to be fulfilled. Isaac had done nothing to deserve death. Such an act seemed illogical and unjust. It did not fit in with Abraham's theological system. The command to sacrifice Isaac stood in diametrical opposition to all that Abraham had come to know about God. Abraham had every reason to disbelieve that the command really had come from God. There was no *objective evidence* to support the conclusion that the command to kill Isaac was a divine imperative. There was no way that Abraham could be sure, as scientists are sure about the formula for water, that it was Yahweh who had addressed him.

Nevertheless, Abraham did what he was asked. Against his logic and theology, against the implications of the promise of Yahweh, and without any objective verification that it indeed had been God who ordered him to murder his son, he prepared to carry out the order.

Kierkegaard points out that Abraham did what he did because he had experienced Yahweh within the depths of his being. While there was no objective evidence that God had spoken to him, there was a subjective knowledge. There was the reason that reason cannot know. There was a personal encounter with Yahweh within the deepest recesses of Abraham's heart. There was an inward experience with God too subjective to have any objective validity. There was a soft, still voice in the depths of his being. And Abraham responded in faith to what he had experienced within his subjective self. It was there, in the secret place of the soul, that God had spoken to Abraham, and Abraham obeyed God.

Kierkegaard marveled at the willingness of Abraham to have faith in the God he had experienced so inwardly. This God was not the Hegelian *Geist* who could be discerned so obviously by the detached, enlightened philosophical mind as He wove His way through the annals of history, expressing Himself in successive cultures. Abraham's knowledge of God fit no theological system. It complied with no dictates of knowledge. It lacked the certainty that we scientific bourgeois people require before we act. For this individual, Abraham, there was only obedience fraught with uncertainty. Abraham, in accord with Kierkegaard's favorite Bible verse from the Epistle to the Philippians (2:12), worked out his own salvation with fear and trembling.

With Kierkegaard, no one is Christian until he/she has encountered God after the manner of Abraham's experience. Living in accord with middle-class morality is not Christianity. Believing theological doctrines does not save the soul. Being baptized into the institutional church is to no avail in this matter. Only a personal encounter in the depths of one's being; only an intimate relationship with God in the utmost subjectivity of the self; only the voice from within can utter saving grace. Kierkegaard scorned the authority of the church as established by Roman Catholics, because no one and no group can affirm what one must believe alone and by oneself. He rejected the bibliolatry of those fundamentalists who would make the Scriptures the ultimate authority for faith. Even though he would agree with those who hold to the doctrine of the inerrancy of Scriptures, he refused to put the Bible in a higher place of authority than the inward encounter with God.

Kierkegaard's total commitment to the subjective experience with God as the ultimate basis for Christianity has caused much upset among more rational theologians. The desire for objective authority has brought forth in our time the so-called "battle for the Bible." The orthodox, with whom I number myself, claim that there is no way to have an authoritative witness to the validity of salvation unless the Bible, which declares our salvation, is beyond the possibility of error. The Scriptures, say the orthodox, are the foundation of faith and salvation. Kierkegaard was not impressed with such arguments. He made us aware that even if a person knew that every fact in the Bible were true, this would not make him/her a Christian. It is a subjective knowledge of God, experienced inwardly, that really matters. If someone can gather irrefutable facts validating that a man named Jesus lived 2,000 years ago and was crucified and resurrected from the grave, that does not make that person a Christian, according to Kierkegaard. Something more is needed. An inward subjective encounter with the Christ is what saves the soul. When an individual has such an encounter with the Jesus who has become a personal contemporary of every one of us, then he/she is a Christian. Furthermore, only Christians can get any true meaning out of the Bible. Kierkegaard does not doubt the veracity of Scripture, but he does not believe it has any authority except for those who already know Christ inwardly and in absolute subjectivity.

Kierkegaard believed that God deliberately withholds the kind of evidence that would force us to accept Him as a fact. Instead He entered into history incognito so that only those who already had met Him inwardly and subjectively would recognize Him. Kierkegaard tried to provide some help for understanding the incarnation of God through one of his most beautiful stories:

> The king loved the maiden and would have her be queen at his side, but how can the king win the maiden? The first and most obvious thing which would come to mind is that the king should simply show himself in his regal glory and declare his intention. However, this would not do because if the king reveals himself to the maiden she will be overwhelmed and dazzled by his presence. She will give glory to the king but the king does not seek his glory, but hers. We might think that the king would simply elevate her to his side, but she will never be able to overcome the fact that she was a lowly maiden and was simply picked up and clothed in unfamiliar garments and made the object of a strange ceremony. He knows she will never be at home or at ease in such a situation. How then can the king reveal himself? Perhaps we could suggest that he put on the clothes of a peasant and visit her as a lowly man, poor and hungry, but that would not alter the situation—he would still be the king. Up to this point the analogy of the revelation of the god is accurate. If the king will win the maiden he must become a peasant, and there the analogy breaks down because most kings will not become peasants. This is the glory and humility of the god, because he did descend in the form of a servant. The only way that the god can reveal himself is to appear as an humble man among men.*

This God is only recognized by those who have already come to know Him inwardly. Objective knowledge is detached and unemotional.

---

* Robert L. Perkins, *Sören Kierkegaard* (Atlanta: John Knox Press, 1969), p. 12.

Subjective knowledge can only come from inner suffering and painful self-surrender. Kierkegaard calls each of us to abandon the posture of the Hegelian philosopher whose religion is a theological system that can be demonstrated with logical and historical proofs. He asks us to set aside the religiosity of middle-class morality and its reduced version of Christian expectations.

Kierkegaard invites us to try to become Christians because we have to. After we have come to realize the eventual emptiness and boredom of living for pleasure; after we have discovered the hopelessness and futility of trying to live out the demands of the gospel; and after we have experienced the despair which he calls "the sickness unto death," he calls upon us to make the leap of faith into a true subjective relationship with Jesus.

The Relevance of Kierkegaard

During the time of my theological studies, wherever my intellectual travels took me, I met Kierkegaard coming back. None of my theological excursions took me more into his style and method of seeking salvation than my trip into the mind-set of the great Swiss/German Karl Barth. If it can be said that Augustine provided a theological version of the works of Plato, and that St. Thomas Aquinas provided a theological version of the works of Aristotle, then it surely can be said that Karl Barth brought Kierkegaardian thought into the mainstream of twentieth-century theology. The radical nature of sin, the subjective experience with Christ as a prerequisite to interpreting the biblical message, the condemnation of cultural religion, and the necessity of an absolute decision for Christ as the basis for Christianity are all emphases which Barth derived from a careful reading of the works of Kierkegaard. It might be said that the post-World War II theological movement named "neo-orthodoxy" was simply a delayed reaction to the Disturbing Dane.

Many evangelical Christians criticize Kierkegaard for some of the same reasons that they attack the theology of Barth. They claim that he undercut the importance of the biblical relation, that he made Christianity far too subjective an experience, and that he failed to see much value in Christian community. However, for any shortcomings he might have, there is one thing for which I will always thank him: he reintroduced passion into Christianity. He made being a Christian something other than intellectual contemplation of eternal truths. He made Christianity into a passionate experience that required an absolute commitment to Christ. With Kierkegaard, being a Christian was a state of surrender to the grace of God into which the individual is driven because his/her life has been empty and meaningless when lived for pleasure alone. His Christianity was a commitment made by the individual who in despair is incapable of going on in life without salvation. Becoming a Christian, for Kierkegaard, is never the result of that cool intellectual reflection in which faith in Christ seems to be the most reasonable option. Instead, it is the desperate act of a person who has turned to Christ because there was nowhere else to turn. It is the leap of someone who surrenders to Jesus because going on without Him is impossible. It is a passionate act that the individual commits because he is suffering from "the sickness unto death" and there is no other cure. There is no a priori evidence that there will be salvation through this inward total surrender of the subjective self. There is no objective proof that Christ waits to be encountered in the depths of one's being. But the sufferer is willing to risk all in hope and faith.

Kierkegaard condemned the society of his day, and he would condemn this society of ours, for not being willing to adopt a religion so fraught with emotion. The well-ordered lives of the bourgeois left little room for the passions that lead to Christ. When people in this present age experience angst, they go for counseling. When they experience despair, they call on a psychiatrist, rather than on Jesus. Kierkegaard says that this lack of passion will be the death of our present age.

> Let others complain that the age is wicked; my complaint is that it is wretched; for it lacks passion. Men's thoughts are thin and flimsy like lace, they are themselves pitiable like the lace-makers. The thoughts of their hearts are too paltry to be sinful. For a worm it might be regarded as a sin to harbor such thoughts, but not for a being made in the image of God. Their lusts are dull and sluggish, their passions sleepy. They do their duty, these shopkeeping souls, but they clip the coin a trifle . . .; they think that even if the Lord keeps ever so careful a set of books, they may still cheat Him a little. Out upon them! This is the reason my soul always turns back to the Old Testament and to Shakespeare. I feel that those who speak there

are at least human beings: they hate, they love, they murder their enemies, and curse their descendants throughout all generations, they sin.*

If we do not learn from Kierkegaard, it may be that what we do not know will kill us.

---

* *The Witness of Sören Kierkegaard,* pp. 36–37.

5

The Freudians: Those Who Tore Away the Masks

THE MIDDLE CLASS of the nineteenth-century Western world maintained a façade of propriety that enabled its members to think of themselves as superior to all other peoples. Outsiders never suspected that beneath a veneer of manners and morality, those who had been steeped in the Victorian tradition had sexual hungers and fantasies that in decent circles were not even whispered about. That hypocrisy and deception was not to last. Sigmund Freud, the founder of modern psychoanalysis, revealed the truth. His theories and writings destroyed forever the pretense of the haughty bourgeoisie. The "decent" middle class banished the word "sex" from its parlor talk, but Freud declared that its thinking was preoccupied with sexual fantasies. The bourgeoisie had claimed to be motivated by such lofty values as altruism and justice, but Freud made them face up to his claim that sexual cravings gave birth to most of their actions.

According to Freud, all human beings are bundles of sexual energy that he called "libido." In each person, no matter how sanctimonious, there is a craving to release that energy through ecstasies enjoyed with specific sexual objects. Freud taught that if there were no social restraints, every person would act out his or her fantasies and fulfill desires for debauchery that would defy the imaginations of even the wildest purveyors of contemporary pornography. Furthermore, Freud believed that we humans become sexual animals at infancy rather than at puberty. The child at his/her mother's breast is seeking much more than nourishment, said Freud. The child, from the earliest stages of development, is sexually motivated in everything that he/she does. Needless to say, the theories of Freud sent out shock waves that reverberated from his Vienna circle and reached around the world.

According to Freud, repression of these natural sexual impulses is essential for social order. If humans were allowed to act out all their sexual fantasies without inhibitions there would be chaos. The fulfillment of sexual wishes would bring to an end not only monogamy, but also the incest taboo. The family, as we know it, would cease to exist as a social institution and, with the collapse of the family, there would come the collapse of civilization. In short, civilization, according to Freud, is built on repression. Social order and all of its benefits are dependent upon keeping the lid on the seething, boiling, volcanic sexual longings that constantly threaten to erupt within the psyches of even the most proper men and women in the drawing rooms of middle-class society.

Repression has its price to extract from the civilization it allows. According to Freud, repression creates neurosis. Hence, the more civilized the people, the more repressed, and the more repressed, the more neurotic. If his theories are true, then no society has ever been more neurotic than that which emerged among the Germanic peoples that were glorified by Hegel. The Western society that was grandly lauded as the epitome of civilization might consequently be considered to have been the one most repressive of sexuality. It was a sick society *because* it was so civilized. Its people, so placid on the surface, were, of all peoples, the most discontent.

Freud's theories were condemned everywhere. From the halls of academia to the halls of national parliaments they were debated and labeled dangerous. His views were seen as promoting a libertinism that could give vent to the vilest urges inherent in *Homo sapiens*. His theories were put down as ideologies of the demonic. According to Freud, the cure for the neuroses of the modern Western middle class seemed to lie in overcoming the inhibitions that frustrated the sexual longings of its members to act out their lustful desires regardless of social consequences. Psychic health for the individual, in Freud's view, was possible only at the price of a terrible toll on the social order. Those who believed in the virtues of the Christianized civilization of the Western world had to oppose his beliefs about human nature. To such protests and criticisms, Freud sarcastically said that people might deny what he said by day, but would dream of the things he described by night.

Ironically, the Freudian description of human nature that elicited so much opposition from the leaders of the bourgeoisie, and particularly from its clergy, is in many ways simply an updated version of a biblical description set forth nineteen hundred years ago by the apostle Paul. The Christian middle-class society that reached from the capitals of Europe to the Westernized colonies and settlements around the world claimed the Bible as its ultimate authority. Yet its citizens refused to face the fact that Paul's depiction of human nature, apart from the miraculous transformation possible only through the grace of God, is every bit as lurid as that set forth by Sigmund Freud. Paul writes in Galatians 5:19: "Now the works of the flesh are manifest, which are these; adultery, fornication, uncleanness, lasciviousness. . . ." Paul describes the character of fallen, sinful humanity in terms that more than equal the language of Freudian psychology.

> Wherefore God also gave them up to uncleanness through the lusts of their own hearts, to dishonor their own bodies between themselves: Who changed the truth of God into a lie, and worshipped and served the creature more than the Creator, who is blessed forever. Amen. For this cause God gave them up unto vile affections: for even their women did change the natural use into that which is against nature: And likewise also the men, leaving the natural use of the woman, burned in their lust one toward another; men with men working that which is unseemly, and receiving in themselves that recompense of their error which was meet.
>
> Romans 1:24–27

It seems that the rejection of Freud occurred only because the gentile bourgeois society of the West never did grasp the meaning of human nature set forth by the biblical revelation which was claimed as the basis of all of that society's truth.

Unfortunately, the negative reactions elicited by Freud's early writings prevented many people, especially those who defended middle-class values from church pulpits, from discerning ways in which his insights could be integrated with a Christian understanding of human nature. Not only the apostle Paul, but Augustine, Calvin, and Luther would have found much with which they could agree in Freud's writings. While they would have held divergent opinions as to the value of religion and the origins of theology, they nevertheless would have found common ground in Freud's revelations about human nature. The scholarly giants who gave birth to the intellectual tradition of the Christendom of the last two centuries would have concluded that Freud was "partly right." What is more regrettable is that the prejudices of Freud's religious detractors kept them from grasping some of his later thoughts and insights which, in many ways, provide some of the most important perspectives on human nature available in our time.

As Freud matured in his thinking, he did not reject his earlier views concerning the sexual nature of personality, but he did perceive complexities about human nature that are not far removed from the insights of twentieth-century existentialist philosophers. He came to see that, related to humanity's fear and repression of its own sexual hungers, was a fear and repression of death. Freud, in his more advanced writings, argued that in the psychosexual development of the human being, there was not only a repressed consciousness of sexual hungers, but also a repression of mortality. It is the Freudian interpretation of the meaning of death and the consequences of the awareness of death for all of us that provide profound insights that must not be ignored. What Freud said about the ways in which we handle death is of crucial significance to any of us who seek help in understanding our own inner workings, and in grasping hitherto unprobed dimensions of the biblical message. Freud provided important contributions for both, as strange as such a claim may seem to Christian defenders of middle-class culture.

The Freudian trek from sexual psychology to existential philosophy begins with the psychoanalyst's understanding of the developmental stages through which a human being passes on his/her way to maturity. The first stage, according to Freud, is called the oral stage. In it, the infant has delusions of omnipotence. According to Freud, the child sees no limits to his/her powers. To the child, it seems that whatever the child wants, the child can get. The need for food or for physical warmth can be satisfied simply by crying. The longing for tactile gratifications or sexual fulfillment (which in the oral stage comes from being at the mother's breast) is met at will upon demand. Freud teaches that in the earliest stage of psychosexual development, the infant has a godlike consciousness. Since the mother is not perceived to be a distinct and separate entity, but rather an extension of the self, and since the mother provides all that the infant needs, whenever the infant expresses the desire for gratification, he/she has a sense of being totally self-sufficient.

The second stage of development, according to Freud, destroys this delusion of godlike omnipotence, and in it the child discovers the dark underside of his/her nature. This second stage is the anal stage, and it is in anality that the infant begins to gain the awareness of his/her physical nature with all of its limitations, filth, and mortality. During the anal stage, Freud explains, this would-be god gradually realizes that on the bottom of his/her body there is a hole which, from time to time, emits a brown and smelly substance. At first the child plays with the feces, pretending that it is totally separate from and not part of his/her humanity. But the pretense cannot be maintained, and sooner or later the child comes to see that there is a dimension of his/her humanness that is fraught with decay and which elicits disgust. Over and against the child's consciousness of his/her godness is the growing awareness of this decaying, disgusting dimension of a physical nature. Consequently, there is the beginning of the awareness of the duality of human nature. The child is thrust into the existential awareness that there is one part of his/her personhood that is lofty and divine, but there is also another side that "stinks" and is subject to decay. The child realizes that there is a part of the self that is likened unto the angels, and another part that is akin to the animals that live and die all around him/her. The biblical psalmist may have been trying to express this perplexity when he said:

> What is man, that thou art mindful of him? and the son of man, that thou visitest him?
> For thou hast made him a little lower than the angels, and hast crowned him with glory and honor.
> Thou madest him to have dominion over the works of thy hands; thou hast put all things under his feet.
>
> Psalm 8:4–6

Norman O. Brown, a philosophical psychologist and modern interpreter of Freud, provides us with the clearest insights into the religious dimensions of what Freud discovered during his investigation of anality.

It was Brown who delivered Freudian psychology from a reductionistic biologism that made human behavior seem to be the result of instincts and allowed us to see its profound implications for religion and philosophy.

In his book *Life Against Death,* Brown spells out the ramifications of what Freud teaches about the human condition. Brown makes clear the ultimate questions about life and death which become part of the human consciousness as the result of anality. We must thank Brown for keeping Freud's teachings alive in the midst of contemporary religious discussion.

According to Brown, the later writings of Freud represent something of a shift from the emphasis evident in his earlier writings. While Brown contends that in the later writings of Freud, repression is still the basis of civilization, he believes that in these later writings, Freud considered the repression of what is discovered in the anal stage of human development to be more important than the repression of sexual cravings. The repression of the decaying physical side of human nature and the awareness of encroaching death is what makes life tolerable and civilization possible, according to Brown's interpretation of Freud.

Consciousness of mortality would drive us mad. Thus we propagate a denial of death which in itself is an act of madness. But it is a madness that prevents that greater madness which overtakes us when we grasp the truth about our lives and the ultimate despair associated with dying. What follows is a summary of Brown's interpretation of Freud. This interpretation by Brown can provide Christian theologians with a new basis for dialogue.

Freud's Death Doctrines in Religious Perspective

We are delighted with the sense of immortality developed in our oral stage, and we find that the mortal side of our humanity as evidenced in anality is too painful to accept. Fortunately, society conspires with us to perpetuate the lie of our immortality. Society helps us to construct a variety of instruments and belief systems to facilitate our escape from the ultimate truth about existential reality.

When we attend funerals we expect the corpse to be properly attired and laid out in dignified repose. We want the corpse resting in a cushioned, satin-lined casket surrounded by flowers. We desire the illusion that the person in the box is not dead, but only sleeping. We try to evade the fact that the corpse is all dressed up with no place to go. We want to pretend that death is not the end of life. We cry at funerals, not for the dead, but for ourselves. We deceive ourselves if we think otherwise. But such are the deceptions that make our lives tolerable. We weep because we know that each of us will come to a similar end. And all of us wonder what it will be like when we take our places in caskets. We wonder if others will say of us what we are saying of the dead one, "He looks as though he's sleeping, doesn't he?"

We admire those who can face death with courage, and we have doubts about how we will handle death when it comes. When we hear of someone dying while sleeping we have a certain strange envy. Each of us thinks, "I hope that when my time comes it will be just like that. I don't want to think about dying and I don't want to know when I die."

Eastern religions pretend that people do not want to live forever. They say that each person's desire to go on living as a distinct individual is an illusion, but they lie. Hinduism and Buddhism pretend that we do not want what, in reality, we want the most. They try to tell us that dying is good and natural, but deep inside, each of us knows that death is evil and that it confronts each of us as the most unnatural and ugly event possible.

Christianity has been structured to make death unreal. Preachers tell us that on the other side of death there is a new life awaiting each of us. We are told that death is only "crossing the bar" and that after death we, as individuals, will live forever. But there are times when even the most faithful of believers wonder if that message is simply wishful thinking.

Apart from Christianity, humanity works out a variety of strange and macabre ways to deal with death. For instance, many sociologists point out that peasants in agrarian societies along with the underclasses of modern urban societies escape the consciousness of death by bickering. They use arguments over trivial matters as preoccupations. By focusing on the inconsequential, they drive what is ultimate from their minds. Arguments over the mundane are excellent ways to avoid the reality of death. Even middle-class people employ the technique from time to time. Often, arguments over heirlooms and legacies are nothing more then subconscious attempts to evade the ugly truth about ourselves which the death of a loved one thrusts upon us. If we can argue over who inherits what with sufficient passion, we may be able to forget that death is stalking the labyrinth of our brains reminding each of us of our eventual fate.

Far more desirable is the attempt to escape death by embracing life. Like the main character in Nikos Kazantzakis's novel *Zorba the Greek*, some of us try to dance in the face of life's absurdities and laugh at what makes others tremble. Surrendering to the lusts of the flesh and the ecstasies of sensuality, some seek to escape from what the higher side of our humanity finds unthinkable—our mortality.

Sooner or later these and the other techniques and schemes fail, and the truth erupts through our efforts at repression. Death eventually charges into our consciousness and in the face of death, we find that life loses its joy.

To some the truth comes sooner than to the rest of us. They are the ones who go insane and must be hospitalized. They are the ones who learn too soon the intolerable truth. Others of us are not so smart, and to us the truth comes slowly. Fortunately we lack the cleverness to see through the deception games society has taught us, and we go on playing and working, hoping that the end of life will overtake us by surprise.

Society at its best makes deceptions about life and death so real that its people seldom grasp the significance of death. So properly socialized into a cultural mind-set that makes "nonbeing" unreal are its citizens that the anxiety about death is almost absent among them.

However, sometimes society's deception structures erode, and there is a breakdown of the belief systems that usually repress the awareness of death. When that happens, a social sickness breaks loose and despair invades the consciousness of almost everyone, including young people.

We live in such a time. The truth about death is asserting itself, and morbid thinking is evident everywhere. Teenagers are committing suicide with dramatically increased frequency, confessing to the meaninglessness of life. A "cool" generation rocks and rolls to music groups with names like "The Grateful Dead," and other groups on television videos glorify decadence and pain. For so many, the teenage years are no longer the "happy days" depicted by the Fonz, but are years of despair in the face of existential questions too heavy to bear. The generation now coming of age in America is not made up of bad kids. They simply know too much too soon. When society no longer provides techniques for repressing death, then people, old and young alike, must seek new ways to salvation. They must find their own routes of escape from the intolerable truth. They must have their own private Nirvanas.

Sometimes the escape routes are called mental illness; sometimes, religious devotion; sometimes, art appreciation; and sometimes, heroism. Whatever value judgments may be made of these private mechanisms of repression, they all have one thing in common. Each is an attempt to deal with what is ultimate about life, and that is the reality of death.

Delusion as a Defense Mechanism

Schizophrenia is one way to escape mortality. Through schizophrenia persons try to overcome the duality of their humanity by taking flights from reality. In these excursions into the worlds of make-believe, they lose the side of their nature discovered through anality and imagine themselves to be superhuman. The most extreme cases are those of people who think of themselves as gods or messiahs. Others choose less grandiose personas and escape into the roles of the immortals of history. Becoming Napoleon, Julius Caesar, or Alexander the Great offers some possibility for escape from the insignificance "we petty men who creep about finding ourselves dishonorable graves" experience. To assume the identity of one who has done things of monumental importance can create the illusion of immortality.

Schizophrenia is too extreme an escape for most of us. Instead, we seek limited and harmless fantasies that allow us temporary departures from the too-heavy burden of the truth about death. Many of us, like Walter Mitty, have secret lives of fantasy in which seemingly impossible feats are accomplished and magnificent deeds are done. What high school basketball player has not taken temporary flights into make-believe situations wherein he/she scores the winning field goal just as time runs out in the championship game? Who of us has not daydreamed about performing an act of nobility that elicits the admiration of the whole world? Who has not longed to do something worthy of a standing ovation from all of humanity?

Those who work with young people are well aware of such delusions of grandeur among teenagers. There are cheerleaders who are so taken with their own selves that they believe themselves to be worthy of worship. There are "jocks" who take a bow every time there is a clap of thunder. There are many in the high school subculture who are so "stuck" on themselves that they honestly believe that everyone notices everything they do, say, and wear. They seem to be inviting us to commemorate their birthdays by sending their parents notes of congratulations.

But perpetuating the delusion that we are only divine, while we ignore or forget that side of our humanity discovered during anality, does not always work. For most of us, delusions of grandeur are only temporary excursions from the horror of our animal nature. Most of us do not take those permanent flights into fantasy that cause people to whisper that we have lost touch with reality. For most of us, delusions of grandeur are only short-lived experiences.

Fantasies seldom become realities. However, even if a person does actually get to live out a fantasy, the benefits are limited. All of us know of someone who once did something that gained the admiration and applause of others and who then spent the rest of his/her life trying to relive that experience. There is the football player who caught the

winning pass at the Rose Bowl game; the violinist who got to play at the
White House; the preacher who once inspired huge throngs. All of them
remember these experiences with longing and find it intolerable that
people have so quickly forgotten their moments of greatness. They make
the rest of their lives postscripts to their flashes of stardom. The rest of
us say with pity, "They're living in the past," and we wonder whether or
not it might be better never to have tasted of the fame that makes ordinary living so unacceptable.

To forget our own mortality through delusions of grandeur seldom
works, except for those who are extreme schizophrenics. Most of us seek
other paths of escape from the duality of our nature.

Forgetting Our Divinity

Far more common than escapes through delusions of grandeur are
escapes sought through self-degradation. While some may deceive themselves into thinking themselves so divine that they ignore the underside
of their personalities, far more overemphasize the truth discovered about
themselves through anality. Our world seems overpopulated with people
who forget that there is something about them which likens them to gods
and degrade themselves by seeing only their corruptible nature.

People in the counseling profession report that they have far more
cases of depression resulting from self-contempt than they do cases of
megalomania. People silently think of themselves as worthless. They
understand all too well that there is a side of them that is deserving of
reproach and condemnation. Unfortunately, many people think that
there is nothing more to them than those despicable traits comparable to
excrement or, using the terminology of the apostle Paul, "dung." They
forget their divinity. They forget that they are made in the image of God.
The doctrine of total depravity is embraced in such an exaggerated manner that they believe there can be nothing good or worth loving about
themselves. Psychoanalysts and psychotherapists tell us that most of
the people who come to them have such low self-images and poor self-
concepts that self-hatred seems to be their only option. Sometimes such
sick self-contempt masquerades as an expression of Christian humility.
Its victims forget that they were created "a little lower than the angels"
and that the eternal and majestic God of the universe loves them and
knows them by name. They ignore the biblical declaration that they have

been predestined to be sons and daughters of God. There is something within them that hints of such greatness, but they ignore these inklings of divinity and preoccupy themselves with the filthy side of their humanity. Without their divinity, they are devoid of inner conflict. They see themselves only as being perverse.

Recently I was reviewing some of the writings of Martin Luther. I was surprised to discover how many times the Great Reformer used words that would shock most of us in the religious community. Words that supposedly should be removed from the vocabularies of the "righteous of the Lord" reappear with startling regularity in Luther's works. No four-letter word appears as often as the one the Reformer uses to describe himself, his life, and all his work. He compares himself to excrement so often that writers in the field of psychology have utilized him and his writings to illustrate the personality who has an "anal complex."

Luther is not the only one who saw himself in such despicable terms. The hymn writer who taught us to sing "Amazing Grace" was all too ready to call himself a "wretch." The entire reformed tradition provides an interpretation of the Pauline epistles that looks at all of us as totally depraved and completely perverted.

There is nothing wrong with admitting to the dark side of our lives as long as we keep that truth in balance with the opposite truth, that we are people who are in the image of God and to whom God has imparted His Light. "That was the true Light, which lighteth every man that cometh into the world" (John 1:9).

It is hard to maintain belief in the divine side of our humanity, particularly in an age that increasingly buys into a secularized version of humanism. If, as the secular humanists say, there is no God, then we cannot say that we are in His image. If there is no God, the truth about ourselves discovered through anality is the only truth that there is. Then we are *only* dung; we are *only* worms. The most negative consequence of secularism may not be that people do not believe in God, but that they do not believe in themselves. Without God, what are human beings? Are not these creeping, crawling creatures that copulate like monkeys simply dung?

Forgetting our divinity and overidentifying with our anal humanity is responsible for a host of maladies that plague our contemporary society. For instance, the brutalization of wives, in part, results from self-contempt. Wives who endure obscene and violent beatings from their husbands often think that for some reason they deserve such treatment. They are deluded into believing that they are so worthless and despicable that the beatings are their just punishment. The most difficult task for counselors of such victims is to convince these women that they are not unworthy creatures for whom beatings are the just due. Counselors must go on to help such women to redefine themselves, to view themselves as persons of worth. They must rediscover the dignity associated with their divinity and recognize that, as children of God, they deserve respect. "There is therefore now no condemnation to them which are in Christ Jesus" (Rom. 8:1).

Too often, religious leaders have encouraged the mentality that has contributed to the brutalization of women. On the one hand, they have overemphasized the dark side of humanity which makes women feel deserving of the most degrading forms of punishment. On the other hand, they have preached that wives should submit to their husbands no matter what the consequences.

Obviously, such messages have no affinity with Christian truth. The Bible affirms the dignity and infinite worth of each and every person, male or female, Jew or Gentile, slave or free. The apostle Paul, contrary to many accusations made against him, was not a sexist male chauvinist who called for the degradation of women. Quite the opposite, Paul affirmed the dignity of women and recognized that there were some marriages that would best be ended. Paul taught that there were occasions when spiritual and physical self-preservation might require a wife to leave her mate (see I Cor. 7). Unconditional submission to husbands is not a biblical requisite. To twist the Scriptures in a way that encourages women to endure brutalization is not only sick, but it is also blasphemy.

Another social sexual problem associated with self-degradation is promiscuous adultery. Many people with low self-images look for affirmation of their worth by seeking out relationships with persons who deem them attractive even if such liaisons take them outside the limits of marriage. Subconsciously they think that if they are able to achieve sexual conquests with new partners, they can prove to themselves that they are worth something despite their inner feelings to the contrary. The sexual partners sought for in such relationships are not persons to be loved as much as they are objects to be used to affirm the desirability of the conqueror who has serious doubt about his/her self-worth. In short, there would be less adultery and sexual promiscuity if people thought more of themselves. Those who sense their divinity and know their self-worth do not have a need to use others as sexual objects to bolster their self-images.

Another despicable consequence of the self-degradation so common in an age in which people forget their divinity can be found in the business of prostitution. Studies of women who work in this profession reveal that they, more than most women, are persons with very low self-images. There is some evidence that this low self-esteem not only allows them to debase themselves with "Johns," but it also causes them to need the gratification they receive from knowing that they are desirable enough to be able to make others pay to be with them. The willingness to endure humiliation at the hands of their pimps results from their sense of worthlessness on the one hand, and the vicarious gratification they get from allowing their pimps to feel like "somebodies" on the other hand.

Self-condemnation and self-contempt can often aggravate already painful situations. Interviews with cancer victims often reveal that they believe they are being punished. In many cases they think that God has afflicted them with the disease because they are despicable people deserving of suffering and pain. Sometimes people are ashamed to let anyone know that they have cancer because, subconsciously, they feel that then others will know they are despised by God. Cancer is horrible enough without the guilt and self-condemnation that is too often associated with it.

Unfortunately, there are "pop" theologians, particularly some who articulate their views on religious television shows, who have contributed to the guilt associated with cancer. In one case, the father of a friend of mine was dying of cancer. My friend wrote to a prominent media preacher and asked for prayers for healing. The preacher responded by saying that if all of the members of the family would get right with God and pray, their father would be healed. The family members went through the prescribed routines of rededicating themselves to God and praying for healing for their father. However, in spite of all their spiritual exercises, my friend's father did die. Another letter was sent to the TV evangelist for guidance and for an explanation of the father's death. In the answering letter, the family members were told that their father died because of unconfessed sin in their lives. That letter sent all the family members into despairing self-condemnation. Each was convinced that he/she was responsible for the father's death. After all, who is so holy and divine, besides Jesus, that punishment is not deserved?

The idea that God would kill a man with cancer because his children have unconfessed sin dishonors God. I detest profanity, but I prefer the street variety to the kind that makes God into such a despicable, unjust culprit. The God of Scripture has no relationship to the god of that TV evangelist. The God of Scripture is not mean. It is too easy to propagate a theology that plays upon people who have a tendency to resolve the duality of their character by seeing themselves only as filthy mortals. It is too easy to accentuate the discoveries made through anality and forget our divinity. It is too easy to lead people to believe that God hates them even though the opposite is true.

A Christian Understanding of Human Nature

When it comes to establishing a balanced view of personhood, it is hard to beat the Bible. The Scriptures never let us lose sight of our sinfulness, nor do they allow us to forget our divine potential. In the Bible it is never a matter of either/or. Within the Christian perspective on human nature, *both* the glorious and the despicable sides of personhood are declared.

The balance in Scripture is not always maintained by those who endeavor to preach its message. I am amazed at how many people think they have heard the good news about God when all they have heard is the bad news about themselves. I am intrigued with the way so many are attracted to preachers who hold up the worthlessness of the congregation while giving little time or effort to holding up the beauty of Christ and declaring the good news that Christ has for us all.

Those who understand that the tendency of most people is to view themselves as worms and dung should not be surprised that preachers who articulate these images of human nature gain large audiences. Those people are simply finding a resolution of their dual natures by affirming their sinfulness while forgetting their divinity. They seem willing to ignore the fact that the word "gospel" means "good news." They have learned to revel in the bad news about themselves and have made this bad news the essence of their religious faith. No wonder William James, the modern founder of the psychology of religion, called most religious people "sick minded."

A great deal of criticism has been leveled at the popular television preacher, Dr. Robert Schuller. He has been accused of distorting the gospel and making it into a Pollyanna religion filled with smiles and optimism. Personally, I think most of the critics are jealous of his gifts.

I have listened to Schuller speak on numerous occasions. He never denies the frailty of human nature or the dark side of our personalities. However, unlike many contemporary preachers, he convinces us of our potentialities and our possibilities. He never lets us forget that we have a divinity about us and that as sons and daughters of God we are capable of great things.

Some insight into the importance of Schuller's message for our day can be gleaned from the theories and writings of Abraham Maslow. This leader in the field of humanistic psychology has argued that most human beings are afraid of their own potentialities for greatness. Maslow suggests that the awareness of divine potentialities is too much for most of us. We are so afraid that we will not live up to our possibilities that we seek to escape from them by recognizing only our frailness and weaknesses. If we deceive ourselves into thinking that we are nothing but worms and dung, then we will not be haunted by our possibilities for wonderful things. Maslow argues that if we affirm only our evil nature and weaknesses, we need not face up to the awesome challenges of our potential for greatness.

Schuller will not let us get away with our little game. He reminds each of us that God has endowed us with great possibilities and that God has high expectations for each of us. Schuller affirms our divinity, yet does not deny our humanity. For most of us his message seems too good to be true. But after all, isn't that what the gospel is? Isn't God's message to sinful humanity that He sees in each of us a divine nature of such worth that He sacrificed His own Son so that our divine potentialities might be realized? The good news is that to all who receive His "Word," He gives the power to become sons of God (John 1:1–12).

For ten years I taught at a large Ivy League university. A significant number of my students were Jewish, and I often attempted to influence them with the message of Christianity. On one occasion, during a discussion of social problems, I thought I had found an excellent opportunity to talk about Jesus and to quote some Scripture. We were discussing the problem of prostitution in modern urban America. After some time of give-and-take with my students, I asked, "Have you ever wondered what the great religious leaders of history would have said to a prostitute? Have you ever asked what Buddha would have said had he encountered such a woman? Have you ever wondered how Mohammed would have handled such a conversation?" Then I thought I had them ready for the set-up question, "Have you ever wondered what Jesus would have said to a prostitute?"

To my surprise one of my Jewish students shot back with the answer, "He never met one!" I was about to correct him and show him from the New Testament that Jesus indeed had met prostitutes and that He had had some gracious things to say to them, when I realized what he meant. Jesus never did meet a prostitute. He certainly met women we would call prostitutes. But He never saw them as such. When He looked upon Mary Magdalene, He did not see a prostitute; he saw a woman with divine potentialities. He was aware of the filthy side of Mary and her sisters in the world's oldest profession, but He also saw their divinity. When He looked at Mary Magdalene, He saw holiness and loveliness and in the way He viewed her, He changed the way she viewed herself.

Erich Fromm, one of the most popular psychoanalysts of our time, recognized the diabolical social consequences that can come about when a person loses sight of his/her own divinity or the divinity of others. In his book *Escape from Freedom,* Fromm reminds us that forgetting the divine side of human nature is what leads to fascism. Ignoring the divine side of a certain race of people was a precondition for the persecution of the Jews and the propagation of the holocaust under the Nazi regime. Fromm points out that only by viewing Jews as devoid of godlike qualities could destroying them become possible. He saw that if the belief is perpetuated that only the elect who trust in Christ as Lord and Savior possess divine qualities, the persecuting of those outside the Christian community becomes permissible. When the destruction of non-Christians is seen only as the destruction of persons who are totally depraved, the ovens of Dachau become a possibility. Fromm argues that the Lutheran and Calvinistic view of the Jews as a totally depraved people, quite apart from God, created a disposition toward Jews that tolerated one of the most horrendous crimes against an ethnic group in human history.

It is a terrible mistake to forget that each of us is holy and sacred. On the other hand, it is foolish naiveté to ignore the mortal, corruptible side of our humanity. The tension between the awareness of our divinity and the discoveries we make about ourselves during our anal stage of development has to be resolved. But we must find a better way than to repress either our godlike qualities or the filthy corruptible underside of our humanness. We must face up to our eternity without denying our mortality. There are ways of doing just that. It is these positive ways of resolving our duality and overcoming our mortality that require our utmost attention.

6

The Neo-Freudians: New Options on the Road to Greatness

NEO-FREUDIANS have delivered Freud's work from the parodies and misconceptions that have accompanied it for decades. Norman O. Brown, in particular, has demonstrated that Freud, especially in his later writings, recognized dimensions of human nature that modern existentialist philosophers have only begun to grasp in their entirety. Brown shows us that Freud discovered that to be human is to have a corruptible body and, eventually, to die. Brown helps us to see that Freud understood that to be human is to be oriented to death and that the awareness of impending death is too ugly a truth for any of us to admit into our conscious minds. In the face of this terrible truth about human existence, we all seek ways to evade it or to repress it. According to Brown, the creating of a technique for repressing the truth about our mortality is a major responsibility of society. Without effective repression techniques, all of us would go mad in the face of the despairing realities that await us at the end of life.

The insights into Freud provided by Brown are invaluable. But there are implications to Freud's theories that even Brown, his best contemporary interpreter, did not recognize. Consequently, we must move on to consider the works of Ernest Becker, another neo-Freudian, in order that our attempt to separate Freud's writings from their most typical distortions be more complete. Only with this additional perspective can Freud's works and theories be recognized as having real significance for Christians seeking insight into human nature and human behavior.

Brown helps us to see that Freud recognized the seriousness of death in his understanding of the human situation. However, Becker goes beyond Brown by helping us to see the ways in which we humans endeavor to overcome death and to cure the anxieties that come from facing the threat of nonbeing. He outlines a variety of techniques that humans utilize in their efforts to conquer their mortality. Reviewing these techniques is essential to our self-understanding because most of us find some consolation in one or another of these means to salvation. An understanding of the various escape routes from death will help us to comprehend more fully a great deal of human behavior. This, claims Becker, is because most of what we do in our everyday lives is a covert attempt to overcome the consequences of our mortality.

In his most important book, *Denial of Death,* Becker outlines some of the cures for the ultimate sickness of our soul's angst, better known as the fear of dying. The following is not only a summary, but a Christian interpretation of what Becker states in that book.

The Transference Cure

One means of escaping the consciousness of one's finitude and mortality, according to Becker, is by identifying with a person who conveys an impression of immortality. Suffering from angst, many people seek out someone who appears to them to be superhuman. When such a person is found, they identify completely with this hero/heroine. By losing themselves in such a leader and by making that person their messiah, they gain a sense of power and significance that they would not otherwise have. Through a total identification with their seemingly divine leader, they gain a sense of participation in the messiah's apparent divinity. The need to escape the awareness of death moves them to transfer their selfhood to a charismatic leader who seems to be beyond their own limitations and shortcomings. Of such psychological needs dictators are born.

We fool ourselves if we think that a leader like Hitler imposes himself upon people or forces them into submission to his will. Neo-Freudians such as Becker believe that in most cases people crave domination by a Fuhrer. Becker says that they seek to be swallowed up by the seemingly all-powerful leader in the hope of sharing in his/her apparent immortality. The passion to overcome death has vast political implications.

If the neo-Freudians are right, then modern atheism with its emphasis on the temporal nature of human existence has prepared the way for the totalitarian regimes of the twentieth century. Becker's theory makes it easy to explain why the German people, who lost faith in themselves and in their God because of the breakdown of their society following their defeat in World War I, willingly embraced fascist dictatorship. Living in the midst of a society so disorganized that the usual techniques for repressing the truth about human nature were no longer effective, they sought immortality through the transference of their identities to one who to them seemed to be godlike. Hitler was more than a political leader to them. He was their savior from death.

Those of us who live in contemporary America, with its democratic institutions, are not beyond being tempted into the kind of leader worship that led to the fascism of the Nazis. If we are to escape such a future it will be wise, even necessary, to overcome the fear of death in a more constructive manner.

It is important to note that transference objects need not be totalitarian dictators. Positive wholesome leaders also can elicit high levels of identification from people, and provide for them the comforts of transference. Certainly, John F. Kennedy is an example of one to whom people transferred their hopes and dreams for immortality. His vitality and idealism touched a host of us Americans and we found in him a promise of glory. Many of us thought him to be endowed with a destiny for greatness, and we longed to share in that greatness. To numerous Americans, Kennedy embodied a quality of transcendence, and many, especially in the youth culture, overcame their sense of insignificance by losing themselves in him. He represented for more than those who will admit it the eternal greatness that we long to gain as a defense against the consequences of death.

The murder of John Kennedy affected most of us in a surprising manner. Many who ordinarily found it hard to weep cried openly at the news of his assassination. The outpouring of emotion at his funeral demonstrated that his death was more than the loss of a president. The bullets in Kennedy's skull not only killed him; they also crushed the hopes for immortality among the millions who subconsciously identified with him. Kennedy's death was their death, and when they cried for him they cried for themselves also. They had transferred their longings for transcendence over death to one who seemed immortal, and his death betrayed their trust.

Freud, according to Becker, points out that there are others, outside of politics, who also can serve as transference objects for those who need a savior from death. Becker shows us that Freud himself recognized that as a psychoanalyst he often served in such a role. He realized that his patients had a tendency to so identify with him during their time of treatment that ending the intimacy that accompanied psychoanalysis often left them in the depths of despair. To his patients, the psychoanalyst sometimes gives the impression of being omnipotent and omniscient. Freud realized that this could lead to a subjective transference. In counseling situations, there are many who try to escape their existential limitations by identifying with a person who symbolizes immortality.

Transference is so common that it is easy for psychoanalysts to exploit the process. Without too much effort psychoanalysts can turn transference into dependency, fostering relationships in which their clients become addicted to weekly visits at very high fees. Clients often beg for such dependency, and far too many professionals encourage it for their own aggrandizement. Exploitation can take even more ugly forms, as is readily revealed by statistics on the incidences of the sexual seduction of clients by counselors. So anxious is the client to be lost in the personhood of the seemingly omnipotent counselor, that no price proves too high to continue the relationship. It takes an ethical professional to avoid the temptation to exploit transference tendencies among those who come to his/her office.

Lest religious leaders get too haughty in their condemnation of the dependency relationships engendered by some professional counselors, let me hasten to point out that the clergy is often guilty of similar practices. With counseling becoming more and more a part of pastoral ministry, many of the clergy are unpleasantly surprised to find themselves in potentially dangerous relationships with parishioners. Church leaders who feel ineffective in their ministries may find that the adoration of their counselees provides some compensation for their sense of failure. And clergy persons who feel put down by unresponsive congregations can gain euphoric ego-lifts from persons who come to them for counsel and who are more than willing to make their pastors into their gods.

Transference tendencies of parishioners in counseling situations often have disastrous consequences. The scenario goes something like this: A woman is experiencing bouts of depression which are the unconscious result of death fears. She goes to her male pastor for counseling. He seems so wise, so caring, and so godlike that she feels secure when she is with him. She visits him often, and finds that she looks forward with intense longings to her time with her pastor. With each visit and conversation she becomes more dependent upon the inner peace she gains while with him. She subconsciously loses her identity in him, and he becomes her hope, joy, and life. Not sure she can live without her increasingly precious times with him, she has now reached a state of almost complete transference. She escapes her sense of mortality by feeling at one with this man who speaks of eternal things and seems to hold the secret of immortality. For his part, the pastor has entered into the counseling relationship with this woman not only for her sake, but because of his own needs. He is experiencing a sense of defeat in his ministry. When first he came to the church, he had dreams of being a prophet of God who would fill the sanctuary weekly with people who would gain new perspectives on life from his preaching. He imagined his church becoming a model of avant-garde ministry, charting new directions for Christendom even as its accomplishments were being written up in denominational publications.

But things have not worked out that way. Instead, he looks out upon the same old group Sunday after Sunday, and they are more interested in sermons of consolation than challenges to Christian activism. His new programs have not worked and he finds that most of his time is consumed by religious bureaucratic functions. At this point they come together—the woman who wants a godlike person through whom she can escape from the increasing evidence of her decaying body and growing consciousness of her approaching death, and the pastor who longs for adoration and worship that will establish within him a sense of glory. Their needs make for a symbiotic, mutually gratifying relationship. At first the relationship is all innocent, but she seeks deeper identification with him in every visit, while he desires more and more adoration from her. The counseling session begins with an embrace of affection (after all, the seminary taught him about the holiness of tactile experiences), but soon it moves to more intimate caresses. Transference leads to sexual intimacy and soon two marriages are destroyed and a pastorate ruined. This escape from death has become a most deadly enterprise. It takes a very "together" pastor to handle counseling.

Transference occurs on an even grander scale for the evangelist. While the process is not as direct or intimate as that which occurs in pastoral counseling, it is no less intense and, in different ways, every bit as dangerous. The evangelist, who is most often a male, and who has seeming charismatic authority, projects a quality of fearlessness as he challenges evil and the Prince of Darkness. Strutting back and forth across the platform of the tabernacle, the evangelist appears powerful enough to stand up to and defeat any and all spiritual enemies. With index finger pointed to the heavens and with fist pounding the pulpit, he seems to be an invincible prophet of God.

It is no wonder that so many of his listeners will become his followers, and that many will identify with him so completely that they will lose themselves in him. Anyone who has ever attended a mass gathering in which an evangelist does his "thing" is well aware of the transference that is taking place. The evangelist appears awesomely daring to those who have deep feelings of cowardice, and invincible to those with fears of failure. To those who feel like dung he seems like a god who dares for them, triumphs for them, and is virtuous for them. He seems to live out the greatness that they fear is trapped within them, and by living out that greatness delivers them from the guilt of not expressing it in their own lives. They do not have to dare anything. They only have to conform to the group which the evangelist has brought into being through his oratory and to lose themselves in the movement which he seems to be creating. He convinces them that they are part of a mighty movement which will drive back evil, purify America, defeat communism, and bring forth the kingdom of God. It is easy to understand how those of us who are filled with anxieties and fears about what we are and what we might become can so readily give ourselves over to the seemingly godlike personage who promises us eternal significance if we join him.

My deepest fears about mass evangelism are not based upon what the evangelist does to the crowd. Instead, I fear what the crowd does to the evangelist. Seeing in him the embodiment of their dreams for immortality, they lay upon him burdens that are too heavy for him to bear. It should come as no surprise that some evangelists who cannot bear it chuck the whole business and run off with some adoring sexual partner to live out the antithesis of their spiritual public personas.

I do not condemn evangelists. I myself am one of them. I find that answering the call to be an evangelist is a good way to carry out the Great Commission of Jesus to preach the gospel to all nations. I simply am calling attention to the seduction into transference that characterizes a great deal of what goes on subconsciously in evangelistic meetings. There are times when I have finished my evangelistic preaching only to wonder whether I have brought glory to God or brought glory to myself. And far more dangerous than I are those evangelists who are not even aware of the potentialities for transference that are inherent in their ministries. These are the ones who are most likely to be destroyed by it all. Evangelists have not all been men. From Aimee Semple McPherson to Katharine Kuhlman, a growing number of them have been women. And women are in every bit as much danger of these pitfalls as are their male counterparts.

True Christianity as Transference

Freud has led many of us to think that transference is a basically bad thing, without redeeming qualities. He has caused us to assume that transference is something done by psychologically sick people, leading us to the faulty assumption that there are others of us who are not psychologically sick. Freud leaves us feeling that we should do something to cure people of their tendencies toward transference. It remained the task of his successors to demonstrate the positive potentialities in this process. Otto Rank, one of Freud's successors, helps us see how transference can be turned into something creative and humanizing, particularly within the context of religion. Feeling a kinship with "The All," he shows, can have therapeutic consequences for troubled and fearful humanity.

According to Rank, only by having a "god-ideal" outside of the self is human existence possible. Only through believing in a transcendental reality can persons gain a sense that what they do and who they are has some ultimate significance. Some may say that believing in a God who gives meaning to life and importance to what we do is a delusion. If it is, argues Rank, it is a delusion without which life, for most of us, would be impossible. Freud saw our hunger for God as immature and selfish, but Rank saw it as a "reaching out for a plenitude of meaning for life." Rank said that through religious transference we are reaching out for more of life; each of us seeking to discover what makes each of us special; each of us seeking to discover the unique gifts that God has designated for all of us.

In the final analysis, becoming a Christian is basically an act of transference. Salvation is experienced when individuals receive eternal life by identifying with God through Christ. Losing ourselves in Christ is the essence of the Christian faith, and the biblical message is filled with invitations to do just that. To those of us who are weary with the burden of our mortality, the fear of death, and the guilt associated with the failure to realize our potential greatness, Jesus says: "Come unto me, all ye that labour and are heavy laden, and I will give you rest. Take my yoke upon you, and learn of me; for I am meek and lowly in heart: and ye shall find rest unto your souls. For my yoke is easy, and my burden is light" (Matt. 11:28–30).

For those of us who want to become new and glorious persons, the apostle Paul has stated that this can happen if we are willing to lose ourselves "in Christ": "Therefore if any man be in Christ, he is a new creature: old things are passed away; behold, all things are become new" (2 Cor. 5:17). A careful reading of Scripture will help us to see that losing ourselves in the cause of Christ is the only way to hold onto life and live it abundantly. "Then said Jesus unto his disciples, if any man will come after me, let him deny himself, and take up his cross, and follow me. For whosoever will save his life shall lose it: and whosoever will lose his life for my sake shall find it" (Matt. 16:24–25).

As one who spends most of his time endeavoring to communicate the gospel to college students, I have often focused on answering the question of what actually happens to persons who become Christians. I have rethought with intense concern the meaning of conversion. I have sensed the ultimate significance in exploring the essence of the Christian experience in social and psychological terms. More and more I have come to believe that what is involved in being "saved" is to undergo a process, akin to what the Freudians might call transference, in which persons so identify with Christ that His victory over death becomes theirs. As Christians, the "saved" enter into His heroic mission for the salvation of the world. They share in His courageous sacrifices for humanity. Like the apostle Paul, they pray that they "may know Him, and the power of His resurrection, and the fellowship of His sufferings, being made conformable unto His death" (Phil. 3:10).

Christians are people who completely identify with Christ, and through Him sense a oneness with God. They are encouraged into this transference by Christ Himself who prayed "that they all may be one; as thou, Father, art in me, and I in thee, that they also may be one in us: that the world may believe that thou hast sent me" (John 17:21).

Through identification with Christ, the fear and guilt associated with unrealized potential is overcome. Christians are able to say: "I can do all things through Christ which strengtheneth me" (Phil. 4:13). The act of transference is a prelude to heroism. By identifying with God through Christ, all things seem possible (Mark 10:27). The apostles, who, following the capture and trial of Jesus, seemed cowardly and weak, gained incredible courage and strength when they were able to "enter into fellowship" with the resurrected Christ. Peter, who had been threatened by a sole inquiring girl by a campfire, was able to declare the gospel of Christ boldly before thousands, after he had entered into a state of spiritual and psychological oneness with the resurrected Lord. Disciples who hid themselves during the trial of Jesus were able to risk their lives as His witnesses after they had experienced the transformation of their psyches through identification with the eternal Christ. From their time to the present, persons have been transformed from frightened, despairing, guilty souls into courageous, hopeful crusaders for the kingdom of God.

Religious transference in which one gains a sense of worth, significance, and immortality by identifying with a person who becomes one's god is a delusion, because the person who stands for God is an impostor. That is not the case for Christians. They believe that God is, and they are sure that Jesus is their God expressed in human form. They know that their Jesus is not simply a historical figure who lived and died a long time ago, but is a living, resurrected person mystically available to them for personal relationships. I know something of these relationships, for I am in one. I can affirm to a personal involvement with Christ. I encounter His presence. I live with a consciousness that I am "in" Him and He is "in" me. Call it transference if you like, but in my relationship with Jesus Christ I know that I have eternal life. I can personally testify to the fact that "he that hath the Son hath life" (1 John 5:12).

Freud argued that there is no God and that transference encourages immaturity and psychological sickness. Christians affirm that there is a God who expressed Himself fully in Jesus and is present with us now as the Holy Spirit. We believe that being in Him enables us to achieve a higher level of humanity and to acquire a psychological wholeness that enables us to live with joy.

Romance as Salvation

There are many in our secular age who cannot find salvation through identification with Christ because they find believing in God intellectually impossible. This is not because there is evidence that there is no God or that Jesus was just an ordinary man, but because these persons have been conditioned socially into a secular mind-set that has no room for such beliefs. These secularists are not people who have no need for religion, no fear of death, and no need for transference. They are simply people who have no God to whom they can give themselves. They are victims of a modernity that confines belief to the empirical and logical, and the gospel is neither of these. Secularists too need salvation. They too need deliverance from the reality of their mortality. They look, as do we Christians, for transference objects that can bear the burdens they find too heavy.

One commonly adopted transference object in a world that has grown cold because of the "death" of God, is a lover. Someone who finds religion unreal may choose a flesh-and-blood member of the opposite sex to be an instrument of salvation. It is possible for a person to "fall in love" in such a way as to make his/her partner into a messiah who provides deliverance, at least temporarily, from the pangs of human existence. In such a case the lover is imputed with divine qualities and is viewed as possessing the capacity to meet every emotional need. It is fair to say that when a lover becomes an object of transference, the lover functions as a god. Understandably, most love songs in our culture depict lovers in sublime language and utilize a vocabulary traditionally reserved for religion. The music of romance is prone to have such phrases as:

"I can't get along without you, baby . . ."

"Ah, sweet mystery of life . . ."

"You're my everything . . ."

"If they made me a king, I'd still be a slave to you . . ."

"I'm nothing without you . . ."

"I'm in heaven with you . . ."

Lyrics of love songs leave little doubt about the significance of a lover. Dedication and willingness to sacrifice for the lover are so great that they can only be compared to the dedication and sacrifices that the saints of the church have offered up to God. The person is completely lost in the lover and believes that there is no meaning apart from being with that person forever.

The process of transference to a loved one can result in heroic accomplishments. Throughout time there have been stories of feats of courage and sacrifice in the name of love. For lovers, dragons have been slain, suicidal missions undertaken, and lives recklessly spent. Like Hotspur, many of us long for dangerous opportunities that will allow us to display our willingness to sacrifice our lives for love. There is no way of knowing how many of us secretly seek to be heroic knights willing to fight to the death for the sake of our lovers.

Making lovers into transference objects poses a variety of problems for all concerned. First, the lover is bound to be a disappointment, for, after all, he/she is only human. Sooner or later the lover's image of perfection is going to be broken. Marriages break up because wives complain that their husbands are not the men they thought they were. Husbands become disillusioned when they grasp the fact that their wives are corruptible and mortal.

Unfortunately, lovers almost always betray our idealization of them. They are too available for scrutiny. It is much better to have a god we cannot see. It is better to love from afar—much better. The tragedy of Don Juan is to be found not only in the brokenhearted women he used and left behind, but in his failure to find in any of them the salvation he desperately sought. With each lover he had hoped to find the one who was worthy of worship, capable of giving him immortality and deserving of his greatest sacrifices. To his disappointment, he discovered that they were all too human, and that he was seeking salvation where it could not be found. No one, save Jesus, is capable of maintaining the image of divinity upon close inspection.

I wonder how many marriages fail because people expect too much of their partners. I wonder how many partners grow disillusioned because they discover that they are not married to gods. Perhaps a good reason for being religious is to create good marital relationships. If you have a transcendent God, there is no need to make your lover into one. If you worship Jesus, there is no need for your partner to be worshiped. If you are a Christian, you free your lover to be herself/himself and nothing more. Only then is a creative relationship possible. Only when we see each other face to face rather than through a glass darkly is it possible to know each other. Only when we encounter the person who really is, rather than the person we establish out of our need for transference, is it possible to have humanizing affection. We all need to worship a transcendent God lest we destroy those closest to us by forcing them to be gods for us.

Whenever I hear someone say, "I worship my wife; I need no other commitment," I pray.

The Creative Cure

I have tried to demonstrate that for most of us psychological survival is possible because we have bought into a lie about our human nature. We have repressed the truth about death and we go on about our daily affairs as though we will live forever. Logically we know that we will die, but the truth that logic affirms nearly always seems unreal. Society undertakes the task of providing sufficient diversion from the truth about existence to keep us from grasping the significance of our mortality. Each of us is able to say with detached logic,

> All humans will die.
> I am a human.
> I will die.

But the truth of the logic does not impinge upon our consciousness. The existential reality with its despairing message is pushed into the subconscious. The "healthy" people of the world are those of us who are deluded into ignoring our mortality.

I have also endeavored to point out that there are some exceptional people who see through the deception and the distractions that society employs to keep us "together" lest in solitude we grasp the truth. These are the individuals who for the most part become neurotic and, at times, psychotic. Often the people we call "sick" are none other than those who have understood the significance of death and find the truth too burdensome to bear.

Our bourgeois world provides fewer and fewer effective mechanisms for delusions into immortality, but there are some escape routes from its neuroses and psychoses. Among those escape routes is art, which brings us once again to the work of Otto Rank. This semi-religious neo-Freudian was unique in his explorations of the role of art as a technique for handling existential reality. It was Rank who recognized that the difference between a "sick" person and an artistic genius is talent. Whereas the neurotic internalizes his/her suffering and makes the truth about death a cancer that destroys the joy for living, the artist has the ability to externalize agony and creatively work out despair.

Nietzsche once said that through art it is possible to make suffering into something beautiful. Rank recognized in Nietzsche's comment a possible escape route from the destructiveness of existential truth. The artist, contends Rank, is able to "work out" the agonies of his/her soul on the canvas or the music page, or in a manuscript. Like the scapegoat of the ancient religions, art is a vehicle for carrying that which the artist finds too heavy to bear. The artist hangs his soul on his art and gains relief through the externalization of his/her sufferings. The works produced are more than "pretty things" to be used to decorate walls, stand in hallways, or otherwise provide for public entertainment. It is true that what the experts call "folk art" may merely decorate, but art at its best is therapy for the fear of death.

We should not be surprised that Salvador Dali and Pablo Picasso were reluctant to sell their paintings. They, like all true artists, felt that something of themselves was incarnated in what they had created. They had no desire to witness their souls being dissected by critics who all too often talked about color schemes and balance.

True art tends to communicate a melancholia to its sensitive viewers. A certain unpleasantness, a strange weariness may overtake us as we wander through the halls of masterpieces, whereas folk art exhibits make us happy. The kind of stuff offered for sale at novelty shops generates delight. But there is something haunting about most true art, because it stimulates an awareness of the agony of the artist's soul. Van Gogh's *Starry Night,* Bosch's visions of the afterlife, Beethoven's *Fifth Symphony,* and Milton's poems all elicit "groanings which cannot be uttered." Oh, there are many exceptions—the childlike joy expressed in Picasso's painting of *Three Musicians,* Tchaikovsky's ballet suite *The Nutcracker,* and Walt Whitman's odes to life. But these are temporary excursions from the real agonies of art which relate to the ultimate truths about life.

Most of us typical and, for the most part, mediocre people have attempted to create something artistic—perhaps a poem or a painting. It is interesting that, as we recall such occasions, we usually discover that they were associated with life's tragedies. They may have followed a time of failure. They may have been associated with the death of a significant other. They may have been a result of unrequited love. You can probably recall, as can I, staying up into the wee hours of the morning and scribbling poems to give vent to feelings. Our creative juices flowed, and we sensed that we were expressing something of ultimate importance. It made no difference that the world would not see what we were creating. We were creating for ourselves, or perhaps for God, which is the case with all true art.

Among the greatest fears of artists is that they will lose their skills. Most of them have nightmares that their talent will suddenly be taken from them. Painters often delay starting on a new canvas for fear that they do not "have it" anymore. Writers, too, often shy away from getting started on new works. Musicians suffer from the same malady, citing all sorts of reasons for not composing new scores—the weather, their lovers, the food, the lighting. Each of these creative individuals fears awakening, as did Samson after his head was shorn, to discover that his/her particular gift has departed. To lose their talent is to lose the ability to externalize their sufferings, to be without a means of unburdening their souls. Held inside, their suffering might become too much to bear, even to the point of causing them to commit suicide.

Middle-class culture and middle-class religion have never handled artists well. They do not like most art because it makes them uncomfortable. The culture and religion of the middle class are designed to maintain psychological comfort and a happy-minded adjustment to life. True art disrupts this pleasant state and forces the comfortable members of the bourgeoisie to give up their illusions concerning life. In his book *One-Dimensional Man*, Herbert Marcuse wrote that by reminding us of what is absent, art makes us discontent with what is. Marcuse understood all too well why we middle-class types so often ridicule and reject art. As it brings to consciousness what our bourgeois social system has been constructed to conceal, it stirs within us the inklings of the truth and, consequently, makes us unable to enjoy the "good life" that we have learned to expect.

Art reminds us of that which even our religion has tried to conceal. Religion's homilies on being nice to the postman, its focus on contemporary social issues, and its programmed encounter groups have all evaded the ultimate religious truth—that we all die. The artists will not let us off the hook so easily. They break through our religious activism and our busy committee meetings and remind us of what is absent from our religion—the awareness and the conquest of death. We would rather not hear from them. Middle-class religion delights in being positive and happy. But the artists will not let us go. They constantly remind us that in the shadow stands Thanatos. And once we are reminded of what we have tried so hard to forget, that which is, our bourgeois culture and its religious legitimation seem intolerable. We want didactic art that depicts scenes from the life of Christ, paintings showing Him holding baby lambs or preaching on a lovely hillside. We don't want pictures of our souls. We don't want music or paintings that carry us unwittingly into the truth about life and death. We middle-class types want distraction in music and paintings, not reality.

Middle-Class Religion as an Escape

It may seem strange that religion is one of the most common escape routes from religious questions. However, it is quite easy to make a case to substantiate this thesis. The church of middle-class Protestantism is designed so as to keep people from ever having to face the ultimate questions of human existence. A survey of what is said and done in typical middle-class churches will reveal that the people there deal with everything except death and its significance for life. Religion in affluent middle-class America has developed a positive optimistic attitude toward life that allows little room for the seemingly morbid discussion about death. It is interesting to note that courses on death and dying have become part of the curriculum of colleges and universities while middle-class churches shy away from such subjects.

One of my responsibilities is to teach men and women the skills of youth ministry. In acquainting my students with books and program materials available for the development of youth groups, I am disheartened, at times, by the fare available. Those who prepare material for youth ministry essentially provide entertainment ideas. Plans for cookouts, camping trips, parties, and games are carefully delineated. Bible games and discussions of subjects relevant to everyday life are commonly suggested topics for youth group meetings. Programs include guidance in how to choose a college, a mate, a vocation, and places to go on dates, but little is done to confront teenagers with the ultimate questions of the meaning of life, the significance of death, and the nature of our humanity. Claiming that youth are not interested in such subjects, that they are concerned with other things, we cop out by addressing young people where we imagine "they are at." What Freud and his successors have endeavored to make clear to us is that the frivolous ways of the young and the noise they make are only cover-ups for the despair about life and death that is at the core of their personalities. Those in the tradition of Freud have told us quite clearly that, from the time these young people passed into the anal stage of sociopsychological development, they have been troubled by the paradoxical nature of their humanity and have been threatened by the specter of death. Freud, and especially the neo-Freudians, have contended that from the earliest stages of consciousness we are all morbid existentialists.

Why are we surprised when we learn that suicide has reached epidemic proportions among high school students? We should realize that there is more despair in their subculture than first appearance would suggest. When some of the brightest young people of our middle-class churches join religious cults or westernized versions of Eastern religions, we are perplexed. We should not be. At least these new religions, as true or false as their answers may be, deal with the ultimate questions. They talk about death, and they ask what is the mission for the individual in the midst of life lived in the face of death. They make young people feel that they are dealing with that which is of ultimate importance.

What is true for young people is even more true for the adult population. People want to know exactly what will happen to them when they die. They want to know if there is enough meaning to life to keep them from assuming the libertine philosophy of "eat, drink, and be merry, for tomorrow we die." They want to know if life has some ultimate meaning that would warrant the abandoning of extramarital affairs or the pursuing of the gratifications stimulated by media advertising. To paraphrase the words of Scripture, the hungry people look up for bread and receive a stone. They belong to churches preoccupied with building programs, social action committees, and encounter groups. They hear sermons on race relations, disarmament, and liberation theology. Their preachers assure them that they are hearing things that are really important, even as they sense that what is really important to them is being left unanswered. "Who am I?" they ask. "How can I hold on to life?" "How can I stay young?" "How can I go on working at a job that I hate even as I feel my life ebbing away?" "How can I face the disappointment that my life has turned out to be?" "How can God love somebody with such a filthy sex life as mine?" "How can I stop being scared and filled with anxiety?" "How can I overcome this pervasive depression I feel about life?"

It seems to me that the churches of middle-class Protestantism are justifiably condemned for their evasion of what is ultimate about life and death. The techniques that they employ are manifold but nearly all of them center on one principle: make ultimate that which is trivial. If people are preoccupied by thinking that they are dealing with ultimate questions, when in reality they are dealing with trivial matters, they can ignore, at least temporarily, what *is* of ultimate concern.

Consider the things that become major issues among middle-class church people. Do any of them relate to that which is ultimate? Churches go through schisms over issues like whether or not the return of Christ will occur before or after "the seven years of tribulation" (Dan. 9:25–27) referred to in the Gospel of Matthew. Major conflicts arise in local congregations over such matters as whether or not young people should be allowed to hold dances in church buildings. People leave some churches and join others because the music is not what they think it should be. Seminaries raise to a level of urgency such questions as whether the pastor's wife should have to belong to the ladies' aid society or teach the women's Bible class. Bible study often degenerates into a religious version of Trivial Pursuit, as the church places major importance upon whether or not Paul wrote the Epistle to the Hebrews, or Jonah was really swallowed by a whale.

Recently I learned of a church that had gone through great agitation and division over the question of whether or not children should be taught to believe in Santa Claus. Some argued that Santa was taking the place of Jesus in the minds of the boys and girls, and that they were being good for the sake of Saint Nicholas rather than for the sake of the Lord. Others argued that the spirit of Santa was what Christmas was all about, and that the jolly man about whom Virginia inquired in her famous letter to the editor incarnated Christian virtues. The pastor of the church who wrote to me about this matter stated with seeming wonder, "Many of the people in my church do not realize just how important this question really is." I am sure he would have been offended if I had told him that he should be concerned about more important things. To him and to the people of his congregation, the Santa issue was of ultimate concern.

By making trivial matters into major concerns, the churches of the middle class are able to keep their members preoccupied, diverting them from the hard and ugly questions about human existence. Once people believe that what is trivial is of ultimate importance, they feel justified in spending all their time and energy pursuing these concerns. Ultimizing the trivial creates the preoccupation that delivers the bourgeois Christians from the ugly questions of existence. Thus, religion becomes an escape from the religious issues of life.

Heroism as an Affirmation of Humanity

So far as Ernest Becker is concerned, the best way to overcome the dilemmas of human existence is through heroism. Furthermore, he argues that religion is failing in our day because it has failed to provide models of heroism for young people. That, says Becker, is why young people turn from religion and even despise it. They, like the rest of us, seek to do with their lives something that will justify their existence. They want to do something that will establish their immortality, something that is so wonderful that they would find dying in the process of attempting to do it worthy of their highest aspirations. According to Becker, young people despise a culture that promises them comfort, and they shun a church that seeks to entertain them. Youth, contends Becker, is made for heroism, not for pleasure. Youth rejects a religion that only invites them to imitate the roles created by society to ensure culturally defined success.

Those of us who have aged somewhat also have a thirst for glorious heroism. We too long for the opportunity to realize our potential for greatness. We feel that we can face death only if we have done something magnificently heroic with our lives.

Once when I was at a theater in New York City, enjoying a performance of the award-winning musical *Man of La Mancha,* a most revealing thing happened. The woman next to me began to scold her husband. "John!" she said, "John, stop that! You're exposing yourself. You're exposing yourself." Seated next to her was a middle-aged businessman, dressed in a proper three-piece suit, crying uncontrollably. It took me only a moment to figure out the cause of his emotional breakdown. Don Quixote was on stage, singing the lyrics of the theme song, "To Dream the Impossible Dream."

As I glanced out of the corner of my eye at this sobbing man, I wondered what long-suppressed dream was now being remembered, what great thing he had planned to do that had been set aside as he carried out the more mundane concerns of life. I wondered what he had hoped to be but had never become. I had the feeling that this ordinary man had once hungered for greatness and that he had let the time for greatness pass him by.

Heroism meets the requisites of human existence. It enables each of us to achieve a sense of immortality and it provides for each of us the opportunity to realize the awesome potentialities we feel within. Only humans can be heroes. Animals lack the sense of divinity which the Freudians say is generated in the oral stage of human development. It is the awareness of the divine side of our personalities that drives us to do things worthy of gods. Angels cannot be heroes because they do not have our weaknesses, and therefore do not possess our probability for failure. Angels do not know what it is like for those with the limitations of mortals to attempt godlike feats. Heroism involves the probability of failure and destruction. The best heroes are the tragic figures who have defied their human limitations and attempted, like Icarus, to fly to the sun.

In heroism we affirm both our humanity and our divinity. Both dimensions of our paradoxical personalities come into play. We affirm our divinity by doing what is worthy of gods, and we affirm our humanity by taking risks only available to mortals.

God had to become one of us before He could be heroic. He had to take on the likeness of our humanity before He could attempt the impossible. In Jesus, God took on the weakness of human flesh. In Jesus, God could have failed. He might have bowed down to Satan in the temptation experience, but He did not. He might have come down from the cross when Satan mockingly called upon Him to display His powers, but He did not. He was tempted in all ways as we are tempted, yet He remained without sin. In Christ, God heroically challenged the powers of darkness. In Christ, God went through the valley of the shadow of death. In Christ, God, with human weakness, challenged the Prince of Darkness. He is the ultimate hero, and as such provides the example for us all.

Christianity offers the best opportunities for greatness. Through faith, each of us can come to believe that our creatureliness has meaning to the Creator. The leaders of Campus Crusade, one of the most dynamic Christian movements on university campuses today, attract collegians to Christ with the simple declaration: *God has a wonderful plan for your life.* They know that there is no greater turn-on for young people than the good news that there is some ultimate purpose to their lives, and that for each of them there is something heroic to do for God. If the churches of the middle class lose their members while such parachurch organizations as Campus Crusade grow, it is because they have made Christianity too easy and have failed to provide the challenge of heroic missions which characterize biblical Christianity.

Heroes assert their divinity in the face of their humanity. They do not passively surrender to their weaknesses, nor do they remain silent dreamers. They plunge into great undertakings and find their fulfillment in tasks that seem worthy of them. Christ enables them to achieve their heroism as they sense that what they do is done for Him and through Him. Serving God leaves them with the sense that even if they fail they do so in a cause that will ultimately win. Acting in the spirit of Christ, they sense an empowering Presence that enables them to attempt things that will realize their greatness. In the hands of Christ, their earthly bodies are transformed into the likes of Prometheus. As heroes they can cry out, "O death, where is thy sting? O grave, where is thy victory?"

The Failure of Freud

Freud rejected the possibilities of Christian heroism. He viewed people who lived for God as infantile, still needing a father to carry them through the ultimate struggles of life. Freud believed that people too weak to stand alone had created an imaginary heavenly father to take over from their biological fathers the task of being their protectors and sustainers. He himself thought that he was strong enough to face death without God. Freud, according to Becker, thought that he could achieve immortality through his works. He believed that his discoveries about human nature would carry him into the age to come. Freud was convinced that the field of study he initiated would, in some sense, keep him alive after death.

Becker tells us that toward the end of his life, Freud became aware of the fact that his basis for immortality was shaky at best, and perhaps even worthless. On two occasions Freud became so upset that he fainted. According to Becker, the fainting spells were the results of events that signaled to Freud that his work would not continue intact. On both occasions, the fainting occurred when Carl Jung, Freud's most favored student, defied him and offered theories of his own to explain human behavior. Freud, contends Becker, realized that Jung would not take the place of the son he had never had. In these confrontations, Freud realized that after his death even his most devoted follower would not treat his theories as sacred. Jung would modify them and reach greatness through his own achievements, rather than by simply carrying on the work of his mentor. Freud realized the truth about Jung and could not tolerate the idea that his own immortality was at stake, and he lost consciousness at the certainty of his own demise.

Freud avoided religion even though his theories had religious dimensions. He shied away from the dreams and visions of religious crusaders because he believed them to be unreal. He hoped that he could achieve immortality another way. He believed his significance would be established through academic accomplishments. Freud failed to understand that the visions and dreams that we all need in order to make life tolerable are generated by the belief that there is an ultimate meaning to life. He failed to grasp the truth that there could be no hope in the face of death without God.

Part Three

The Attack from Below

7

Marx: Good Intentions Gone Astray

THE ATTACK upon cultural middle-class religion by the socially disinherited proletarian class had its most significant expression in the works of Karl Marx. Seated inconspicuously in the library of the British museum, this brilliant philosopher (although he called himself a scientific historian) analyzed human history from an economic perspective. He contended that, rather than the Hegelian *Geist*, the economic requisites for human survival were the driving forces of history. He taught that all social institutions and cultural products were created by people seeking ways to meet their real and artificially created economic needs.

The writings of Marx proved to be the most challenging critique of Christianity to emerge in the twentieth century. More intellectuals were lured away from religiosity by the seductive logic and clarity of Marx's arguments than through any other scholarly instruments. The appeal of the social movement generated by his thinking captured the allegiance of more oppressed industrial workers and impoverished serfs than any option of hope provided by democratic capitalism. Ironically, Marx's revolutionary ideology eventually came to be integrated with the Christian belief system which he so much despised, to form one of the most dynamic theological movements of our time—liberation theology.

It is fair to argue that the Communist movement has provided the most serious threat to the continued existence of traditional Christianity since Mohammed led his Moslem hordes out of Arabia and marched them to the gates of Vienna. And it is also fair to say that Marxist thought has provided the most popular ideological alternative to the Christian faith since the Renaissance.

Many Christians have seen in the Marxist proletarian soldiers the evil "armies of the north" which the Bible predicted would arise "in the last days" to challenge the armies of God at Armageddon. The onslaught of communism has been called the work of the Antichrist, and Marx himself has been labeled as a Satanist come to blaspheme the name of Jesus.

Whatever the concerns surrounding the threats that Marx's philosophy and the Communist movement pose for Western democratic capitalism and for middle-class religion, it is foolish to believe that this ideology and its followers could spell the death of Christianity. For those who believe in the sovereignty of God there can be no doubt about the survival of Christ's church and the outcome of history. Any who have read the Bible know how the world ends—Jesus wins! In the words of Isaac Watts's great hymn, "Jesus shall reign where'er the sun does its successive journeys run." However, the coming Kingdom of our Lord may be vastly different from the utopia envisioned by middle-class churchgoers, and the future shape of Christian doctrinal expressions and cultural institutions far different from those that exist today. I am sure that Marx was wrong when he predicted that humanity would outgrow all forms of religion. But I am convinced also that the forms of Christian thought will be influenced significantly by dialectical tensions with Marxist ideologies. For better or for worse, the institutional forms of middle-class Christianity will be changed through conflict with its most formidable enemy of the twentieth century.

As we Christians face the future, we must understand the nature of Marx's attack. We will do well to use the valid aspects of his critique of bourgeois Christianity to purge ourselves of those accretions to our faith that are alien to the essence of the biblical message and only serve our social-class interests. We must be prepared to defend ourselves against a seduction by Marxist philosophy that would make Christianity into nothing more than another form of the Communist revolution. If we do not recognize our enemy, we will be conquered before we realize what is happening. If we do not learn from our enemy, we will fail to avail ourselves of the insights of our most honest critics.

The Struggle between Classes

First and foremost, Karl Marx believed that the history of humanity was a history of struggles between social classes. He rejected as mystical nonsense the Hegelian concept of the *Geist*. Marx did not believe that there was a God or any other spiritual power controlling the historical process. According to Marx, an understanding of history is to be found, not in religion or philosophical idealism, but in the everyday struggles of human beings as they try to eke out their survival in a world with limited resources for their sustenance.

In every society since the dawn of civilization there has been a class struggle. Ever since that early time when humanity emerged from the primitive socioeconomic conditions which Marx called "primitive communism," there have been those with a disproportionate and unfair share of the economic resources necessary to sustain life, and there has been an oppressed class of people who have had less than enough to survive. The ruling classes, in their immoral selfishness, have used brutality and trickery to hold onto what they have had while the dominated working classes have submitted to an unending array of injustices and schemes of exploitation. Marx committed himself to the task of explaining to the poor peoples of the world the ways in which they had been misused and denigrated by the ruling classes, and to calling them to rebel against the social systems that had made them into chattel and slaves.

Those who have seen in Marx's philosophy and plan for the oppressed peoples of the world a humanistic version of the Christian gospel are quite correct in their analysis and conclusion. If there had not been a Judeo-Christian tradition, there would not have been a Marxist movement. Marxist philosophy is a twisted Christian heresy. Marx's hope for the world is a secularized version of the biblical kingdom of God. His beliefs about the final struggle between the bourgeois class of the capitalist society and the so-called exploited proletariat has its parallel in the biblical imagery of the battle of Armageddon.

Marx, like the New Testament writers, looked forward to a time when this present social order would pass away and be replaced by a new kingdom in which justice and goodness would prevail. Like the apostle Paul, he believed that the present age, with its wars, sufferings, and inequalities, was about to pass away, and that we could be said to be living in "the last days." In the future age there would be no ruling classes; no rich elitists lording it over the oppressed; no evil political systems denying people freedom. As in the early church that is described in the Book of Acts, every person would receive what he/she needed and each would contribute to the welfare of society in accord with his/her abilities. Marx looked forward to a time when the nations would be unified into one world so that there would no longer be Greeks and barbarians, Gentiles and Jews, or males and females: there would be only comrades. He anticipated the liberation of women, the demise of racial discrimination, and the end of human selfishness.

According to Marx, it is the present economic system that is responsible for the sin and evils of our world. He was convinced that the new socioeconomic order he envisioned would so structure human relationships that what he perceived to be perversions of basically good humanity would fade away. As he saw it, it is the system, not our hearts, that makes us do evil things to one another. According to Marx, human behavior is not distorted by original sin as the Christian theologians have said. Instead, human behavior is determined by the social system, and when the social system is changed to a just and benevolent order, human beings will be conditioned to be just and benevolent. Marx would say that it is our present capitalistic system, with its emphasis on competition, the private accumulation of wealth, and the maintenance of the class structure, that has generated the envy, selfishness, greed, and covetousness that mark the people of our age. In Marx's communistic society of the future these emotions and attitudes will disappear.

Marx believed in the kingdom of God without God, and that was his mistake. Without God, anything is permissible, and so it has been with the movement generated by the philosophy of Marx. The means to achieve his envisioned kingdom of total freedom has fostered more enslavement and mind control than all the totalitarian movements that have gone before it. His plan for camaraderie among all peoples has led to more bloodshed and death than resulted from the actions of both Hitler and Genghis Khan.

The revolution that Marx envisioned would not necessarily have to come about through violence. In some places, his brave new world could be brought about through free elections. It could be achieved by participating in existing bourgeois governments and gradually influencing them to become more and more socialistic. The Communist movement could gain control of the labor unions of a particular nation and negotiate its demands for a change from that source of social power. However, the means and the goal must be the same: there must be created an entirely new social order in which a classless society replaces the present class society with all its inequalities and forms of exploitation. Marx saw the need to control the governments of nations in order to bring about his new socioeconomic order but, strange as it might seem, governments frightened him. He hoped that, once the Communist society was established, these political entities would pass away.

Marx also assumed a very negative attitude toward the existence of the state. In this respect, he must prove an embarrassment to those socialist governments that have developed extensive self-perpetuating bureaucracies. He condemned the tendency of the state to usurp the prerogatives of society and to give them over to a small elite of government officials. Marx contended that people are forced to regard such officials as their masters when in reality they should be humble servants, if they exist at all. Civil servants, he said, inevitably become masters who dominate the workers. The power that belongs to the people becomes invested in bureaucratic clerks who exercise control over those who should have the right to determine their own destinies. Decision-making, which should be the right of the working people who create society's wealth, becomes the province of bureaucrats who produce nothing.

Marx's Hope for Society

It was Marx's hope that the state would wither away following the creation of a socialist system. Needless to say, that has not happened in the nations of the socialist bloc. Instead, the governments of these countries have become increasingly bloated bureaucracies, primarily committed to their own perpetuation rather than to serving the general public. Marx had feared that there would be a perpetuation of the state in socialist systems, and toward the end of his life wrote one of his most scathing denunciations of government, outlining its inherent tendencies toward totalitarian tyranny.

It was Ferdinand Lassalle, an early organizer of the Communist movement, who was the culprit who conceived of the state as a primary instrument for promoting social progress. In his not-so-famous Gotha declaration Marx condemned Lassalle and called the Communist party away from its increasing commitment to the utilization of a proletarian government as the instrument for promoting social change. Marx saw that the state would allow only changes that did not threaten its own domination of society and would prohibit changes that might render itself dysfunctional. Marx realized that there would be little advantage to the proletarian workers if their domination by industrial capitalists was displaced by domination by bureaucratic clerks. In his last days, he cynically predicted that Lassalle would win the argument and that the movement which he had hoped would bring freedom would instead bring about new forms of oppression.

Whereas Hegel had assumed that the state was society's greatest invention, Marx saw it as a selfish instrument to serve the interests of the ruling class. From Marx's perspective, the state was created for the express purpose of controlling society in favor of the interest of the bourgeoisie. The political/economic system which the state represents only makes legal the unfair distribution of material goods. The state justifies the concentration of wealth and of limited resources for sustenance in the hands of the capitalists. Resources and wealth are limited, and the capitalists, using the instruments of government (i.e., the courts, the lawmaking bodies, the police) are able to ensure their own disproportionate ownership of these things.

It was Marx's hope that in the near future the technological capabilities of society would be so greatly improved that more than enough of everything could be produced. There would then be no need for connivers to use the state as an instrument to further their own interests. Each person in society would produce according to his/her ability and would receive everything essential to meet his/her needs. If society could produce such an abundance of goods, the state would wither away because it would have no function.

According to Marx, the state always serves the interests of those who control the means of production and who own the wealth. His golden rule can be cited simply: Those who have the gold, rule. We who live in a democratic capitalistic social system may attempt to argue against this Marxist cynicism, but we have a difficult time doing so. Much as we try to promote the idea that in America one person constitutes only one vote, giving all of us equal capability for influencing government policy, we know that this is not the case. In 1976 when I was a candidate for the U. S. Congress, I learned, much to my regret, that politics is controlled by people who have money. To stage an effective congressional campaign requires approximately $150,000. A huge amount is needed every two years by those in Congress when they must stand for reelection. Unless the candidate has vast personal wealth, he/she must turn to special interest groups for support.

Republicans usually find ready supporters within the corporate and business community to underwrite their campaigns financially. The political action committees of the corporate world are all too readily available to make contributions to candidates who serve their interests. Democratic candidates do not lack for support either. Labor unions traditionally have been their "sugar daddies." Of course, if you are part of neither corporate America nor the labor union system, you may wonder if you have any representation in Congress to champion your concerns. I am not saying that you are without representation, but I am saying that the sources of a candidate's campaign funding will have a significant influence upon how that person, once elected, will vote on legislative issues. Over all, I think most of us would agree that even in the American democratic system, which we seem to believe is the best of all possible systems, money rather than idealistic philosophical principles seems to determine how things go.

Marx believed that only when the people (not an elite group of capitalists) own the means of production and derive the benefits from production, will the government of society be responsive to the needs of all of the people. Only when the masses have economic power will they have political power. Only when the factories, machines, and farms are owned collectively will the proletariat have control over their political destinies. Marx looked forward to the day when the proletariat would seize these things from the industrial capitalists and usher in a new era of true democracy.

Ideologies as Instruments of Oppression

Every political/economic system, according to Marx, creates an ideology to legitimate its existence. The most common ideology is a theological system that makes the ruling elite appear to be ordained of God and decrees the government which serves its purposes to be of divine origin. Marx does not believe that people construct societal structures and cultural institutions out of the insights and wisdom of great philosophers and theologians. Instead, he argues just the opposite. He claims that philosophers and theologians are instruments who serve the ruling class by creating philosophies and theologies that seem to give to the ruling class the right to exercise power and exploit the working class. Forinstance, the theologians of the Reformation produced treatises on government which made it clear that the rule of political leaders was ordained of God. Since these leaders were empowered by the rising bourgeois to serve their interests, submission to the political leaders constituted submission to the new class of industrial capitalists. Marx had absolute contempt for the theologians of the church and for the clergy who interpreted their teachings to the working class. He was convinced that they represented a major barrier to human freedom, in that acceptance by the proletariat of the religious doctrines of the Reformation theologians meant that they would accept an ideology contrary to their class interests. As underpaid, exploited workers, they should have been at war with their capitalistic oppressors. Instead, the "wretched slaves of the industrial machine," as Marx called them, regarded the ruling class capitalists as being justifiably in positions of power and entitled to their unfair claims on the profits of production. The Reformers convinced the oppressed that the apostle Paul's teaching in the Epistle to the Romans was inspired by God Himself, and required total submission to those who were in positions of power, regardless of how tyrannical they might be. Paul wrote:

> Let every person be in subjection to the governing authorities. For there is no authority except from God, and those which exist are established by God. Therefore he who resists authority has opposed the ordinance of God; and they who have opposed will receive condemnation upon themselves.
>
> For rulers are not a cause of fear for good behavior, but for evil. Do you want to have no fear of authority? Do what is good, and you will have praise from the same.
>
> For it is a minister of God to you for good. But if you do what is evil, be afraid; for it does not bear the sword for nothing; for it is a minister of God, an avenger who brings wrath upon the one who practices evil.
>
> Wherefore it is necessary to be in subjection, not only because of wrath, but also for conscience sake.
>
> Romans 13:1–5, NASB

It is easy to see how such a passage could be used to legitimate an oppressive political/economic system.

Ideologies are of great significance in that they not only convince the ruling class of its right to rule, but they also convince the oppressed social class that the political/economic system is functioning in its best interests. The workers actually believe that the exploitive, humiliating treatment which they receive at the hands of the ruling class is part of a

God-ordained plan that will ultimately provide blessings for them. While they may be poor and downtrodden, they are led to believe that they are members of a society which a good God has planned for their benefit. Even though everything that happens to them in their daily lives belies such deceptions, they go on believing that they live in the best of all possible worlds. The clergy promote this ideology; its members function as agents of the middle class. Through the use of liturgical symbols middle-class religion generates awe and reverence for a God that has been created in their imaginations. Marx claims that, through theological teachings, the exploited peoples of a society come to believe that their wretched conditions are better than they might be and thereby are made to be thankful for their poverty. Time and time again, exploited people hear proclaimed from the pulpit that they should be grateful for all that God has done for them—in spite of the fact that they lack the means to live with dignity. They are constantly told to be mindful of the fact that there is someone more wretched. When they have no shoes, they are reminded that there are those who have no feet.

According to Marx, the greatest virtue set forth by Christianity is to be the most grateful when you have the least. Preachers love to tell the stories of impoverished people in places like Haiti who have nothing to eat, and yet sing songs of thanksgiving to God. The people in the pew are made to feel like the ungrateful rich by comparison. The sermons end with such condemnations as, "If they can give praise to God when they have so little, why are you not more grateful when you are so much better off?" The workers compare themselves with the desperate people in Haiti and feel guilty that they are not more thankful for the so-called blessings of God that they enjoy. They leave the church singing the praises of God and the wonderful nation that He has given them. It does not matter that they receive unfair wages, that they have no power to make the decisions that determine their destiny, that they do not get even the monetary benefits from the products of their labor—they still believe that they are benefactors of the grace of God. Religion has made a virtue out of not having things and still being grateful.

Marx considers this religious "manipulation of consciousness" that gets people to accept their oppressed condition as a blessed state to be one of the greatest evils that has ever been perpetrated upon society. The wealthy capitalists actually are pitied by the poor working class. The clergy tells them that riches turn people away from God and endanger their souls.

Thus, when the poor see the rich in their conspicuous displays of wealth, they whisper among themselves and say, "Those poor rich people. They don't realize what wealth does to them. They don't know how wealth destroys their faith. They don't understand that 'it is easier for a camel to go through the eye of a needle, than for a rich man to enter the kingdom of God' " (Matt. 19:24). So thoroughly do the clergy convince the oppressed that the rich must pay a heavy psychological price for possessing wealth, that the oppressed end up pitying the oppressors. No matter that sociological studies prove conclusively that the rich have better and more stable marriages; members of the oppressed class still believe that the rich cannot have happy family lives. (There are always enough movie stars with long lists of divorces to which the clergy can point in order to support their myths.) No matter that the poor know that the rich are vacationing on the beaches of the French Riviera, sending their children to the best schools, driving fantastic sports cars, and living in magnificent houses. The poor still believe that they are better off and they tell each other, "I wouldn't want all of that money. Look what it does to them!" And, finally, according to Marx, the poor accept their wretchedness as blessed, while the clergy, knowing that the deception is complete, wink at their rich capitalistic sponsors.

Marx contends that religion is a con job, so thorough that the proletarian poor are willing to die to preserve the system that oppresses them. When duty calls, they heroically go off to war and offer their lives as cannon fodder in order to preserve a political/economic system that denies them power, wealth, and dignity. The sons of the rich get deferments from military service—after all, they must go to college. The poor are duped with television ads promising technical training and preparation for skilled professions. They believe this propaganda, in spite of the fact that they can see all around them veterans of the Vietnam war who cannot get jobs, who are ridiculed as failures for being unable to win an unwinnable war, and who, on top of all of that, are cancer victims of Agent Orange. But the ideology of the system has such a powerful hold over the consciousness of poor people that they continue to volunteer for military service. It is the poorest of the poor who join, and the members of minority groups who are overrepresented in the ranks of the army. Those who are most despised by the ruling class go off to die on its behalf. And it is those who have experienced the greatest economic discrimination who get blown apart in some

Middle East bunker to defend the interests of capitalist investors who would have offered them no jobs if they had happened to return.

The Marxists point out that there are chaplains to bless all of these obscenely indoctrinated members of the armed forces as they go into battle, and that there are prayer meetings in their home churches to uphold them. And should they die in battle for causes they do not understand, the leaders of the clergy will hold memorial services making the living envious of the heroism of the dead. In churches memorial plaques will be nailed to the wall to classify them for nationalistic sainthood. And when a crying mother blurts out, "I didn't raise my son to be a soldier! I didn't raise my son to die like this," she is hushed up and told not to mar the death of her son with such unpatriotic heresy. The clergy brace these weeping women with such words of comfort as, "Now, now! Don't be like that. Be strong in the Lord!"

It was against such support of an unjust political/economic system that Marx railed. It was the legitimation of oppressive psychological conditioning that raised his ire. Marx would point to the American flag displayed in the typical Protestant church and claim that it was evidence of the real purpose of the church—to lend support to the ruling political order. In spite of the church's claims to worship a universal God, for Marx, the presence of the flag would demonstrate that no division between religiosity and chauvinistic nationalism exists.

Philosophy as an Ideology

Religion is not the only means of legitimating a social order or integrating citizens into the dominant values of the political/economic order. Marx points out that philosophical systems can do the same. There are experts in the sociology of knowledge, a specialized discipline that analyzes the origin and function of ideas within societal systems, who would argue that Marx destroyed the possibility of ever again taking seriously the writings of philosophers. Marx made a strong case for the claim that all philosophical systems are, like religious theologies, only inventions on behalf of the ruling classes to make their control of the societal system and their unfair appropriation of the wealth generated by industrial production seem reasonable and right.

Marx's book *The German Ideology* was written with the express purpose of showing how Hegelian thought functioned as an ideology for the

German bourgeoisie during the nineteenth century. In that work, Marx shows how the philosophical principles of Hegel provided justification for the rights exercised by the ruling class at the same time that they concealed the fact that such rights were only available to the wealthy middle class. The philosophical system of Hegel and his followers concealed the fact that those without economic power were left with no rights at all. Marx points out that the free enterprise system and political philosophies that base having freedom on the ownership of private property cover up the fact that people who own nothing lack the opportunity to participate in the decision-making processes of society. The children of the oppressed workers are told that they are free to take risks in the free enterprise system and to make something of themselves. They are indoctrinated with such beliefs while in school (because the ruling class controls the teachings in the schools as well as in the churches) and thus grow up believing that they are free to actualize their highest potentialities.

How long will black ghetto children be deceived before the truth is given to them? They do not have a fair chance to succeed. They are not free to be all that they can be, regardless of what their teachers tell them. The opportunities for developing the vocabulary, the style, and the dispositions so essential for success in the social system have been denied them. The children of those who control the means of production will have easy and favored access to social success, while the children of the socially disinherited are duped into thinking that they have an equal chance to achieve the goals that symbolize success. These deprived children are told that they live in a free society in which anybody can do or be anything. They are told that they have as much of a chance as anybody of realizing the culturally prescribed dreams for achievement. In reality, however, the children of the ruling class are the only ones who have a good chance of actualizing their potential. It is increasingly obvious to those who work with oppressed minority groups in America that the children of these groups have the cards stacked against them.

Marx saw that the same kind of unequal opportunity for achieving success existed among the German people of the nineteenth century. He recognized that the children of the proletariat were denied the freedom to become what their personal gifts and intelligence would allow. Marx pointed out that, in spite of this absence of equal opportunity, Hegelian philosophy perpetuated the myth that everyone had an equal right to gain wealth, power, and prestige within the German society. Hegel had taught the German people that, as the *Geist* emerged through successive cultures, it expressed greater and greater possibilities for human freedom. The Germans, who were heirs to the Hegelian philosophical tradition, were led to believe that as the *Geist* unfolded within their culture the possibilities for freedom were nearing perfection. They were convinced that in Germany all people were equally free and equally able to actualize their potentiality.

Hegelian philosophy served ideological functions every bit as much as the theologies of the Reformers had done in earlier times. It was unthinkable to rebel against a system which Hegelian philosophy had made to appear just, fair, and radiant with freedom and the opportunities that freedom provides. If people were failures and lacked access to power or to the profits of production, they were led to believe that it was their own fault. The German ideology made the poor and wretched workers blame themselves rather than the social system for their lack of social success. The workers ended up experiencing personal guilt instead of anger at the injustices inherent in the social relations and the structures of the political/economic system. They did not see rebellion against the system as a means of improving their lot. They came to believe that they could be better off only if they were more clever or harder working. These downtrodden workers admired their capitalistic oppressors because the workers were convinced that all people had had equal freedom to achieve success and that those who did were simply superior people.

Thus, Hegelian philosophy indoctrinated the masses with the belief that the way to wealth, power, and prestige did not lie in creating a new social system. The ideology of Hegel had entrapped the middle class into believing that a social system which served only the interests of the ruling class provided just opportunities for all.

8

Marx versus Christian Economics

As a student of Hegelian philosophy, Marx gained some of his most brilliant insights from Hegel's writings. Nevertheless, Marx came to regard the Hegelian interpretation of human history as an expression of all that he found oppressive in bourgeois society. He saw in Hegel's works an ideology that glorified and justified a political/economic system that exploited the proletarian worker and denied the masses their human dignity. As Marx endeavored to demonstrate how a tyrannical ruling class could twist the perception of social reality so as to cause oppressed people to accept their oppression as just, he articulated a severe critique of Hegel's philosophy and the German ideology it had created.

Marx's Attack on Hegel

To begin with, Marx totally rejected the Hegelian concept of the *Geist*. For Marx there was no room for an interpretation of human history that had as its essence the unfolding of a spirit or an idea. He argued, instead, that the basis of all social history and cultural development was to be found in humanity's struggle for survival. He believed that the securing of material means for human existence was the cause of all social inventions, and that any interpretation of human history that did not acknowledge this proposition lacked scientific validity.

According to Marx, not only human inventions but social relationships came into existence as a part of humanity's struggle for survival. For example, in the effort to survive against the threat of inclement weather, humanity discovered how to use fire. As people invented ways to start fires and to control them for their own purposes, they gained the ability to insure their existence in the midst of physical conditions that would have otherwise killed them. People discovered that they could have more animals available for food by raising them in herds than they could by hunting for them in the wild. They invented the techniques of agriculture because they realized they would have more to eat if they planted and harvested crops than if they simply gathered the food that grew wild in the forests. For Marx, it was obvious that the driving force in all of these inventions was the desire to meet material requisites for physical survival, not the developing of some *Geist* or intellect. One by one, ways were invented to increase the productivity of those things essential for physical well-being. Nothing more mysterious than the need for sustenance was required to explain why human beings came up with these inventions.

Marx Explains the Evolution of Ruling Classes

As the means of producing the things necessary for sustaining human life improved, social classes evolved. Those who controlled the means of production became the ruling class while others became oppressed workers. Those who took control of the land, of the inventions that improved economic productivity, and of essential natural resources (such as the water supply) were able to exercise domination over those who did not have access to these things. Innovations in the means of producing goods essential for survival resulted in more being produced than were needed for simple survival. This surplus in production Marx labeled *capital,* and those who controlled it, *capitalists.*

As time went on and the inventive capabilities of humanity became more sophisticated, people not only invented new *ways* to satisfy their real physical needs; they also invented new "needs"—things not essential for physical survival but which were, nevertheless, strongly desired. Human beings seem to have a fantastic capacity for creating things they do not really need in order to live, but which become so important to them that they are convinced they cannot live without them. Automobiles and television sets have become for many just as important to have as food, clothing, and shelter—things that satisfy their real needs. Regardless of what is produced, one principle remains a truism: Whoever controls the means of production constitutes the ruling class. Whoever controls the technology and resources to produce what people need and want dominates the society.

In different periods of human history, different kinds of people controlled the means of production and, therefore, were able to dominate others. At one time it was the chief of the tribe or the king. At another time, feudal lords were in control of the lands and farming equipment required for food production. More recently, a new breed of owners has gained control of the means of production—the industrial capitalists. Under their domination, we have come to be dependent not only upon the essential food staples required for bodily sustenance, but upon a host of industrially manufactured things which we have been psychologically conditioned to crave. Those who control the means of producing these desired goods have become the new rulers of society.

With the invention of money, and its use to purchase the surplus goods produced through increasingly more efficient means, the domination of the working class took on a new dimension. Money became the symbol and instrument of capitalistic power. It determined not only the worth of manufactured goods and agricultural products, but also the value of human labor. Ironically, although the capitalists, who owned the means of production, produced nothing, they were the ones who appropriated for themselves the huge financial benefits of production. On the other hand, the workers, who were the real producers of goods and services, received a mere pittance for their labor. And because in a capitalistic society money decrees the value of things and even of persons, those who worked deemed themselves to be of little worth.

The followers of Karl Marx ask some probing questions of those of us who support the capitalistic enterprise. They ask us, what do industrial stockholders produce that makes them worthy of the profits of production? At least such industrial giants of the past as Andrew Carnegie, Daniel Drew, and John D. Rockefeller had had the genius to organize huge factories and distribution systems. At least these legendary captains of industry had taken risks and made bold moves in giving birth to the modern systems of production. But the modern capitalist is simply a stockholder whose labors consist of making telephone calls to the stockbroker after reading the *Wall Street Journal* and clipping coupons from his or her stock receipts. Ironically, these non-producers dominate society; they constitute the ruling class, yet they are of no value to society. As far as Marx was concerned, all oppressive, worthless, nonproductive capitalists should be abolished. The time had come, he said, for the real producers, the workers of the world, to cast off the yoke of the capitalists, to unite, and to rebel against the system of capitalism. They should realize, he said, that "they have nothing to lose but their chains."

Marx envisioned a time, not far off, when the industrial workers and the farmers, led by certain progressive members of the academic community, would carry off a revolution. This revolution, he believed, would result in the seizure by the proletariat, or working-class people, of the means of production, and the declaration of themselves as its proper owners. From that point on, Marx claimed, the profits of production would belong to the workers and farmers who produced them, rather than to the nonproductive capitalists. The profits of production would be shared justly among those who deserved them, bringing an end to economic exploitation. The economic system that Marx envisioned would provide for every person what was needed for a good life, and every person would be expected to contribute to society according to his or her ability.

Marx also believed that when the proletariat seized control of the economic system, the things that were produced would be changed dramatically. Goods produced by a capitalistic economy are designed to maximize profits. Profits are always the only concern of capitalists, according to Marx. He taught that the profit motive is the only motive that capitalists understand. In the world of the future, Marx believed that the proletariat would create a new economy that would have as its purpose the production of things that people *need*. In a capitalist system, he said, vast resources are used up to produce large quantities of consumer goods that nobody needs, simply because, under the influence of advertising, the rich bourgeoisie will want to buy them. While a small group of people will spend vast economic resources to get things that they have been manipulated into wanting, the masses, according to Marx, will suffer privation and starvation. However, said Marx, in the communistic world of the future all of this will change. The proletariat masses, he pointed out, will own the factories and the farms and will use them to produce those things which they themselves need to sustain and improve their lives.

A Christian Response to Marx's Economic Theories

It is difficult to survey the conditions of our world without giving some validity to Marx's view of economic arrangements. There is little doubt that the advanced capitalistic nations are using up the world's resources in order to gratify the artificially created wants of their middle-class populations. For instance, vast amounts of land in Latin American nations are being used to grow cash crops for people in the more affluent Western nations. Land that is desperately needed to grow food for Latin American people is being used to grow sugar, coffee, and tobacco for people in the United States, Western Europe, and Japan. It is more profitable to grow and sell sugar, coffee, and tobacco among the middle classes of rich countries than to produce essential food for malnourished indigenous people. And in capitalistic systems, what is most profitable is what is done.

The questionable nature of capitalistic practices arises not only in reference to the ways in which land and natural resources in Third World nations are exploited, but also with regard to what capitalism does to the poor, socially disinherited peoples who live within the United States, Western Europe, and Japan. For instance, serious concern is being expressed over such products as video games. While the inventing and constructing of video games has produced multibillion dollar profits, there is doubt as to whether they serve any real need. Nevertheless, millions of teenagers are lured into spending a great deal of money as they play these games. Time that should be spent in study is consumed in video game arcades. There are some sociological studies showing correlation between video games and declining school grades among the poor youth in urban areas. Attempts to curtail the deployment of video games are greeted with protests that such actions would hinder the free enterprise system.

In addition to video games, numerous other unnecessary items, including cigarettes and beer, are produced to make profits even though they extract a huge cost in the destruction of human lives and the wasting of natural resources.

Christians cannot remain indifferent to the possible economic injustices that can result from the exercise of unrestrained capitalistic interests. Furthermore, there is evidence that throughout Christendom criticisms of capitalistic abuse are being heard. In late 1984, the Roman Catholic bishops of the United States issued a proclamation to America's churches declaring that capitalism that was only concerned about profits and therefore unresponsive to the needs of the poor is contrary to the will of God. A significant segment of the evangelical community, led by such groups as the Sojourners community in Washington, D.C. (publishers of *Sojourners* magazine), and the recently organized Evangelicals for Social Action, have begun to raise serious questions about the biblical legitimacy of laissez-faire capitalistic practices.

Is capitalism "Christian"? Is socialism more Christian than capitalism? Is there a third kind of economic system that is more Christian than socialism? Questions like these are being raised increasingly among Christians, whenever there are conclaves and conventions called to discuss ways to help the poor and the oppressed of the world. The good news is that some answers to such questions are beginning to emerge from the Christian community. It is interesting to discover that these answers are providing strong alternatives to the philosophy of Karl Marx. However, to the chagrin of many Christians, they are also providing alternatives to the economic system proposed by Adam Smith, the classical theorist for capitalism.

Fortunately, Christianity need not be wed to pure capitalism. It is quite possible for Christians to develop free enterprise alternatives to pure capitalism which will satisfy not only the Marxist's cries for a more just and humane system of economics, but will also comply more fully with the teachings of Scripture. Furthermore, such alternatives are already evolving within Christendom. Around the world today, new models for economic production are being developed which embody biblical concerns for human dignity and which are manifestations of the ethical requisites of the kingdom of God. Most of these new experiments in Christian economics are taking place overseas in Third World countries. They are being sponsored by evangelical missionaries who are attempting to find ways to help the people in poor, struggling nations to escape the grinding poverty that has become far too normative. Allow me to cite and comment on two such experiments:

CASE I   Tom had a deep commitment to minister to the poor and oppressed people of the world. This commitment led him into missionary service in the Dominican Republic. He set up a small factory in one of the worst slums in the capital city and taught several previously unemployed young men the skills necessary to work in that factory, which produced sandals. Tom asked boys and girls in the slum to gather up discarded automobile tires from the dumps and trash lots of the city and bring them to the factory. He paid the children fifty cents for each old tire. The young men whom Tom had trained used very simple tools to cut up the rubber to make the soles for sandals. By adding leather thongs, very durable footwear was produced. The boys and girls of the barrio then sold these sandals on the streets of Santo Domingo.

On several occasions I visited that factory so ingeniously established by Tom. Each time I found a dozen young men hard at work. When they saw me, they always stopped what they were doing to talk with me. Pride was evident on their faces as they showed me the sandals they had produced. With each successive visit I noticed improvements in their skills. Eventually they were able to make decorative designs on the leather, transforming very utilitarian products into things of beauty.

As I watched these young men work, I was impressed with the good time they were having in their work and with each other. I sensed a growing affection among them. I sensed their satisfaction in being able to provide financial support for their families. When they walked through the barrio, they seemed to walk taller than the other young men who were not so fortunate as to have jobs.

I have often asked Tom questions about this missionary project of his. Do you make a profit? Wouldn't it be better if machines were brought in to replace the simple tools that are difficult to use and do not allow for rapid and efficient production? Couldn't more money be made by producing souvenirs for tourists?

Tom tolerated my questions with smiles and answered me with patience. "Look," he said, "I didn't organize this business to get rich. I organized it to create some jobs for poor people. We make enough money to provide each of the guys who works here with a decent living. There's enough left over to keep me fed and clothed. So, what else matters? We could bring in machines, but I don't think the guys would have as much fun running the machines as they have making the sandals by hand. They feel good about what they make and that's important."

On many occasions, I have reflected upon the level of productivity at Tom's little factory, and I have come to see that he has developed a philosophy of economic development that is superior to the philosophies of both Marx and Adam Smith. Furthermore, Tom's philosophy encompasses insights from both Marx and Smith.

First of all, Tom's experiment was an expression of the free enterprise system. It was not government-sponsored; it was a privately owned business and it was initiated with private capital. I believe that the free enterprise system is the will of God and is essential for a Christian economic system. My reason for being such a strong advocate of free enterprise is because of the convincing arguments of two ideologists, diametrically opposed to each other: Michael Novak and (strange as this may seem)

Karl Marx himself. Novak, who is head of the American Enterprise Institute in Washington, D.C. and a professor at Syracuse University, is one of the most respected conservative spokespersons in the discussion surrounding the development of a Christian economic system. Novak argues that economic freedom is the basis for all other freedoms. If freedom means the opportunity for an individual to make those decisions that determine his/her own destiny, people must be economically free to realize this opportunity. What a person does in order to earn a living will condition most of the other activities of that person's life. Family life, educational opportunities, religious life, etc., will all be influenced by the economic employment and financial income of an individual. If a person cannot make decisions that will affect the kind of work he/she will do and how much income he/she will earn, then that which most conditions his/her life is being determined by others. Novak's point is well taken, and furthermore, Marx provides ample support for the same argument. Marx never advocated nor even envisioned the kind of totalitarian state which has become all too common among the nations of the Soviet bloc. Marx wanted to see people able to control their own economic destinies, and he saw in such circumstances the possibilities for genuine human freedom. It was capitalism that Marx opposed, the exploitation of workers by investors who produced nothing themselves. He would have approved of the kind of small village industry developed by Tom.

Second, the product produced was designed to meet a need. People in Tom's community needed something to wear on their feet. Producing the sandals from worn-out automobile tires also used up materials that would otherwise be junk littering the area. The workers could be satisfied that they were producing things that were of real benefit to others. This created a sense of pride and self-worth among them. Furthermore, there was an opportunity for creativity in the work. Those who made the shoes were able to get the kind of emotional satisfaction that is essential to keep people human as they labor. In contrast to the repetitious, monotonous work that too often faces assembly line workers in modern industry, creative opportunities in the process of production were offered to the workers in the sandal factory.

Third, the process of production in the sandal factory encouraged a sense of community among the workers. They did not see each other as competitors, each trying to outdo the other, but instead developed a sense of mutual affection as they viewed their factory as a place that required cooperative friends.

Last, Tom's motivation for starting the factory was not profit. Tom knew all too well that for Christians the primary motive in economic activities, as in all other activities, is love. Through love, Tom was motivated to meet a need. In this case, the need was to create some jobs for poor people that would enable them to have an income while producing something of essential value for others. His motivation for production was to bless people in the name of Christ. Profits were important to Tom because he knew that a factory that did not make profits would not last long enough to help the workers meet their needs on an ongoing basis. However, Tom was motivated by love; profits were only a means to help him achieve what was really important to him employment for his brothers in Christ. Tom would not fit into the capitalistic scheme of Adam Smith. Smith's system required that its participants be self-interested persons bent on maximizing profits for their own gratification. To Smith, Tom would be a deviant. But then, that's what Christians are supposed to be.

CASE 2   Joan was serving as a missionary in Southeast Africa. She loved the people of the area and wanted to stay among them as a servant of Christ, but she lacked the financial resources to remain on the mission field. While the mission boards of mainstream denominations provide guaranteed income, health insurance and program funds for their missionaries, "independent faith mission boards" do not. Joan was a missionary with one of the latter type of organizations and was responsible for raising her own financial support. That meant that she had to contact friends and relatives to ask them to pledge monthly support for her missionary activities. Joan despised raising her own support because she did not feel right about asking people for money for herself. "I don't mind begging for money to feed starving children, but when I have to beg for money in order to take care of my own needs, I'm embarrassed." Her response to an inquiry about her fund-raising responsibilities was, "I just can't make myself do it."

Another problem was that the support she was able to generate was not sent to her in a consistent manner. Sometimes supporters would forget to send in their monthly contributions. Sometimes her friends and relatives faced circumstances in their own lives that forced them to cut down on the amount they could send to Joan. Every few years, she would have to take a furlough from her work, return to the United States, and try to rekindle enthusiastic support for what she was trying to do for Christ and for the native people whom she was committed to serve. For several years, Joan tried to make her mission board's system of raising financial support work for her, but eventually it became too oppressive to endure. One day, she thought to herself, "There has to be a better way to undergird my service. There has to be a better way to establish a support base for my ministry." Thoughts like these provided the impetus for Joan to become a missionary entrepreneur.

When Mary, who had been her college roommate, visited her in Africa, Joan shared her thoughts. Mary came up with a very promising idea. A jar factory, located in Indiana, had developed a food processing system that could be bought and set up in Africa for less than $20,000. The system, utilizing jars which the company produced, could process and preserve vegetables and fruits that were being grown in the region of Africa where Joan was serving.

The farmers in that region desperately needed some sort of food processing system. Lacking the infrastructure to transport their produce to market, they had a difficult time maximizing their profits from the sale of their crops. They did not have trucks and there were no adequate roads. The farmers had to carry their produce to market in ox-drawn carts, and a large part of it spoiled in transit. Furthermore, there was not a steady flow of buyers even when they were able to get the food to the city markets. Often the food spoiled after sitting for days without buyers. A food processing plant would enable the farmers to preserve their produce in their own community. None of the food would be spoiled in transit to the city and none would rot while they waited to sell it. Their profits would be increased, and the amount of food available for sale to the city people would be significantly greater.

Joan went to the African church where she worshiped and worked out plans with the pastor to establish the food processing plant. She wanted those who worked in the plant to be members of her church. This would create employment for her Christian brothers and sisters. Also, it would enable these church members to have the means to support their church and to provide financial resources to expand its ministry. With the money these workers could earn, they could contribute to the church's plan to establish a school and a medical center for their community. Members of the church who were teachers and nurses could be employed and supported.

Joan and her pastor called a meeting of the farmers of the area and explained the plan to them, asking them to invest in the cannery. Almost one hundred farmers invested $75 each in the project. Several had to mortgage their land to come up with the money, but somehow they were able to raise the necessary capital. The church provided an investment of $5,000 and Joan borrowed the rest of the needed capital from some of her friends in the United States.

The food processing plant was purchased and put into operation within nine months. Profits from the plant soon produced income for the investors. Within two years after installation of the plant, the owners were able to pay off the loans provided by Joan's friends. The church received a steady income from its investment that provided the means for expanding its evangelistic outreach.

Joan, who was the manager of the processing plant, had a steady income that enabled her to support herself as a missionary. She started a Bible study with the fifteen people who worked at the plant, and made a special effort to teach what Christ had to say about money. She wanted the people who worked in the plant as well as the farmers connected with the project to recognize that all of their newly acquired income was a trust from Christ and was to be used as Christ would use it if it were in His hands. She prayed daily that they would follow these teachings, lest their money seduce them into a materialistic lifestyle like the one she had left behind in America when she went to the mission field.

On her next visit to her home in the United States, Joan was honored on several occasions for her innovative economic development program in Africa. She was the speaker at a meeting of her home town Rotary Club. When she finished describing her work, the audience gave her a standing ovation and the president of the club congratulated her: "Joan, you've demonstrated that capitalism is the way to help Third World peoples. When private investment is employed for economic development, there is success!"

Two weeks later, Joan was asked to speak to a group of students at an Ivy League university. She was concerned about how they would receive her since these students were known for their politically leftist views. To her surprise, they too greeted her story with a standing ovation. Afterwards, one of the students pointed out that her project illustrated the

viability of a Marxist model for economic development. "After all," he
pointed out, "the workers owned the means of production. When the
profits of production belong to the workers and not to capitalists who
contribute nothing to the actual production process, economic progress
is inevitable."

Joan reflected on these two reactions and said to herself, "The project
was capitalistic because there were shareholders and private investments.
On the other hand, the project was Marxist because the farmers, whom
the students called proletarian workers, owned the plant and shared its
profits. But maybe it's neither; maybe in following the leading of the
Lord, we created an economic model that has the advantages of each of
these systems, but goes beyond the materialism inherent in both capitalism and Marxism."

While the project developed by Joan did not as clearly exemplify an
alternative to capitalism and socialism as did the project developed by
Tom, it did have some features that are significant for our discussion. As
stated earlier, a Christian economic system allows people to control their
economic life and make the decisions that determine their own destinies.
That was very much the case as Joan developed the food processing plant
among the people of Africa.

The cost of the machinery necessary for the plant was within the range
that allowed the farmers and operators to become its owners. Too often,
building factories and buying equipment is so expensive that only those
with vast financial resources can afford them, usually either very rich
private owners (as in capitalism) or a national government (as in socialism). The cost of Joan's food project was small enough to enable the indigenous people who would operate the plant and depend upon it for the
processing of their produce to be the owners. They were in a position to
make the decisions about how the plant should be operated and who
should benefit from its productivity.

Undoubtedly, this kind of arrangement would be impossible if the
project required high technological equipment or intensive capital investment. Low-cost, technologically simple production systems like the one
utilized in Joan's project could never be used to build automobiles or
television sets. But perhaps it would be better if Third World peoples
built their economies on producing things that are simple and will meet
their common everyday needs. Neither modern capitalism nor modern
socialism offers freedom to the common people in Third World nations.

Each of them has an expensive technological production system. Only economic arrangements that *really* put the means of production in the hands of the producers allow them to make the decisions that determine their own economic destinies. Marxists claim that this will happen when Marxists control the economy of a nation, but any examination of the national economies of the nations that they do control will reveal otherwise. In reality, the common workers are controlled by a state bureaucracy that leaves them more powerless than the so-called "slaves" who work in capitalistic industries. Joan created a production system that provided the kind of freedom about which the ideologists of both Marxism and capitalism only talk.

Joan's food processing plant made another major contribution to the community by helping to lessen the seemingly constant migration of rural and village people to the large urban centers of East Africa. Urbanization is a horrendous problem of Third World nations. Most programs for economic development and job creation are initiated in the cities of the Third World because they are the places where unemployment is the greatest. The jobs created in these metropolitan centers tend to attract significant numbers of poor people from the villages and countryside. On a worldwide basis, it is fair to say that ten people are drawn to urban areas for every new job created. This migration of poor people into the cities of Third World nations is causing suffering and subhuman living conditions that defy description. For instance, one capital attracts 50,000 new inhabitants per week. There is no way that Third World cities can provide the housing, food, social services, and employment essential to meet the influx of population that has become all too typical.

Slums are growing up at incredible rates around these cities. Shacks made of scrap wood and cardboard are becoming the homes of countless thousands of poor peasants who have traveled to the urban capitals of their nations hoping to find economic opportunities. Most who migrate to the cities find emotional and social disasters awaiting them. Their dreams for economic success seldom, if ever, are realized, and their rich familial ties have been destroyed. In their struggles for survival, often the children become beggars and the women become prostitutes. In desperation, many husbands desert their families.

Joan's project provided economic opportunities for people in their rural home village and community. Because employment was available there, there was no need for them to migrate to urban areas and abandon familiar cultural traditions. Unless there are thousands of economic development projects like Joan's, the cities of Third World countries will continue to be hell-holes of congestion and despair.

Finally, it should be noted that Joan devised a means of supporting herself and her missionary work. In so doing, she freed up financial resources that could be used to establish pioneer missionary work in other places in the world. It is essential that such new ways of supporting missionary ministries be established. Presently, almost 90 percent of all funds raised for foreign missionary work is used to support already established ministries and churches in Third World countries. Only if missionaries and the churches they establish in these places become self-supporting will those funds be released for new work among unreached peoples.

Toward a New Missionary Strategy

There are many who would question the relationship of missions to economic development. Such persons would view the church as a social institution incapable of promoting extensive programs to eliminate unemployment and deliver large numbers of people, particularly in Third World countries, from poverty. Such doubts and questions are understandable. For years, missionaries understood their mission as doing exclusively religious work. Missionaries "saved souls" and started churches. They believed their sole mission was to prepare people for life after death by engendering faith in Jesus Christ. Missionaries have done this job well over the last century, and the vast expansion of Christianity and the establishing of tens of thousands of new churches around the world testify to their success. During the last few decades, however, missionary strategy has changed. More and more missionaries are turning over the leadership of native churches to indigenous leadership. Missionaries realize that native pastors can communicate the gospel more effectively than foreigners. When there were no indigenous church leaders, the missionaries had to do the preaching, but once some natives were converted and trained, the missionaries realized that it was time for them to step aside. Why should thousands of dollars be spent to sponsor a preacher who preaches with an accent when indigenous leadership that could communicate in the native idiom was available?

This realization allowed missionaries to move into new styles of missionary work. Many of them became specialists and technicians, serving in auxiliary roles while indigenous pastors assumed their earlier roles. Missionaries became teachers, doctors, nurses, and agronomists. They provided a variety of services that were desperately needed in conjunction with already established churches. As a matter of fact, many governments of Third World nations would not allow missionaries to remain in their respective countries unless they were capable of rendering some necessary social service to the native peoples.

Countless stories of sacrifice and achievement can be told about missionary doctors and nurses. There is no question that for many years missionary teachers provided the only education available for vast numbers of people born and raised in Third World nations. Missionary agronomists have worked wonders in developing crops and farming programs among poor people in places like Africa and South America. However, while such specialists are still needed in most places in the world, there is evidence that the time has come for missionary strategy to evolve to still another stage.

More and more missionary strategy has focused on economic development. This is especially true in the face of the vast needs of Third World peoples for food and sustenance. Increasingly, missionaries have sought to find ways of assisting the poor peoples of the world through projects that will provide jobs for the poor. They initiate agricultural programs that will enable economically oppressed people to grow food for themselves. They constantly seek ways to bring hope to people who seem to have no means of being economically self-sufficient and living with dignity. Presently, hundreds of millions of missionary dollars are being spent on economic development programs, as Christians increasingly grasp the message of Christ who commanded His church to find ways to feed the hungry and help the oppressed.

Some members of the faculty at Eastern College, where I teach, initiated a master of business administration program to train a new kind of missionary, committed to serve in economic development programs in the Third World as well as among the urban poor in the United States. The students in this program call themselves "entrepreneurs for biblical justice." They plan to go in among the poor and establish small businesses and cottage industries not unlike those developed by Tom and Joan. These men and women are being taught by some of the outstanding leaders in the newly developed field that studies Third World economic needs and seeks ways to alleviate them. The faculty includes Ron

Sider, the evangelical author of *Rich Christians in an Age of Hunger*, and Al Whittaker, founder of a missionary organization that has created over 800 small businesses in Third World settings.

Hundreds of young people have inquired about this program, and scores have applied for admission. They believe that they can become a major force in shaping a new economic system among the poor people of the world. By creating enough jobs they not only help indigenous people escape from personal poverty, but also provide a way for them to have the financial resources to support their own churches. Furthermore, these students believe that they can help end the brain drain that rich nations now exercise on poor nations. Then trained professionals who graduate from Third World universities will not have to go to rich countries in order to find a clientele who can pay for their services. If indigenous peoples can earn the money to finance their own schools and hospitals, then highly trained Third World people will be able to find employment within their own nations. It is possible, and likely, that over the next few decades the Christian church will become a primary agency for economic development in the Third World. With an army of missionary entrepreneurs, along with the financing provided by churches sensitive to the needs of the poor, the Church can become the hope of the downtrodden proletariat.

Marx would not know how to handle this new force in the economic development of oppressed peoples. He consistently maintained that the church was always an instrument the bourgeoisie utilized to oppress the poor. To Marx, the only role that Christianity could ever serve was in legitimating the domination of the proletariat by the ruling bourgeoisie, and calming the revolutionary tendencies of the poor by convincing them that they would be rewarded after death if they would just behave themselves. A church that generated altruistic entrepreneurs whose concern was to provide economic opportunities for oppressed peoples was beyond Marx's imagination. Yet what Marx was sure would never happen is taking place. The Christian response to Marxist economic theory is not in the reaffirmation of a capitalistic ideology with which the Church has too often and too long been socially aligned. Instead the response is coming from programs and projects for the poor which defy the ideological expectations of both Marx and Adam Smith. While the programs and projects may seem pragmatic in nature, they are really expressions of a new Christian economic system that transcends capitalism and socialism in its radical commitment to biblical principles. These principles have been stated or implied in what already has been covered in this chapter but it may be useful to outline them here in summary fashion.

1   A Christian economic system promotes free enterprise because economic freedom is essential if people are to be able to make the decisions that determine their own destinies. The Bible is clear in establishing the fact that God wills such freedom for all people, regardless of the negative possibilities inherent in it.

2   The motivation for production in a Christian economic system is love. Christians are never motivated by profits, although they are aware that economic activities that do not produce profits do not endure to meet anyone's needs nor do they provide the capital needed to initiate new programs designed to serve others.

3   A Christian economic system is designed to meet needs. Rather than asking how profits can be maximized in production, Christian entrepreneurs ask if meaningful work has been created and useful products produced. Christians are well aware that in a capitalistic system, vast resources can be used up producing great profits while creating the fewest jobs possible, extremely routinized dehumanizing working conditions, and products that cater to artificially created wants, instead of meeting needs.

4   A Christian economic system is designed to allow every worker to have a sense of personal significance, unlike the economies of many socialist nations which make individuals into instruments of the state.

5   A Christian economic system utilizes appropriate technology in production. It utilizes, whenever possible, a means of production that allows the workers to own the machinery they use in the production process. This runs contrary to the designs of both advanced capitalism and advanced socialism, which take the ownership of the means of production out of the hands of the workers.

6   A Christian economic system builds a sense of community among the workers. This transcends the competitiveness of capitalism, as well as the absence of fellowship that exists in a socialistic system that denies the mystical basis for fellowship.

7   A Christian economic system employs the resources of the church. There is recognition that biblical imperatives can inspire

altruistic entrepreneurs and provide needed investment capital to serve the poor.

8   A Christian economic system is committed to initiating programs among the poor. It rejects "trickle-down" theories in both capitalistic and socialistic forms. There is the belief that the kingdom of God begins like a mustard seed (i.e., small). There is the belief that if enough can be done on the micro level, the benefits will "trickle up" and permeate the entire socioeconomic order.

Evangelical Christianity answers the Marxist critique not with theory or hypothetical propositions. Instead it answers with biblically inspired principles, empirically realized in programs that are beginning to help the poor and oppressed in ways that transcend the imaginations of both Marxists and capitalists.

9

The Marxist Doctrine of Alienation

MARX'S VIEWS on alienation offer one of his most significant insights into the human condition. The term *alienation* and its related concepts have become objects of every condemnation of the modern industrial process and its effect upon those who run its machinery. Alienation has come to be thought of as synonymous with dehumanization and, as such, is the major psychological sickness of urban society. It is viewed as the root of most social evils, from juvenile delinquency to political apathy. It plays a major role in the development of the psychological theories of Erich Fromm, the formulation of the theology of Paul Tillich, and the political explanations of Daniel Bell. Alienation has become the dominant explanation for the maladies of our times.

The basic meaning of alienation is separation, a sense of being "cut off." A synonym for estrangement, it refers to a social/psychological condition that leaves people with a sense of powerlessness, emptiness, and psychic deadness. Alienation destroys the capacity to love or to enter into any kind of subjective empathy with others. It destroys humanity's zest for life.

The conditions creating alienation were carefully examined by the writers of the Romantic movement during the early part of the nineteenth century. They sensed that the disposition toward nature generated by science and its empirical approach to things had destroyed something that had been emotionally gratifying to humanity. Prior to the advent of scientism, people tended to view nature in a very personalistic manner. Trees had personalities; animals had souls; the rivers and mountains had consciousness. To primitives, everything in nature had a "subjective" side. This so-called primitive consciousness is evident among present-day Hindus who also believe that there is a sacred personal presence in every living creature.

The Romantics viewed nature in a nonscientific fashion. They encountered nature with a sense of wonder and believed that it was alive with magical powers. In such an enchanted world, human beings believed that they could have relationships with the nonhuman inhabitants of their world in ways that seem inconceivable to those living in our modern times. Pre-modern peoples believed that it was possible to enter into empathetic relationships with animals; subjectively interact with trees and flowers; and commune with the physical setting in which such "personalistic" creatures make their home.

The "scientific" approach to nature destroyed such a religio-magical and mystical interpretation of the world. Science taught us to view nature objectively and to regard the anthropomorphizing of animals and plants as a childlike delusion. With science as a teacher, men and women in the modern world came to look at members of the animal and plant kingdoms as "things." The "sophisticated" mind-set, generated by scientific discoveries since the Enlightenment, regarded flies, spiders, rats, and worms as devoid of a subjective consciousness. Human beings saw themselves as alone in the world. There was no subjective side to the creatures that were lower on the phylogenic scale. Only humans had souls. Only humans had self-awareness. Only humans were capable of being partners in friendship. Science taught us that everything in nature was an "it" and that those who treated any creature, other than a human being, as a sacred "thou" was a quaint representative of a childish stage of evolution.

The Romantics observed the ways in which science demystified the world and left it disenchanted. They witnessed the loss of the empathy with nature that had allowed pre-modern men and women to talk to animals and commune with trees. And their response was one of dismay. They knew that humanity had lost more than it had gained through the adopting of a scientific consciousness. They recognized that modern humanity would never learn the inexplicable emotional gratification that the primitives derived from their relationships with nature. The Romantics detected a spiritual dimension in the psyche of those who had a premodern mind-set that was sadly lacking in those who claimed citizenship in the brave new world. Having defined the physical world in objective fashion and having labeled animals and insects as "its," those with modern perspectives on nature were free to kill other living creatures without guilt and to devastate the physical environment in an arbitrary manner. The respect for nature that had rested on the belief that everything alive had a soul was gone. The destruction of an enchanted view of the world was a precondition to the indiscriminate devastation of nature that has produced both the modern urban lifestyle and the contemporary ecological disaster. The Romantics realized that the objectification of nature and the consequent impersonal treatment of nature had robbed humanity of something precious. There was a spiritual ecstasy, a psychic fulfillment, an emotional aliveness and a host of other gratifications that only poets can describe, which modern humanity had lost forever. Modern humanity had lost a oneness with nature that had fed its soul in ways which the so-called sophisticated members of the scientific intelligentsia could never know. In short, modern humanity had become alienated from the rest of the natural world. Modern men and women would live alone. They would be cut off, and estranged from animals. They would never again be able to talk to rivers or empathize with the souls of trees. Something within humanity would starve and die. This would be the price of scientism. Its name is alienation.

While Marx, particularly in his early writings, shared the perspectives of the Romantics, his concerns for humanity were more profound. He was not only concerned with how scientism had left humanity alienated from nature; he also was concerned with the ways in which the economic arrangements of industrial capitalism had alienated human beings from each other. While treating animals and trees as "things" or "its" can leave persons in a psychologically debilitated state, it is ultimately dehumanizing when persons come to treat each other as "things" and "its." Yet this is what happens, according to Marx, in the modern industrial capitalistic system. The capitalistic free enterprise system with its emphasis on laissez faire competition sets persons in competitive relationships with each other. It is a system which requires each member of society to function as an egoistic molecule pursuing a course of action in relationship to others that is wholly selfish. According to Marx, capitalism glorifies selfishness and makes it the essential driving motivation that enables the system to function successfully. Capitalistic theory suggests that as each person acts to serve his/her self-interests, an economic system will emerge that serves the best interests of everyone in society. From Adam Smith (1723–90) and John Maynard Keynes (1883–1946) up to the present, the theorists of capitalism have claimed that the profit motive will provide sufficient impetus for people to create businesses and industries that will provide employment, and products that will bless the maximum number of persons. Ironically, according to the proponents of capitalism, people who are selfishly motivated to maximize profits will produce the greatest good for the greatest number. Capitalists believe that their economic system creates social good out of the selfish motivations of the individual.

Marx was not convinced that "all things worked together for good" within the capitalistic system. He asserted that human beings were not naturally selfish, but, rather, became selfish in their quest to maximize profits. Capitalism did not so much utilize the innate selfishness of persons to achieve public good, as Adam Smith and other advocates of this ideology had claimed but, instead, stimulated selfish dispositions in any who embraced it. As far as Marx was concerned, capitalism was an economic system that corrupted human nature and fostered anticommunal egotism and self-interested consciousness in those who lived according to its principles. It is safe to say that, in Marx's judgment, human beings are not inherently sinful and selfish. Instead, it is the socioeconomic system of capitalistic private property that is responsible for making them into self-interested sinners. He rejects Calvinistic doctrines of original sin and places the origins of personal evil in an economic order that encourages persons to be motivated by their desires to gain wealth and power at the expense of their fellow citizens. Marx does not question the claim that stimulating selfish avarice encourages economic productivity. However, he does question whether or not the resulting prosperity can be considered a sufficient payoff when the corrupting influence of capitalism is taken into consideration. Can an economic system that plays upon, and encourages, the selfishness of persons be considered good? Keynes, the modern-day modifier of Smith's theories, asks: Can a system that accepts evil as good do anything else but destroy the moral fabric of society by corrupting its citizens?

Marx believed that the economic system developed by capitalism encouraged alienation in human relations. Each member of society, in seeking his or her own self-interests, comes to regard every other person as a competing enemy. Each is trying to outdo all others in the effort to achieve economic success. Such competition, claimed Marx, destroys community and camaraderie. Each person eventually comes to regard other persons as "things" to be manipulated for economic purposes. People end up using each other in their efforts to achieve economic benefits. Without consideration for the well-being of others, capitalists use manipulative techniques to get unwary buyers to purchase things that they do not need. People are regarded as the means for achieving economic ends, rather than as the ends for which the economic system exists. People end up serving the system rather than the system serving people. Society, under capitalism, creates egoists who love things and use people instead of persons who use things and love people.

Marx claimed that capitalism results in persons being alienated from persons. When each operates from wholly selfish motivations, regards every other person as a competitor, and places individualistic economic success above communal affection, alienation has reached its most devastating stage of development. Thus, Marx declared himself the enemy of capitalism in the hope of saving humanity.

There is still another way in which Marx viewed modern industrial capitalism as an alienating system of production. Marx believed that the machines utilized in the processes of industrial production had a dehumanizing effect upon human personality. He was convinced that the modern factory system with its impersonal bureaucratic organization destroyed the dignity and self-worth of industrial workers.

Marx did little to refute the claims to efficient production which are made by the champions of the capitalistic ideology. Quite to the contrary, Marx admired the machines of industry generated by the barons of the gilded age. He thoroughly appreciated the capacity of the capitalistic system to exploit natural resources scientifically, organize the labor force, and create artificial wants among consumers. What disturbed Marx was what happens to humanity in this process. Strange as it might seem, the atheist Marx was concerned about what the modern industrial system was doing to the soul of humanity.

Marx recognized that in an effort to maximize profits, the industrial capitalist sought to minimize wages paid to workers. One way to achieve this goal was for the capitalist to use more and more technology in production. As the industrial process became automated, fewer and fewer workers could produce more and more products. Machines could replace workers while increasing the quantity of goods turned out in any given industry.

Marx was greatly concerned not simply with the horrors of unemployment generated by the industrial process, but with what happened to those workers who still had jobs within the context of the modern factory system. These workers ran machines that allowed no exercising of their creative energies or potentialities. Running industrial machines was tedious and boring. Participating in production that was largely automated tended to reduce the workers themselves into machines. If anything, the modern industrial system produces machines that function like humans and humans who function like machines.

Who of us has not recognized the dehumanization that often accompanies assembly-line production? I remember when I was a boy, what pride and fulfillment my father derived from. his work as a cabinetmaker. He was employed by the RCA Corporation to build wooden cabinets for radios. In those days each cabinet was a hand-crafted work of art. My father would burn his initials into the insides of each cabinet he made. In a sense, each of those cabinets was an expression of his creative genius—a manifestation of his personhood, an extension of his ego. He could look at the products of his labor and say with intense gratification, "Look what I made!" When our family went visiting, it was always my task to sneak a peak at the inside of the radio console to see if it was one which my father had crafted. On two occasions I came upon cabinets he had built, and when I yelled, "Dad! This is one of yours!" his face shone with glorious pride and satisfaction.

All of that changed over the years. As production techniques changed, my father lost the privilege of making radio cabinets. Instead the cabinets were produced by machines, and all he did was to run a machine. Something died within my father. Even though his work was physically less demanding, he came home more tired. He slept a lot—more out of a desire to escape the boring meaninglessness of his life than to recuperate from healthy exhaustion. He was never again to experience that gratifying kind of exhaustion that comes from exerting energy in creative productivity. My father no longer worked with tools, which are instruments used by people; instead he ran machines, which are instruments that use people. He came to hate his job. He hated RCA. He was willing to strike whenever the union asked him to, not because he wanted more money, but because of what the company had done to him. Marx would have understood.

There is a story of a man who bought a new car. On the way home from the car dealer, he heard a rattling sound in the door so he drove back to the dealer and complained. The dealer had one of his mechanics remove the panel of the door. Inside were four large bolts and a note that read "Left here by Ralph."

It is easy to imagine an assembly-line worker putting the panels on car doors day after day without any opportunity to express his creative drives. He simply was part of an industrial process that tolerated his presence until a machine could be designed to take over his job. There was no way he could identify with the products of his labor, no way he could feel that he had left his mark on the world. There was no sense of personal achievement in his job. It is easy to understand that one day, he chose to defy the system and to let those who bought the cars he had helped to produce know that he existed; that he had a name; that he had made a difference. On that day Ralph threw bolts in car doors and left notes to identify himself. No matter that he might be caught and fired. No matter that his self-recognition would prove bothersome and childish. All that mattered was that he believed that some people out there would know that he existed and had left his mark on the world. Once again, Marx would have understood.

In the modern processes of industrial production wherein humans become extensions of machines and lose their personhood, alienation reaches its ultimate expression. Herein the workers come to see themselves as things. They become zombielike creatures who experience a slow ebbing of their subjective consciousness and sense of aliveness. Marx recognized that ultimately the workers would become alienated from "the ground of their own being." He saw that they would become hollow empty shells, devoid of the spontaneous aliveness and élan that marks humanity. It was from this horrendous dehumanization that Marx sought to save humanity by creating a new socioeconomic order.

Even if Christians cannot agree with Marx's cure for the maladies of humanity in the modern capitalistic industrial society, there is much in his diagnosis that elicits our sympathy. Even if we cannot believe that the communistic utopia he envisioned approximates the personal fulfillment we believe possible in the kingdom of God, we can discover much truth in his analysis of the evils of our present age. We must provide Christian deliverance from the dehumanization that Marx describes so graphically. We cannot pretend that this evil does not exist.

A Christian Response to Alienation

It is fair to suggest that what Marx had to say about alienation provides a basis for an understanding of sin and evil that is brilliantly viable for contemporary Christian theology. At least the twentieth century intellectual giant of Protestantism, Paul Tillich, used Marx's insights regarding alienation as a crucial component of his system. It is obvious that the meaning of sinfulness and evil in our contemporary social setting has special and unique dimensions. Marx's perspective on alienation helps us to probe these special and unique dimensions. It provides us also with an opportunity to demonstrate how the saving work of Christ can be appreciated and relevantly related to those who are oppressed by the conditions created by a modern industrial economy.

First of all, Christian mysticism can provide the deliverance from alienation so sorely needed by those who have been seduced by scientism. An affirmation of mysticism and mystical experiences does not require that Christians hear voices from heaven or have flights of the soul into celestial realms. Quite the contrary—what is needed is a Christian mysticism that is "this worldly," a mysticism that equips humanity to encounter the physical world in a new and enlivened manner. What is needed is a transformation of the psyches of people so that they are able to experience trees, flowers, mountains, rivers, and animals with a childlike delight and a lover's joy. In the midst of a physical universe in which a sense of mystery has vanished and the world has become all too mundane, there is a hunger for something that will make all things new.

Several years ago I was invited to lead a week of special meetings at a small midwestern college. It was to be one of those "religious emphasis weeks" which all too often have no other function than to feebly convince the trustees of church-related schools that have become secularized that the schools are still Christian. Sitting slouched on the front row of the auditorium were three "counterculture types" who tolerated my ranting and raging as I tried to generate some enthusiasm for the gospel. At the end of my lecture I asked if there were any questions. One of these young men raised his hand and in a casual manner that drew snickers from the crowd asked, "What's it all about, Alfie? I mean—what are you trying to get at with all of this religious jazz?"

I braced myself and evaded the question by saying, "That question is far too broad to be answered tonight. But tomorrow evening I'll attempt to give a specific response to it."

I did not expect that my antagonists would even be present the following evening, so I thought I had escaped what might have been an embarrassing exchange. However, much to my chagrin, all three of them

were back for the next meeting. Sitting in the same seats on the front row
of the auditorium, each of them flashed a "V" sign at me as I took my
seat and waited to be introduced by the school's president. I knew there
was no escape. I also knew that the answer I had to their question would
not impress them in spite of its validity and truth. I searched within
myself and then, surprisingly and unexpectedly, found an answer which
seemed most appropriate for my skeptical antagonists.

"When I was seven years old, I wanted electric trains for Christmas,"
I told them. "My mother suggested that I ask Santa Claus for them. At
seven, I was already suspicious of the Santa who sat enthroned at the
department store. His whiskers were not real and his 'Ho! Ho! Ho!' had
a ring of phoniness. Nevertheless, I knew how the system worked. And
on the appropriate Saturday I went with my mother to visit the local St.
Nicholas and told him what I wanted. I made sure that my request for
electric trains was loud enough for my mother to hear. (It was probably
loud enough for everyone in the store to hear.) On Christmas morning
I stumbled down the steps to the living room, went to the pile of presents
designated for me and picked out the biggest box. With wild anticipa-
tion I tore away the paper, lifted the lid—and found underwear and shirts.
They were gifts from my Aunt Madaline. Totally dispirited, I opened the
other gifts, but now nothing seemed to matter. Then I noticed something. There was another large box that had somehow escaped my attention. I scrambled over to it and lifted the lid. There they were—Lionel
electric trains! I picked up the engine and hugged it to my chest. I was
overcome with joy. A sense of ecstasy surged through me. I loved everything. I loved everybody. The world seemed radiant and wonderful. A
sense of aliveness permeated my consciousness. The world was magical
and vibrant. I stayed in my state of heightened awareness and sensitivity for almost three hours. Then something happened to the trains.

"They didn't break. Broken trains can be fixed. Something far worse
than that happened to them. They became old. They lost the quality of
newness, and when the quality of newness is lost there is no more luster,
no more magic."

I finished my story. Looking into the eyes of my questioner, I said, "If
anyone is in Christ, that person is new. Old things pass away. All things
become new. What this Christian thing is about is that a person can have
an encounter with Christ that makes all things new. The excitement and
wonder that belongs to that which is new seems to radiate from everyone

and everything. You are only twenty-one years old, but I sense that everything has become old to you. Everything has lost the capacity to generate wonder. But the good news is this: Jesus is a mystical presence in this room. You can surrender to His presence. You can invite Him to enter into your psyche, permeate your consciousness, and take possession of your emotions. You can know the unspeakable joy and aliveness that make my boyhood experience with new electric trains pale by comparison.

"I told you the story of my Christmas trains so that you might have some hint of the ecstasy that comes from being in Christ. To be in Christ is to experience renewal, not only of the self but of the world. To be in Christ and to allow Christ to dominate your consciousness generates an awareness of the world that is mystical and filled with wonder. To be 'in the Spirit' is to live in the same old world in a brand new way. It is living life on another level and approaching all things as though they were new. It is encountering the world in a way that enables you to sense something of the eternal in even the most temporal of things. It is the capacity to encounter the world and its inhabitants as theophanies through which the sublime is revealed."

I had gone beyond myself in my answer. It was as though "another" was speaking through me. I had left behind the logical categories of my lecture material, and I sensed myself gloriously transported even as I spoke. I experienced "the mystical" in my words, and so did my counterculture friends. They understood what those who know cannot say, and those who say, do not know.

The possibility of mystical rebirth exists even in the midst of a world that has grown boring through positivism and science. There is the promise of wonder as an individual surrenders to the awesome presence of the great "I AM." It was this that Moses experienced on Sinai. It was this that characterized Isaiah's experience in the temple in the year that King Uzziah died. And it was this that stirred the shepherds and made the wise men gasp. It was this that the three apostles experienced on the Mount of Transfiguration, and again on the day of Pentecost. Phrases like "born again" and "filled with the Spirit" are used to express it. But perhaps most exhilarating to those who encounter the life that results from surrender to the presence of the resurrected Christ, who is called the Holy Spirit, is the overcoming of their alienation. They no longer sense estrangement. Like Saint Francis, they feel they can talk with the

birds. They feel a kinship with the animals. They sense a spiritual oneness with the natural world. They sense that they have "come home."

Jesus once said that unless we become as little children we will in no
wise enter into the kingdom of Heaven. It was the wonder of children
that He wanted us to have. It was the excitement that belongs to those
who live in a world infused with vibrant spirit, a world so alive it seems
to speak to us in a personal way. He spoke to the winds and the waves,
and they obeyed Him. I cannot fully explain it, but I know that there
have been times when I have been so "turned on" by the indwelling presence of God that the world has once again become enchanted and my
sense of separateness from nature has vanished. This is what I mean by
the mystical. This is why I claim that oneness with Christ is salvation
from alienation.

A friend of mine, Philip Yancey, once speculated that God alone
maintains a perfect childlike disposition while all the rest of us have become old and jaded because of sin. If you bounce a child on your knee,
throw the child in the air, then catch the child in your arms, you will
probably hear a delirious, gleeful plea, "Do it again!" Yancey suggests that
when God made His first daisy, He giggled in childlike fashion, "Do it
again!" And He has kept on doing it. He has kept on recreating all things
because they are always new things to our childlike God. The Christian
experience is designed to let the mind of Christ be in each of us. This is
part of our answer to the disenchanted world that has become the dwelling place of modern humanity. This is a hope for transcending a world
that has become strange, indifferent, and filled with alienated people.

Overcoming Alienation between Persons

If evangelical Protestantism is to respond adequately to the conditions that alienate persons one from another, it must rework its ethical
philosophy. Individualism has characterized the mind-set of evangelical Protestantism, which long has gained its membership from a highly
individualistic middle-class constituency. Consequently, it is not surprising that the ethical system governing interpersonal relationships for
evangelicals is overly individualistic in its design and purpose. In fact,
it seems legalistic, composed as it is of rules and regulations directing
the individual's behavior, but often lacking sensitivity to issues regarding interpersonal relationships. Usually proof-texting its doctrines of

morality and justice, evangelicalism provides clear-cut principles to guide its "inner-directed" members. Middle-class evangelicalism sets forth an ethical philosophy that provides clear, crisp answers to questions about personal behavior. Its adherents require absolutes on questions ranging from abortion and premarital sex, to discussions of the free enterprise system and capital punishment. With dispositions that make them legitimate heirs to their Puritan forebears, middle-class evangelicals seldom raise questions about what "legal" and "honest" behavior can do to the dignity or emotional well-being of persons. If workers agree to the wages offered by an employer, then few questions are raised over whether or not they are exploited or dehumanized. If the Bible calls for wives to be submissive to their husbands, then wives should be submissive, even if such submission results in humiliation and degradation. If everyone has the right to vote, then the rule of the majority means justice even if some out-voted minority group is denied recognition and dignity in the societal system. The ethical system of the middle-class evangelical community is a system of principles that at times seems only secondarily interested in the condition of persons.

But there have been signs of change. Perhaps one of the most hopeful of these has been a willingness to learn from the Jewish theologian Martin Buber. At first glance it might seem strange for evangelicals to be open to the teachings of a Hasidic Jew, but the insights of this theologian are so biblically based that it is easy for evangelical intellectuals to find themselves at home in his thought patterns. Above all else, evangelicals endeavor to be biblical, and to them biblically consistent doctrines are acceptable regardless of who provides them.

Buber introduced the categories of "I-It" and "I-Thou" relationships to Protestantism. In so doing he provided an excellent escape from rigid legalism into a theology that is concerned with human relationships. In I-It relationships, according to Buber, the person regards the other as an object or a thing. There is no attempt to enter into the subjectivity of the other in an I-It relationship. Emotional empathy with the other is not something to be sought. The other person can be manipulated or used as one might use any object. In I-It relationships the concepts of right or wrong are determined by whether or not the individual treats the other person in accord with principles of righteousness laid down from before the foundation of the world. The ethical system in the world of I-It relationships is a set of rules and regulations, and as long as they are obeyed righteousness is established. Other participants engaged in social interaction are treated as the rules require. No empathy or emotion is required. As a matter of fact, there is a higher level of morality in I-It ethics if the individual does what *ought* to be done, without regard for feelings.

The ethical system that governs those who relate to each other in an I-Thou fashion represents a bold departure from that which governs I-It relationships. Buber explains that in an I-Thou relationship the other person ceases to be a separate entity. Instead, the other becomes one with the self. It is no longer a subjective self standing over and against an objective other; rather, the two become one. The self enters into the other so thoroughly that alienation evaporates. Each individual experiences life from the heart, mind, and soul of the other. It is as though the self has so empathized with the other that the other enters into the self even as the self enters into the other. There is no need to explain or describe feelings and thoughts to each other because the two have become one. However, Buber is quick to point out that individual identity does not cease to exist in an I-Thou. Quite the contrary, individual identity is heightened and the person begins to actualize potentialities for love and life never before possible. The word that Buber uses to explain this unique kind of oneness is *polarity*. Even as there is a positive and a negative in a single magnet, each making the other possible, so in an I-Thou there is oneness even as the I and the Thou become distinct poles in the relationship. In the polarity of an I-Thou, both the I and the Thou are in absolute dependence upon each other. There is mutual submission in an I-Thou, whereas in an I-It relationship the self endeavors to dominate and control the other.

Any attempt to put the I-Thou into words seems to come across rather like the descriptions of interpersonal relationships of the sensitivity groups of the sixties. Let me assure you that the I-Thou is infinitely different from those "touchy feely" exchanges that all too often represented the so-called "Encounter Group Movement." Martin Buber makes it clear that there is a transcendental and mystical quality to an I-Thou relationship that makes it qualitatively different from what is experienced in any relationship contrived by engineers in the field of group dynamics.

Buber declares that in a genuine I-Thou relationship there is always a revelation of God. Any person in an I-Thou relationship will be strangely and unexpectedly sensitive to a divine presence even as the encounter with the other person is taking place. A mystical euphoria accompanies the I-Thou, making the participants aware that they have not only gained a oneness with each other but have, simultaneously, experienced fellowship with God.

Buber points out that God cannot be known as an object. God is not an "it" or a thing. To objectify God is to commit the sin of idolatry. Those who define God will always construct Him in their own likeness. The objectification of God that occurs as we construct our images of Him will result in His becoming an expression of our superegos (Freud) or an expression of the positive collective values of our culture (Durkheim). Buber declares that God cannot be known by those who try to grasp Him, conceptualize Him and establish His nature in theological categories. Instead, God is unexpectedly in an I-Thou encounter which one person has with another. Buber claims that in the I-Thou the participants experience the mystical presence of "The Eternal Thou." In the I-Thou encounter God is known, not as an objective thing, but as a transfiguring presence. God is known as an event, a happening, a quality of relationship. "Beloved, let us love one another: for love is of God: and every one that loveth is born of God, and knoweth God" (1 John 4:7, KJV).

When Moses came upon the burning bush in the wilderness he discovered that an ordinary bush had suddenly come alive with a divine presence. So it is that in an I-Thou encounter an ordinary relationship suddenly is ablaze with the glory of God. Consequently, we see the truth of the apostle John's declaration, "No man can say that he loves God unless he loves his brother." It is in loving one's brother/sister, that God is encountered, enjoyed, and loved.

We traditional Christians go beyond the mystery and wonder of Buber's I-Thou relationship when we enjoy encounters with each other and with those who are outside our faith commitments. The God whom we allowed to impart Himself to us when we surrendered our lives to Jesus Christ gives to I-Thou relationships a unique quality. Christians are capable of recognizing and sharing Christ in I-Thou encounters in a way that those who are detached from Jesus never can.

Marx failed to grasp the possibilities for divine revelation in seemingly mundane human encounters. He clearly understood that the social relations generated by the capitalistic social system often set persons against each other, causing the emotional privation he called alienation. However, Marx had no grasp of the mystical capacities that were inherent in interpersonal relationships, if they could be transformed into I-Thou encounters. Marx had written off the possibilities of the transcendent. Consequently, he did not seek divine presence in human encounters, and only those who seek will find (Matt. 7:8). He understood the psychic impoverishment experienced in a social system that oriented persons to each other as things and encouraged persons to manipulate each other in their selfish economic efforts to maximize private profits. However, Marx failed to see that persons who surrender themselves to each other, poise themselves in openness to each other, and wait to be surprised by an overpowering spiritual euphoria known as the I-Thou, can abolish alienation and know a fullness of life that can only be called God. Marx saw God as a hypothetical construct of the ruling elite that was used to legitimate oppressive socioeconomic domination. He never experienced the God who came to give life and to give it more abundantly (see John 10:10).

Overcoming Alienation in the Workplace

Alienation in the workplace is all too much a part of the experiences of workers in modern industrial systems. The absence of emotional gratification in work that is done only to get money, and the lack of creativity in assembly-line production are hallmarks of our times. Marx proposed that new economic arrangements created by socialism would help to overcome the alienation experienced by industrial arrangements. But even Marx realized that the problem of alienation in the workplace could not be overcome simply by declaring the workers the owners of the means of production (i.e., the factories), and therefore the owners of the fruits of production (i.e., the profits). Work is still meaningless and devoid of creativity for most workers, and those who labor in socialist societies have realized few, if any, of the benefits which Marx had promised.

Christianity has been slow in responding to the need for a theology that would guide modern-day workers in their efforts to find some alleviation from the emotional emptiness of their labors. Protestantism has provided a work ethic that creates a "drivenness" in workers, making them feel guilty if they are not diligent at their jobs. However, the Protestant work ethic has done very little to help people find emotional fulfillment in work that often fails to utilize the intelligence and creativity that is latent within most people.

What makes matters worse is that many young people who have trained for professional roles which they believed would grant them personal gratification are being shocked by the realization that there are limited employment opportunities for persons with their skills and knowledge. Vast numbers of overqualified people in America are trying to figure out ways to put their talents to work. Thousands of persons with earned doctorates cannot find teaching positions in colleges or universities. Lawyers are being graduated each year only to find a judicial system overrun by too many lawyers. Qualified young people are being turned down by medical schools which cite projections that there will be a surplus of medical doctors in the years that lie ahead. Too many young people who have worked hard to gain necessary qualifications and credentials are facing possible unemployment in a socioeconomic system that does not need them. Society owes every citizen a meaningful job that will enhance his/her humanity. But society seems increasingly unable to pay that debt.

The Bible does make one principle about work abundantly clear. It declares that in work the individual should seek to do things that will bless other people rather than being concerned merely about gaining personal gratification. The Scriptures tell Christians that if they are willing to lose their lives for Christ and for the sake of others in the name of Christ, they will find fulfillment and spiritual satisfaction. Whenever I speak to college students, I tell them that they are desperately needed on the mission field. Just because America has too many doctors and teachers does not mean that there is a surplus of such professionals in other parts of the world. Those who are willing to forgo the financial payoffs and the "good life" provided by top positions in the American society can find places and opportunities among poor and oppressed peoples, who will usually welcome and appreciate them. There are opportunities for heroic missions among the hungry of Africa, the poor of India, and the socially disinherited of Latin America.

10

Dostoyevsky:
The Passionate Free Man

MANY WOULD argue that the finest refutation of the philosophy of Karl Marx comes from the works of Fyodor Dostoyevsky. This nineteenth-century Russian novelist, whose books include *The Idiot, The Possessed, Crime and Punishment,* and *The Brothers Karamazov,* perhaps the greatest novel of all time, hardly can be called anti-Christian. His works contain one of the most brilliant expositions of Christian philosophy ever penned. His love for Christ and his commitment to the Russian Orthodox Church provided the bedrock upon which he built the plots of his novels. He functioned as a Christian prophet in his own day, and he serves now as a model for such contemporary critics of communist regimes as Alexander Solzhenitsyn. We discuss his work, not because he is an enemy of Christianity, but because he is a friend that some church leaders wish they did not have. He is one of the founders of modern existentialism, and that alone is enough to make him *persona non grata* in some evangelical circles. But he is also the most brilliant critic of communist systems and offers us insights which we sorely need. Furthermore, he is intensely identified with the common people of the world.

The Proletariat: Dostoyevsky's Hope for Humanity

Dostoyevsky believed in the proletariat, not as a group as did Marx, but as individuals. Each of the poor Russians who struggled to survive and who grappled endlessly with the meaning of life possessed the qualities he believed essential for the realization of the best that is in the human race. In Dostoyevsky's eyes, each of the most common members of society possessed the vision and the freedom to build the kingdom

of God on earth. He criticized the utopian schemes of the elitist bourgeoisie and opted for a society built upon the free expression of ordinary
people, whom he believed were in the image of God. Dostoyevsky truly
represents a Christian anti-Marxist critique of the bourgeoisie and its culture. His writings represent an attack upon the intellectualism and religiosity of the middle class. Dostoyevsky came before Marx and the
Communist revolution that Marx inspired, but he anticipated both. It
can legitimately be said that the writings of Dostoyevsky represent one
of the most sophisticated Christian arguments against the ideology of the
proletarian revolutions which have shaped Russia and its satellites during the twentieth century.

The bourgeois intelligentsia, on the other hand, is viewed by
Dostoyevsky as a group enamored of their own cleverness and perverted
by their own pride. Ivan, one of the main characters in *The Brothers
Karamazov*, symbolizes this group. He is a sophisticate whose philosophies and ideas stimulate his brother, Smerdyakov, who symbolizes the
less intelligent proletariat, to actions which lead to destruction and chaos.
Obviously, Dostoyevsky believed that the intelligentsia of the bourgeoisie
held little hope for humanity. Through the character of Ivan he expressed
his profound distrust for the elitist mentality of the bourgeois intelligentsia and their conviction that the reins of society should be turned over
to them because they alone know what is best for the masses.
Dostoyevsky did not believe in the capabilities of the middle class, whose
members he viewed as spoiled dilettantes. Rather, he saw humanity's best
hope in the proletarian masses whose sufferings had spiritually purified
them and whose basic character was capable of noble heroics. Thus, he
utilizes his novels to critique the implied elitism of those who believe that
the hope of humanity lies in the utopian plans of secular versions of
socialism. His writings help us to see the dire consequences of a humanitarianism that seeks utopia without God.

In his youth, Dostoyevsky himself had identified with political utopian movements and had joined forces with those who plotted the
overthrow of the Tzars and the establishment of socialism. His political
activism resulted in his being arrested and sentenced to death. As a form
of psychological torture, he was blindfolded, led before a firing squad,
and compelled to listen to the commanding officer give the order for the
soldiers to fire. However, the guns were loaded with blanks instead of real
bullets. The young Dostoyevsky mentally experienced the excruciating

ordeal of dying before he realized that he had not been killed. That experience changed his life. He felt love for those whom he had once hated. He gained a passionate appreciation for life which is readily discernible in his novels. He who had been a political revolutionary longing for a new political order became an intense Christian who saw the hope of the world in the simple faith which the common people have in their God.

Dostoyevsky's novels, which many acclaim as the highest state of the art of the genre, were written to express his mature views on the meaning of being human and to outline his prophecies about the future. In dealing with both of these concerns, he has much to tell us about the nature of freedom. Dostoyevsky considered individual freedom to be essential in establishing a person's humanity, and he feared the coming of an apocalypse that would be followed by the establishment of a sociopolitical system that would curtail freedom and dehumanize the peoples of the world.

Freedom: God's Ultimate Gift to Humanity

According to Dostoyevsky, freedom is God's ultimate gift to humanity. It is freedom, he says, that differentiates us from the animals. The animals are simply conditioned creatures. Anticipating the discoveries of Pavlov, he saw that the behavior of animals was the result of stimulus-response training. Each creature in the animal world learns to associate positive or negative consequences with certain behavioral patterns and, therefore, behaves in ways that will maximize the most positive consequences. Animals do not act; they react. Certain stimuli elicit certain associated responses. There is no freedom or decision-making. This is not the case with humans. We can decide what we do. We are not conditioned or trained. We are creatures with the ability to decide and act on the basis of values and truths that take us far beyond the Bentham pleasure principle.

God took a fantastic risk when He made us free, says Dostoyevsky. He could have made us into robotlike creatures which would have to do the will of our Creator. Instead, God created us as free creatures, capable of living contrary to His will. Dostoyevsky makes it clear that by making us free God created the possibility for evil to exist. Really free creatures can live contrary to the wishes of their Creator, and that means that humans were created with the capacity to sin. However, contends Dostoyevsky, if God had not made us free we would be unable to love Him. Love exists only when persons freely choose to give themselves over to the one who is loved. God, according to Dostoyevsky, was faced with the option of creating us so that we would have to obey Him but could never love Him, or creating us with the capacity to love Him and the freedom to disobey Him. God chose the latter.

Dostoyevsky recognized that human freedom, as presented in the biblical revelation, was absent from the philosophies of the ancient Greeks and the Moslem religion of the Middle East. The Greeks held to the doctrine of fate. Our Hellenistic predecessors believed that all of us were caught up in an inevitable flow of events and though we might heroically struggle against our destinies, each of us ultimately would be conquered by the fates. We might choose to be tragic heroes, as Nietzsche would inspire us to be, but each of us would sooner or later have to face the reality that our individual destinies are fixed and sealed. Among the Moslems there is no freedom, for all that happens has been written by Allah before the foundation of the world. It is the Judaeo-Christian tradition alone that suggests that each of us is capable of making decisions that determine our personal destinies, and it is this freedom that is, for each of us, the greatest of blessings and the most horrible of curses. From a Dostoyevskian perspective, modern existentialism, even in its atheistic forms, must be seen as an outgrowth of biblical religions.

Most of the characters in Dostoyevsky's novels demonstrate the capacity of human nature to use freedom to do evil in opposition to the will of God. One after another, his characters (whose names challenge the pronunciation capabilities of those who do not know Russian) will to act in ways that are sinful. In each case the desire to sin comes from the heart rather than the social surroundings. Dostoyevsky gives no quarter to behaviorist theories which blame behavior on sociological factors. He makes it clear that his characters do what they do because they will it in their hearts. He was able to predict the emergence of the psychological theories of J. B. Watson and B. F. Skinner, who contend that everything people do is determined by environmental factors that condition their behavior. But Dostoyevsky opposes such explanations of the actions of human beings. He believes that theories like these deny us our dignity and humanity. It is in the innermost recesses of the heart that each of us decides what to do. Sin and righteousness are, by definition, according to Dostoyevsky, willed realities. In *Notes from Underground,* one of his most brilliant short stories, he has his main character rebel against behavioristic interpretations of human existence by saying that when scientists figure out what makes people sane, he will go insane just to spite them.

Not only is sin the result of freedom, but so are repentance and righteousness. These wonderful spiritual qualities could never exist without freedom, according to Dostoyevsky. Those who do the "right" things because they are programmed to do so, cannot be considered good in a moral sense. They might be called innocent, or they might be called ignorant, but they cannot be called righteous.

Those who naturally turn from sin cannot be looked upon as having done something pleasing to God. If God had programmed us to repent, that would mean that God had done something to please Himself. That is not repentance, according to Dostoyevsky. In repentance a person who is free to oppose God chooses in freedom to show love for God by turning from the sin that attracts him. The theme of the inward nature of repentance is woven throughout Dostoyevsky's novels. His characters repent, not because they have to, but because they want to. Nowhere is this more evident than in the life of Raskolnikov, the main character of Dostoyevsky's novel *Crime and Punishment.* In this book we learn the inner workings of Raskolnikov's thinking following his murder of his landlady. In a dialogue with his own superego, he tries to justify what he has done, attempting to convince himself that the murder had been a blessing to many and a curse to none. Within the recesses of his heart he tries to rationalize away his guilt, but he is unable to make himself righteous. Finally, he convicts himself and turns himself in to the authorities for punishment. No external constraints determine his action. Raskolnikov repents because he subjectively wills it. He could have escaped the punishment of the state had he remained silent, but his inner convictions were more painful than any punishment that could be meted out by the courts.

Freedom as a Heavy Burden

The freedom that provides the possibility for our humanity can also be a heavy burden for many of us. According to Dostoyevsky, not everyone will view freedom as a blessing. Many will find its responsibilities threatening.

I once read a newspaper story about a young couple in Tallahassee, Florida, who committed suicide. One was eighteen years old and the other was nineteen. In the suicide note they left behind, they gave as the reason for their decision to end their lives that they were afraid of becoming adults. The young couple explained that they did not feel up to making the host of decisions that they would have had to make over the next few years.

Here were two people who were afraid of freedom. They would have preferred that someone else make the decisions that would determine their destinies. They saw freedom as a burden and, therefore, turned away from that which could have made them fully human.

Dostoyevsky saw dire sociopolitical consequences for societies whose people are afraid of freedom. He anticipated the insight of Erich Fromm, who in his book *Escape from Freedom* claims that political dictators do not have to impose themselves on people because, in most cases, people gratefully surrender their freedom. Like Fromm, Dostoyevsky saw that there are many who prefer to turn over decision-making to rulers in exchange for having their basic physical and social needs cared for. It was the awareness of this attitude toward freedom, which is increasingly evident in modern societies, that made Dostoyevsky apprehensive about the future. He feared the emergence of seemingly humanitarian political systems which would benevolently provide what people want and need, but would in exchange expect them to surrender their freedom.

Dostoyevsky foresaw the coming plague of socialistic totalitarianism that has swept across the Eastern bloc nations. His vision of the future set forth the themes that Aldous Huxley would expand in his book *Brave New World*, and which George Orwell would explore in his book *1984*. Dostoyevsky recognized that the political tyranny of the future would not present itself as diabolically brutal but would appear benign and humanitarian. Dostoyevsky predicted that the political totalitarianism of the coming age would feed the hungry, entertain the masses, maintain peace, and enhance the general good of society. It would ask only this— that people relinquish their freedom and allow the state to make decisions for them.

Karl Marx had not yet been introduced to the intellectual discussions of Europe, but other forms of socialism were available and being championed. It was these socialistic options that frightened Dostoyevsky. He believed such sociopolitical systems to be the greatest threat to humanity.

On the one hand, he saw them as offering so much for the poor and oppressed that their advent would be welcomed. But, on the other hand, he feared the tendencies of such systems to take away the personal freedom which is what makes us human beings in the first place.

Dostoyevsky also feared the Roman Catholic Church. As a member of the Russian Orthodox Church, he maintained a suspicion of the power of Rome that dated back to the split of Catholicism in A.D. 1054. Actually, he knew very little about Roman Catholicism, and his understanding of its structure, theology, and designs for the future were based upon the common religious lore that pervaded the Russian consciousness. Nevertheless, Dostoyevsky saw in the Roman church the same dangers of a benevolent totalitarianism which he predicted would result from the socialistic movements of his day. He suggested that this seemingly humanitarian and benevolent religiopolitical order would do all the same things that socialism would do—feed the hungry, care for the masses, ensure peace and security—but would at the same time take away personal freedom. Nicholas Berdyayev, the most prominent interpreter of Dostoyevsky's writings, shows that Dostoyevsky actually believed that Roman Catholicism and socialism would be unified. Furthermore, claims Berdyayev, Dostoyevsky believed that the resulting theocracy would be presided over by the pope, who in time would reveal himself to be the Antichrist described in the book of Revelation. Nowhere is this vision more clearly presented than in "The Myth of the Grand Inquisitor" in *The Brothers Karamazov*.

"The Myth of the Grand Inquisitor"

"The Myth of the Grand Inquisitor" is part of the argument against religion which Ivan, the sophisticated agnostic member of the Karamazov family, presents to his brother, Alyosha, who is a deeply committed Christian. Ivan creates a story in which he describes the Second Coming of Christ.

In the myth, the Second Coming occurs in A.D. 1000 in the city of Madrid. As Christ walks the streets of the city, history seems to repeat itself. He heals a lame man and cures another of blindness. Arriving at the Madrid Cathedral just as a funeral procession is leaving the sanctuary, He approaches the corpse and raises her from the dead. At that point, the Cardinal of Madrid, who has witnessed the Resurrection, orders his soldiers to arrest Jesus. The reader may reflect and say, "There they go again. They did not recognize the Son of God the first time He came, and it appears that they have not recognized Him at His Second Coming either." However, such a conclusion is a mistake, because in the story told by Ivan, the Cardinal, who is the Grand Inquisitor, has Jesus arrested because he knows Him to be the Son of God.

In the next part of the story, the Grand Inquisitor visits Jesus in His cell and asks the Lord why He has returned to earth. He explains to Jesus that it has taken the church a thousand years to undo the damage to humanity which he claims Jesus did during His earlier incarnation. He explains to Jesus that His mistake was to believe in the potentiality of human beings to appreciate freedom. The Grand Inquisitor claims that most people do not understand or want freedom, and that consequently, the plan of Jesus was all wrong. For instance, when Jesus is tempted by Satan to change stones into bread, He refuses (Matt. 4:1–11). The Grand Inquisitor accuses Jesus of having made an unloving and evil decision. He explains to Jesus that the refusal was made on the grounds that to turn stones into bread would destroy humanity's privilege of free choice. According to the Grand Inquisitor, if Jesus had turned the stones into bread, hungry people would have had to become His disciples because their physical survival required it. Jesus would have bought their allegiance at the price of bread, and that, says the Grand Inquisitor, was something that Jesus refused to do.

It is the contention of the Grand Inquisitor that the Lord made the wrong decision. He accuses Jesus of being unconcerned about the untold millions of people who neither understand nor want freedom, but are desperately hungry for bread. He explains to the Lord that only a small number of persons in all of human history ever have appreciated the significance and meaning of freedom, and only a small number ever have grasped the ultimate value of freedom. The Grand Inquisitor condemns Jesus for offering humanity the gift of freedom, which only a sophisticated elite could enjoy, while ignoring the cries of the hungry masses for food. It is these others, who lack the capacity to handle freedom and who are starving for lack of bread, who are the primary concern of the Grand Inquisitor and the church he represents. He claims that Jesus has provided a way of salvation for an elite who could appreciate freedom while he, the Grand Inquisitor, and his church have denied freedom and even eliminated it, but have sought to feed the hungry masses.

The same kind of argument is given with regard to the temptation in which Satan asks Jesus to jump from the highest pinnacle of the temple on Mount Zion and then miraculously to float unharmed to the ground. Once again, Jesus refuses to yield to the temptation of the Evil One. The Lord will not be seduced into winning disciples through miracles and wonders. Instead, Jesus respects the freedom of people. Miracles and wonders would leave them with no option but to acknowledge His lordship, and that is not His way. Once again, the Grand Inquisitor condemns Jesus and points out that, without miracles and wonders, life is unbearable for most of humanity. The masses much prefer miracles and the hopes that miracles generate within their hearts, to the possession of that freedom which Jesus places in such high regard.

The Grand Inquisitor's final accusation against Jesus concerns the final temptation in the wilderness as described in the Gospels. Jesus is taken to a high mountain and shown all the kingdoms of the world. He is told that He can have them all to rule and govern if He will bow down and worship the Devil. Jesus refuses, even though doing so would have enabled Him to bring peace among the nations and to order history in ways that would be beneficial to the entire human race. The Grand Inquisitor condemns Jesus because the Lord would not adopt a system to enforce peace on earth, but rather preferred His way which made peace something that humans would have to choose for themselves. Still again, the question is asked of the Lord: Does He recognize the fact that very few want the freedom to determine their own destinies, and that most would prefer to have a peace forced upon them from on high? The Grand Inquisitor asks Jesus to remember the countless children who have died in wars, the numberless hordes who have lost their lives in battle, and the devastation and horror that have been caused as nations conquer nations. Finally, he asks if it has all been worth it. He asks Jesus if the gift of freedom for the few has been worth the sufferings of the others.

The Grand Inquisitor claims to be morally superior to Jesus because he is concerned, not for the elite who crave the freedom to be fully human, but for the others who suffer in hunger, live in despair and are devastated by the ravages of war. He acknowledges that he, and the church he represents, have bowed to Satan and have become the servants of the Evil One. But he tells Jesus that he gladly accepts the punishment for all of this and will rejoice in the pains of Hell if he is able to feed the hungry, give hope to the hopeless and create peace for the masses. For the sake of the huddled masses of humanity who cannot appreciate freedom, he will accept the torment of the flames. Jesus may be the Savior of an elite, but the Grand Inquisitor declares himself to be the Savior of the others. The myth concludes with Jesus walking across the cell, kissing the Grand Inquisitor, and going back to Heaven never to return again.

"The Myth of the Grand Inquisitor" has become a significant contribution to contemporary theological discussions. At least one of the modern-day God-is-dead theologians has confessed that it was this passage by Dostoyevsky that set him on the course of thinking that led to cynicism and religious doubt. It is easy to see why the story looms important and why it generates questions among theological thinkers. The myth makes Jesus seem immoral. He seems to have chosen to serve the interests of an elite while ignoring the desperate needs of the masses. The Grand Inquisitor, who has yielded to Satan, appears to be more compassionate than does Jesus, who is committed to the principle of freedom.

However, Alyosha the Christian responds to the story told by Ivan by claiming that it glorified Jesus rather than dishonored Him. Alyosha helps us to see that Jesus believes in ordinary people. He shows us that Jesus believes in their capacity to handle freedom with courage, to choose in heroic fashion a destiny worthy of creatures who are made in the image of God. Alyosha wants his brother to recognize that Jesus believes in the potentiality for greatness that lies within each of us and that He believes we ordinary folk crave freedom more than the detached members of the intelligentsia could ever imagine.

Contrariwise, the Grand Inquisitor has no respect for humanity. He sees the masses of humanity as being inferior to himself and to the elite with whom he is identified. In many ways the Grand Inquisitor demonstrates that the skeptical intelligentsia who do not believe in God commit the further sin of not believing in ordinary people.

There is pity in the Grand Inquisitor, but pity is not a humanizing emotion. It leads those who have it to reach down to aid those poor unfortunate creatures who need the help of their betters. Pity creates a kind of "humanitarianism" that diminishes the stature of those who are the benefactors of charity. Pity is what the superior feel for the inferior. It is disguised egomania. It is a curse to those whom the pitying humanitarians think that they bless.

Alyosha calls for compassion rather than pity. Compassion results when persons, as equals, share one another's emotions and thinking. Compassion is based upon love and has no condescending qualities. Compassion enhances the humanness both of those who show it and those who receive it. Compassionate people seem to communicate that they know what you are feeling and thinking because they are just like you.

Jesus was compassionate. Through the Incarnation, He became one of us. He was tempted in all ways as we are tempted. He did not deem himself to be of greater importance than any other human being, but was quite willing to become a servant to the lowest and least. Jesus does not offer us condescending pity. Instead He offers us love and seeks to help each of us to see that He is our brother.

Whereas the Grand Inquisitor demonstrates a contempt for human beings whom he believes incapable of choosing the greatness that is available to them, Jesus confronts us with His conviction that He has great expectations for each of us. To each and every human being, Jesus provides the freedom to choose his or her own destiny and, through the Scriptures, He lets us each know that as many as receive Him to them He gives the power to become the sons and daughters of God.

Alyosha uses "The Myth of the Grand Inquisitor" to champion the cause of Christ which Ivan had designed it to condemn. He reveals, in brilliant fashion, that skepticism leads to elitism, and elitism to the denigration of the masses of humanity which are composed of ordinary folks.

Dostoyevsky employs the myth to attack the growing tendencies toward socialism that he believed would swallow up the Russia he loved. He recognized that the leaders of the socialist revolution, which he believed was about to overtake his native land, had their prototype in the Grand Inquisitor. He saw them as demigods, who could feel pity but not compassion. He saw them as arrogant elitists who believed that they knew better than the masses what was good for the masses. He realized that such cynical elitists would never believe that ordinary people should be allowed to be free; he feared that the rulers of the future would create their own version of utopia in which people would be fed, entertained, cared for, and even given peace, but would be denied one of the greatest gifts of God to humanity—FREEDOM. He was convinced that the future rulers of Russia would not believe in God and, consequently, would not believe in people. Such leaders, Dostoyevsky taught, would not represent the Christ, but the Antichrist. The socialist revolution which he was sure would come to Russia would deny people the basis of their highest expression of humanness and would doom them to a comfortable form of slavery. He declared that the "messiahs" that would take over Russia would be as despicable as the Grand Inquisitor. It is no wonder that many have considered Dostoyevsky a prophet.

The Limits to Our Freedom

While it is clear that Dostoyevsky affirmed freedom as essential to our humanity, he also made it clear that we must recognize limits to our freedom. He let us know that when we aspire to be more than we should be, or other than we should be, there will be dire consequences. We humans, he claimed, sometimes aspire to dismiss God and assume for ourselves the privilege of doing whatever we please. At times we think we can order our lives better than God can, and are able to construct circumstances for ourselves which are better than those which are willed by the Almighty.

Raskolnikov, in *Crime and Punishment,* is a man who might identify with the Nietzschean *Zarathustra.* He thinks of himself as an elitist with potentiality for greatness, and concludes that if one of the nameless members of the gross and common masses must be eliminated in order for him to realize his greatness, then, with regret, that is what must be done. The murder seems even more justified in light of the fact that the victim was a tyrannical, mean person. The woman murdered during the unraveling of the plot seems to be a person without whom the world would be a better place.

If there is no God, the case to justify the murder is easy to make. But Dostoyevsky makes it clear that there is a God and that this God has established each and every person as being immortal. Consequently, murder can never be justified, because a person who is immortal is of infinite worth and can never be seen as expendable in the pursuit of a higher purpose. Without God, anything seems permissible, but if there is a God, particularly a God who establishes infinite worth for each person, then there are limits to our freedom. We can never use or misuse a person to serve our own ends because, as immortal souls, each person is an end unto himself or herself. The so-called Nietzschean superman deludes himself if he thinks that he is beyond the good and evil associated with God's constraints on freedom; he is doomed to horrible consequences if his God-ordained freedom is misused.

Dostoyevsky is cited in this book because, like Christ, he is a believer in the humanity which is often debased by the aristocracy and ridiculed by the bourgeois intelligentsia. He finds that truth is best understood among the simple peasants of Russia, rather than among the sophisticated dilettantes. His writings display a reverence for the common workers and peasant farmers of Russia that makes us aware that he believes them to possess messianic qualities. Dostoyevsky sets forth his belief that in the personal sufferings and struggles which are common to them, these poor people learn to trust God in ways that the comfortable bourgeoisie seldom understand. The common people discover God in their relationships with each other. They find God in their loves and their joys. They find Him in their tears and their agonies. They find Him in their efforts to wrest a living from a society that yields only reluctantly to their needs. Dostoyevsky lets us know that these people have learned to grasp faith and truth in ways that the rational intellectual middle class will never know. He teaches those of us who practice middle-class religion that while our systematic theologies and our well-reasoned homilies may give us some information about God, they can never introduce us to *The Truth*.

Dostoyevsky challenges the not-too-latent snobbery of the bourgeoisie. He points out that the rationality of the bourgeoisie produces cynical people rather than disciples and saints. He makes us realize that as people struggle with guilt and despair, they are more likely to emerge believers than if they struggle with ideas and concepts. The bourgeoisie has opted for the latter approach to God and it is, therefore, far from the heavenly Kingdom. On the other hand, those who are not proud, who are not ashamed to weep tears of repentance, and who are not frightened by passion for God, will have life and will enjoy it eternally.

Conclusion: The Future of the Middle-class Church

M IDDLE-CLASS religion, according to many social and religious prophets of the 1960s, was supposed to die. Books were written, lectures delivered, and sermons preached, declaring that the Western world was about to enter into a "post-Christian era." If Christianity did survive, they said, it would be a "religionless Christianity." The traditional forms through which religion expressed itself (i.e., churches, liturgy, and creeds) would become passé. Religion departments in the most elite colleges and universities began to theologize for the secular men and women of the future who would need the meaning and values derived from religion without a theistic context. But their dire vision of the future never materialized. To the surprise of the liberal intellectual elite, religion has not only survived in the last quarter of the century; it has made a roaring comeback. Churches are filled, religious TV networks have been established, and major evangelistic crusades have been launched.

In the 1976 national election, Jimmy Carter made being "born again" a political asset, and by the 1984 election it had become a political necessity. During that campaign, a minister, the son of a minister, and a President who courted the support of ministers dominated at the polls. The religious community served notice to its cultured despisers, who had treated it in a cavalier fashion for more than a decade, that it was planning to take back the America which seemingly had slipped from its grasp. No more could the critics of the church declare that institution to be irrelevant. (This had been the "in" thing to do among the pipe-sucking sophisticates at the "better" divinity schools.) Politically speaking, there was nothing more relevant than religion. The name "Moral Majority" sent tremors up the spines of liberals, and those who had ridiculed a church detached from political/social action during the '60s bitterly complained that in the '80s the church was gaining control of the American political agenda. After the lull of the '70s, the demonstrators were back on the streets demanding to be heard. But their demands were not the demands of the political left that had typified the '60s. Instead, they had religiously and politically conservative causes to support. The new demonstrators were calling for an end to pornography, a reintroduction of prayer in the public schools, and most important of all, an end to legalized abortion. Bombs were going off, blowing apart buildings and shattering windows; but these bombs were not set by the Minutemen or the SDS, groups almost forgotten among the middle-aged and unknown to the young. These bombs were not planted to destroy symbols of the military defense establishment and the capitalistic economic system. Instead, these bombs were being set by Sunday school teachers and deacons who hoped to blow up the abortion clinics which, to them, symbolized what was wrong with the America that they had allowed to slip into the hands of "secular humanists." As the middle years of the '80s unfolded, it was apparent that, for better or for worse, religion was alive and relevant on the American scene.

This new religious fervor and activism has not expressed itself in all sectors of the religious community. Surprisingly, this vitality has manifested itself in those groups where the futurists of the '60s had least expected it—within the evangelical community. It is the old-time religion that has powerfully broken loose in our world. It is the Christianity of gospel music and revival meetings that is blooming. It is in the churches committed to "saving souls" and sending out missionaries to reach "the lost" that "the action" can be found. Those who contended that evangelical Christianity was a vestige of the American frontier mentality have had to face the fact that this religious orientation has found ready acceptance among the business executives and "yuppies" of the modern urban society. It has attracted the graduates, not only of Bible colleges, but of the Ivy League. It has appealed not only to those whom the prominent sociologist H. Richard Niebuhr called the "socially disinherited," but it has spread like wildfire among the affluent and the powerful.

I live in suburban Philadelphia, in an area that has been labeled the "Main Line." The name comes from the fact that it is composed of communities that grew up along the main line of the Pennsylvania Railroad. Proximity to the railroad enabled wealthy Philadelphians to escape to suburban living long before the age of expressways and family automobiles. The area has maintained its reputation for sophistication and affluence and is a place where the upwardly mobile of southeastern Pennsylvania like to live.

In the early '70s, a bright fundamentalist minister, formerly associated with the California-based Campus Crusade for Christ movement, joined forces with a zealous and intensely committed business executive to start a Bible study for Main Liners. A small group began meeting on Sunday evenings in the ballroom of a local hotel. It organized as Church of the Saviour and moved to an elementary school building to hold Sunday morning worship services and Sunday school. Then something happened that sociologists who study religion would have been unlikely to predict. The church's membership grew dramatically. Wealthy, highly educated professional leaders and their families flocked to its services. In need of more space, the congregation moved to the auditorium of a junior high school. Pastors were hired and land purchased. A decision was made to build a sanctuary that would hold approximately nine hundred people. But before the building could be completed, the congregation exceeded that number. The new sanctuary was too small for the church's needs the first day it was opened. Two services had to be held each Sunday, and both of them were filled. For a time there were three morning services and eventually the sanctuary was enlarged.

The church drew people from the traditional Main Line congregations—Presbyterian, Methodist, Episcopalian, Lutheran. The pastors of many of these churches grumbled and complained. Some of them criticized this new fundamentalistic congregation, calling it an expression of civil religion. But the growth went on. The youth program at Church of the Saviour attracted teenagers by the hundreds. Lay members of the congregation started Bible studies in office buildings and restaurants throughout the area. I find it difficult to eat breakfast at a restaurant in our community without running into a group from Church of the Saviour, drinking their coffee over their Bibles. Philadelphia newspapers have carried several feature articles on the church and its activities. The church is the dominant religious institution in the area.

Similar stories can be told about evangelical churches across the country. There is Willow Creek Community Church in Barrington, Illinois. There is the South Coast Community Church in Newport Beach, California. The list could include hundreds of other congregations that have come out of nowhere to dominate their respective communities. To this list should be added the congregations of the mushrooming American charismatic movement. In thousands of towns and cities, Pentecostal congregations have grown up faster than anyone can keep track of them. Whereas the major denominations have left the urban centers of America, I have witnessed the emergence of a host of evangelical/Pentecostal churches in these deserted areas: the day of the evangelical has come. While the more liberal National Council of Churches and related denominations slowly wither, the evangelical counterparts of these groups, which are affiliated with the Washington-based National Association of Evangelicals, seem to be growing by leaps and bounds. In the face of all the dire predictions of sociologists, in spite of all the angry condemnations from proletarian enemies, and in defiance of the condescending critiques of aristocratic elitists, the bourgeois churches live on.

The Growing Discontent in Middle-class Christianity

Karl Mannheim, one of the founders of a relatively new academic field called the sociology of knowledge, suggested that people could be categorized by the ways in which they think. According to Mannheim, there are two major thought forms that can be found in society, and people will adopt one or the other of these forms as a basic orientation toward life. He called these two forms *ideological* thinking and *utopian* thinking.

Those who are *ideological* in their thought orientation, said Mannheim, are those who have a vested interest in maintaining the existing social system with its political and economic arrangements. These are people who want a religion that legitimates the present government, sanctifies the established wealth distribution, and supports the existing institutions. These are people who want a religion that will do all the things that Marx argued that the church does do. Ideologists are priests who believe that the task of religion is to validate liturgically the way things are in society, and to socialize the young into its dominant values.

What Marx did not see, but Mannheim saw clearly, is that there is another style of religious thinking, which has been labeled utopian.

According to Mannheim, utopian thinkers use religion as a basis for revolution. Their religion provides a revelation of an ideal society which makes the existing social order pale by comparison. The utopian believers have a religion that creates a constant discontent with the society in which they live because they are constantly contrasting it with the revelation they have received of what society ought to be. The utopians are ready to condemn the system in which they live because it falls so far short of the kingdom of God, which they pray will become a historical reality "on earth as it is in heaven." The utopian thinkers are "prophets," calling the people of society to repent of their evil ways and to make their social institutions more just.

Most societies have their share of both ideologists and utopians, both priests and prophets. Some sociologists argue that every society needs both these types. On the one hand, if there are no priests, society will become disorganized and fall into a state of anomie. On the other hand, without prophets, society will fail to see its fatal flaws and shortcomings, and ultimately will be destroyed.

Without priests, there would be no stability, and without prophets, there would be no change. Survival requires a creative balance between the two. Bourgeois Christianity has both priests and prophets. Its vitality lies in the presence of both ideologists and utopians in its churches. Furthermore, its future is dependent upon its ability to keep both of these types in creative tension.

The critics of middle-class Christianity often fail to recognize this balance. They fail to notice the presence of utopian prophets in the pulpits of bourgeois congregations. They are convinced that middle-class churches are totally ideological in their makeup. Consequently, they fail to understand the nature of bourgeois Christianity and, as has been verified by what has happened over the last decade, they fail to predict its future with accuracy.

Ideological Christianity

Sociologists are quick to point out the growing presence of ideological Christianity in middle-class churches. The emergence of the Moral Majority (which claims to be a purely political movement, but is recognized by the larger society as representative of the fundamentalist wing of middle-class Christianity) gives ample evidence that bourgeois religion can easily be utilized to support the existing political/economic establishment. Under the direction of the Moral Majority, there has been an over-legitimation of American institutions and a religious affirmation of middle-class morality. Dr. Jerry Falwell, the pastor of the

Thomas Road Baptist Church in Lynchburg, Virginia, has unintention-
ally merged the political movement he founded to promote "family
issues" with the fundamentalistic Christianity that he fervently
preaches. No one seems to be sure where Falwell the political activist
ends and Falwell the Baptist preacher begins. From both the platform
of his church and the platform of the political arena, his messages seem
to hold one theme: "Let us repent as a nation and return to the values,
lifestyle, and institutions of the glorious American past." Many would
argue that the American past was not as glorious or as Christian as
Falwell imagines it to have been, and that, in reality, he is calling the
American people to an idealized version of their past. It makes no difference, because as every sociologist knows, if things are real in the
imagination, they are real in their consequences.

American people have heeded the call of Falwell with enthusiasm
and in numbers that have surprised the leaders of liberal middle-class
churches. The liberals have treated Falwell and his Moral Majority as
aberrations on the American scene, and have expected them to fade
away at a moment's notice. I have listened to the leaders of liberal
middle-class churches claim that Falwell's movement has already lost
credibility and will be relegated to insignificance in coming political
elections. I believe that their post-mortems on the movement are wishful thinking. I believe that the Moral Majority will be here for a long
time. I believe that Falwell has tapped something deep in the American middle-class consciousness. He understands the convictions of
people who believe that the old-time virtues and the traditional institutions of society are still the best hope for humanity. And he knows
that many Americans believe that the social system that they are sure
existed in "the good old days" was founded on Christian principles and
is therefore "the city on the hill" which all other nations should imitate.

The conservative movement in America, now referred to as "the
New Right," has recognized the fact that Falwell and his movement
have captured a significant following from mainstream Protestant
churches, in which denominational leaders and seminary professors
lean to the liberal end of the political spectrum and to the Democratic
party. The New Right has been gleefully encouraged as Falwell and his
movement have been able to deliver a block vote into the hands of the
Republican party. Falwell is not the only one who has been able to call
forth support for the politically conservative Republican party. Others,

particularly among those who dominate religious programming on television, have done the same.

There is no need for another critique of the religious right and its connections with the political right. And there is no need for another condemnation of the civil religion which is inherent in the proclamations of most television preachers. Criticism and condemnations have already come from capable, unbiased scholars on the one hand and from sociologists with Marxist leanings on the other. Furthermore, enough was said about these matters when I presented Marx's criticisms of bourgeois Christianity in earlier chapters of this book. However, what *is* needed is a review of the positive contributions which the Christianity of the New Right has made to the maintenance of the American society and a revitalization of its institutions.

Many who do not agree with the politics of Jerry Falwell and company and who fear the power of the New Right will have to give the movement some credit, however grudgingly. Falwell and those associated with him have contributed to the necessary corrective of the American self-hatred which began in the '60s. The Vietnam War, the Watergate Scandal, the manipulations of oil companies after the Six-Day War in the Middle East, and other horrendous events of that decade and the first half of the '70s, had left Americans with a sense of shame and a distrust of their basic institutions. The sexual revolution, the feminist movement, and the Supreme Court rulings on abortion all shook the people who lived through those perilous years and gave them a sense that the family, society's most basic institution, had been undone and even might die. The troops of the New Right and their religious compatriots have been major factors in reversing those trends and attitudes.

Today the family is making a comeback. Marriage among young people is growing in popularity. Divorce, for the first time in decades, is showing signs of decline. Crime rates are down. Confidence in America is once again growing. People are volunteering for service in the armed forces in unprecedented numbers. Flag-waving has replaced upraised fists at the Olympics. Business is once again "bullish" on America.

During the late '60s and early '70s, many worried and predicted that the American society would fall apart. There was talk of a post-American era. Now all of those negative voices have faded. There is a new consciousness in America, and it is definitely optimistic. There are restraints on that emerging libertinism that had threatened to undo American sensitivities. There is no doubt in my mind or in the minds of most other observers that, for better or for worse, the Moral Majority and the New Right have been significant forces at work in generating this new consciousness.

W. I. Thomas and Florian Znaniecki, in their classical sociological study *The Polish Peasant in Europe and in America,* pointed out the dangers for a people who become too socially disorganized and who make "bohemian living" normative. These two prominent founders of American sociology warned of the social and psychological consequences of normlessness and anomie. When too much change occurs too rapidly, they said, society becomes sick. There is need for countervailing forces to keep social changes in check, and for our times Falwell and his associates have helped to meet that need. Ideological religion can be positive.

It must be noted that Thomas and Znaniecki also saw the need for creative personalities who would initiate change as society needs it for survival. Every society must have a certain degree of restructuring in order to permit the necessary adaptation to the demands of changing external conditions. In this respect also, middle-class Christianity has demonstrated its genius. In the midst of bourgeois churches, there is a strong prophetic movement that keeps them from becoming ideologically frozen and structurally stagnant. The Christians of the middle class are constantly confronted with voices that challenge the social establishment in which they are imbedded, and call for a new and just social order.

The Evangelical Left

Perhaps surprisingly, the most effective prophetic figures on the contemporary religious scene are also evangelicals. What is even more surprising, is that they have a great deal in common both with those in the Moral Majority and with the television evangelists. They believe in the authority of Scripture, the deity of Christ, the virgin birth, the validity of Christian conversion, the Second Coming of Christ, salvation through the death and resurrection of Christ, and all of the other doctrines that constitute the theological orthodoxy so precious to the preachers of the Falwell stripe. However, there are major differences too. Prophets of the evangelical left may use the same Scriptures employed by middle-class ideological religionists, but they use them to critique the American society and to demand, in the name of God, that it change. They are utopian thinkers who believe that the Bible contains a call for social revolution. To them, America is not seen as the "city built on a hill," but as the biblical Babylon that seduces people into an affluent and destructive lifestyle, which threatens the well-being of humanity.

Those in positions of leadership in this group of evangelicals are sometimes called "closet Communists" by their New Right critics. They tend to oppose the American military buildup, and they call for a redistribution of wealth, welfare programs for the poor, the abolishment of capital punishment, an end to U. S. intervention in Central American nations, and a host of other concerns that are usually on the liberal political agenda.

Perhaps the most overriding concern of the New Evangelicals, as they have been named by at least one author, is for the poor. With a careful exposition of Scripture, they make their case that God has always identified with the plight of the poor and throughout history has championed their cause. The New Evangelicals argue that those who would become followers of Jesus must recognize that concern for the poor and the oppressed is related to the evangelistic mission which goes with discipleship. Jesus, they point out, initiated His ministry by bringing good news to the poor and by promising deliverance for the oppressed (Luke 4). And to be a Christian requires imitation of the Master.

The New Evangelicals charge that the social system is designed to serve the interests of the rich and the powerful, and therefore must be challenged and changed. They call for basic changes in the structures of American social institutions so that oppression might be ended and justice instituted. They want an end to male chauvinism in marriage and a change in the role prescriptions for husbands and wives. They call for a new economic order in which production will be designed to meet basic human needs, rather than to have a primary orientation to maximize profits by producing things that meet artificially created wants. They demand a government that is more committed to human rights at home and abroad than it is to the preservation of its own political and economic self-interests. They argue that the basic value system of the United States is in conflict with the value system presented in the Scriptures. The New Right views the New Evangelicals as a dangerous enemy—and all the more so because of the conservative theological stance which its members embrace.

Among those who belong to this prophetic left wing of evangelical Christianity are Jim Wallis, editor of the influential journal *Sojourners*; Ron Sider, author of the controversial book *Rich Christians in an Age of Hunger*, and leader of the organization Evangelicals for Social Action; Tom Sine, author of the award-winning book *The Mustard Seed Conspiracy* and a popular speaker on the evangelical circuit; Tom Skinner, author and leader of many black coalitions for social action; and a long list of significant others. These leaders all build their cases on the biblical revelation. They could all sign the creed of the conservative National Association of Evangelicals, and none of them is closely associated with a major mainline denominational organization.

We would have expected liberal and prophetic leadership to come out of the National Council of Churches and its affiliated denominations, but apparently that is not where the action is. These organizations have fallen upon hard times. Their membership rolls have dropped off considerably. Their influence with young people and programming for youth is pale compared to parachurch organizations that have emerged out of the evangelical sector of Christianity. The programming of the National Council of Churches and its affiliates has become bogged down by the countervailing influences of special interest groups that sometimes are more concerned about their particular issues than the overall programs of their respective denominations. Perhaps this situation simply reflects the fact that the decade of the '90s belongs to the evangelicals, and evangelicalism has not been too popular in mainstream denominations, resulting in their having been left out of the onrush toward religion that, of late, has marked the middle class. It is difficult to say why or exactly when it happened, but the prophetic cutting edge seems to have moved into the hands of others.

It may be that the New Evangelicals simply picked up the issues of older denominational leaders, but articulated them from the perspective of a very high view of Scripture. Because they appealed to Scriptures and could say, as Billy Graham does, "The Bible says . . ." they were able to gain the support of mainstream Americans who, regardless of their flaws and weaknesses, always endeavor to be faithful to the written Word of God.

It must be firmly stated that the New Evangelicals, like the Moral Majority and the New Right, are entrenched in the American middle class. The movement is part of the bourgeois church. Its appeal is to theologically conservative mainstream Americans. It is a movement that has come to coexist in the same religious community that has embraced the politics of the evangelical New Right. The tension between these two groups has been evident for some time, but has become extremely overt of late through the books and sermons of Franky Schaeffer, son of the prominent evangelical philosopher/theologian Francis Schaeffer. He openly has declared war on the New Evangelicals and has predicted that unless they are driven from the ranks of middle-class churches there will be, as the title of one of his books states, *The Great Evangelical Disaster.* Schaeffer can be criticized for his sometimes intemperate attacks, but he merely has brought to the surface the polar extremes of thought and practice that have always existed within evangelical Christianity.

Schaeffer will not succeed in his program, in my opinion, because the left will not be driven from bourgeois Christianity. The middle class, in a mysterious way, seems to recognize the need for the New Evangelicals because it has always sensed a need for balance. The creativity and dynamism of middle-class Christianity lie in its willingness to endure creative tension and to evade the tendency to be swept away by the rhetoric of the New Evangelicals on the left or the dire warnings of the Franky Schaeffers on the right. American bourgeois Christianity refuses to be either ideological or utopian, but instead holds both styles in a dialectical tension that promises creative possibilities for its future.

The middle-class churches of America have heeded the call of the New Right for a return to traditional values and a revitalization of traditional institutions. But they also have been sensitive to the concerns raised by the New Evangelicals. Among even the most conservative congregations, there is now an intense concern for the plight of the poor and oppressed. Ron Sider's book *Rich Christians in an Age of Hunger* has had a wide reading in some of the most fundamentalistic circles. On the campus of almost every theologically conservative Christian college (e.g., Wheaton, Houghton, Westmont, Gordon, Eastern), there is a chapter of the national organization Evangelicals for Social Action. These campuses also have a good representation of faculty members who raise the concerns of social justice as viewed by the New Evangelicals. The National Association of Evangelicals, the coordinating body for conservative denominations, has a Christian Social Concerns committee which, while not identified with the New Evangelicals, shares many of their concerns.

Among evangelical Christians, the term "social gospel" once had negative connotations. The title evoked memories of the programs of liberal churches which, during the first half of the century, abandoned traditional evangelism and "soul winning." Evangelical Christians treated discussions on the political and economic implications of the gospel as dangerous and deviant. However, times have changed. Liberalism, as a theological movement, has lost support and waned while evangelical Christianity has demonstrated unusual growth and vitality. With these developments, evangelical Christians have gained a new sense of confidence which has allowed them to reexamine positions and ideas previously held exclusively by their liberal opponents. They have discovered that many of the positions on social issues taken by liberals are biblically sound and legitimate. They have recognized that there is no way to reject these positions or to fail to espouse such biblically substantiated causes without being unfaithful Christians. The net result of this recent revaluation of social concerns in the light of Scripture has been the development of a more holistic view of the gospel within the theological formulations of evangelical Christians. Furthermore, the evangelicals who have become active in the area of social concerns bring fresh zeal and enthusiasm to contemporary efforts to achieve biblical justice. And their zeal and enthusiasm has traditionally made them more lively than the liberals who were previously the sole champions of these causes within the church.

Recently I visited Africa to survey the plight of the famine victims of that continent and to ascertain ways in which American Christians could help. Everywhere I went I found evangelical missionaries engaged in social ministries. They were supervising food distribution programs, encouraging economic development projects, helping indigenous people to dig wells, and sponsoring cottage industries. These missionaries had not neglected the proclamation of the gospel for the purpose of winning converts. However, they had discovered the social dimensions of the gospel and were determined to make social concerns part of their ministries. The representatives of the mainstream denominations and of the World Council of Churches were also there, hard at work, but they were overshadowed by the very number of workers and the vast resources of such evangelical organizations as World Vision and Compassion International.

The concern for the poor and the oppressed which has become crucial to the mission of evangelical Christian churches not only expresses itself in ministries to the victims of calamities but also expresses itself in efforts to effect systematic change when the sources of human suffering lie in social structures. Evangelicals have become convinced that there is a divinely ordained imperative to change the world from what it is into what Jesus intends it to be.

The concern for social justice among evangelical Christians has led some of them into a limited sympathy for the liberation theology that comes out of Latin America. While they reject the Marxist doctrines that so often are interwoven with this theological movement, and while they condemn the violence that seems to be legitimated within the revolutions sometimes inspired by liberation theology, they nevertheless give sympathy to the belief that churches have a spiritual responsibility to inspire oppressed peoples to seek freedom.

Evangelical Christianity experiences tension between the sociopolitical conservatives and the sociopolitical liberals in its ranks, and it is that tension that is the source of its dynamism and vitality. It is that tension that keeps it from either the ideological or the utopian polar extreme. It is that tension that ensures its future.

Middle-Class Heroism

Another reason to believe in the future of middle-class evangelical Christianity is that its program provides the necessary challenges for modern young people. Any survey of the youth programs of American churches will reveal that evangelical churches are the ones with burgeoning youth programs, while the youth programs of the mainline churches seem to be waning and suffering. The reason for this difference is that, consciously or unconsciously, evangelical churches have tapped into the latent hunger for heroism in American youth. Evangelical churches have turned Christianity from a religion into a crusade. They have made church vocations into heroic callings, whereas the perception of these vocations in liberal churches has tended to cause young people to view them as prosaic professions. The neo-Freudians and Nietzscheans would not approve of the goals of the new evangelical would-be heroes, but they certainly would approve of their style.

Inter-Varsity Christian Fellowship, an evangelical movement among college and university students, is responsible, through conferences that it sponsors every three years at Urbana, Illinois, for leading tens of thousands of young people to commit themselves to foreign missions. The prominent evangelical seminaries (e.g., Gordon-Conwell, Asbury, Fuller) are attracting huge numbers of applicants, while the seminaries of the mainstream denominations find it difficult to fill their necessary quotas. These evangelical young people are heroic enough to surprise Nietzsche, socially concerned enough to break the Marxist stereotypes of them, and passionate enough to please Kierkegaard. They represent a new breed of Christians who make the future bright for middle-class Christianity.

A Concluding Note of Optimism and Hope

Evangelicalism is increasingly identified as the religion of the middle class, and the middle class is falling in love with evangelicalism. The holistic gospel of this movement, devoid of fundamentalistic legalism, has given it a great future. This brand of middle-class Christianity is neatly balanced between ideological and utopian concerns. It is challenging enough to provide a meaningful purpose in life for those who need heroism. And most important, its members are able to learn from its critics. The attacks of its enemies are not ignored, but rather are seriously scrutinized. The leaders of middle-class evangelical Christianity treat the writings of its most severe scoffers as a hungry man treats a steak; the meat is eaten and the bone is thrown away. To laud middle-class Christianity may not be common, and it is considered obscene by some. Yet when all is said and done, I believe that middle-class Christianity is on the verge of its greatest days and is capable of making a historical contribution to Christendom.

If it resists seduction into cultural Christianity; if it heeds those within its ranks who disturb its members with calls to radical discipleship; if it has the humility to learn from its critics what are its shortcomings and failures; and if it has the courage to live with the tensions that keep it vitally balanced, it may be that bourgeois Christianity will not be a bad name after all, but a justly honored one.